WISH LANTERNS

ALEC ASH

WISH LANTERNS

YOUNG LIVES IN NEW CHINA

PICADOR

First published 2016 by Picador
an imprint of Pan Macmillan
20 New Wharf Road, London N1 9RR
Associated companies throughout the world
www.panmacmillan.com

ISBN 978-1-4472-3795-2

Photographs on pages 308–311 and 313 copyright © Christopher Cherry
Photograph on page 312 copyright © Lu Ran

1 3 5 7 9 8 6 4 2

A CIP catalogue record for this book is available from the British Library.

Map artwork by ML Design
Printed and bound by CPI Group (UK) Ltd, Croydon, CR0 4YY

For my father

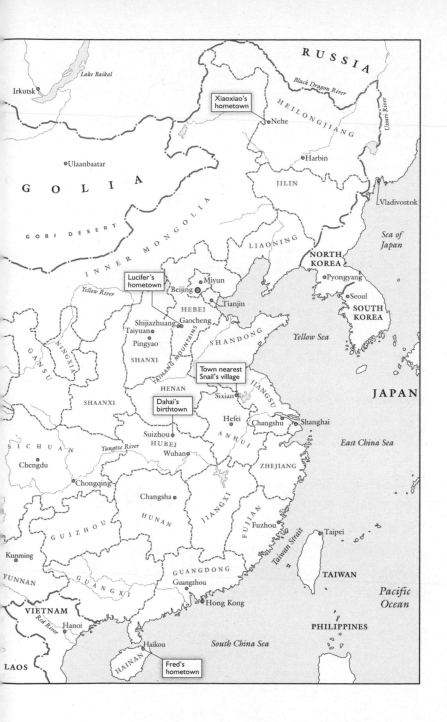

Note on Names

In this book I follow the lives of six young Chinese born between 1985 and 1990, telling their stories from childhood to late twenties. For those who have English names, I use them for familiarity's sake. Dahai and Xiaoxiao don't, so I use their Chinese nicknames instead, which is how their friends know them. Fred is her English name but also serves as a pseudonym, and details about her family have been left out at her request, out of concern for her father's position as a Communist Party official.

Pinyin is used for other Chinese names and words. For terms with a simple English equivalent, I use it, but for some of the more common or interesting terms I give the Chinese too. A few tricks help pronunciation – x is 'shh', q is 'ch', c is 'ts', z is 'dz', zh is 'dj' and js are hard.

Everything in quotation marks is in translation from the Chinese, except where marked as originally in English. All money is in yuan (RMB), which was roughly ten to the pound sterling for most of the period covered, the childhood and early teens of the twenty-first century.

Cast of Characters

Dahai (Yu Hai) – *Military child, netizen, self-styled loser, born 1985 in Hubei province*

Xiaoxiao (Liu Xiao) – *Small-business owner, dreamer, born 1985 in Heilongjiang province*

Fred (anonymous) – *Official's daughter, Ph.D., patriot, born 1985 in Hainan province*

Snail (Miao Lin) – *Country boy, internet gaming addict, born 1987 in Anhui province*

Lucifer (Li Yan) – *Singer, aspiring international superstar, born 1989 in Hebei province*

Mia (Kong Xiaorui) – *Fashionista, reformed skinhead, born 1990 in Xinjiang province*

WISH LANTERNS

It had been a decade since Dahai buried his diary.

The leather journal was waiting in the dry earth beneath a pine tree, at the top of the mountain behind his childhood home. He was eighteen when he put it there, in a dark teak box used for storing tea leaves, along with a pack of cigarettes and some old photos.

Born in 1985, he was a child of new China. His was the first generation with no memory of Tiananmen. A generation of only children born to a country growing as fast as they were. Natives of its hurtling present, inheritors of its uncertain future. In the diary he wrote about worries, wishes, fragile dreams . . . but mostly about a girl.

The May heat frazzled as he topped the summit. But which was the right tree? He unfolded an army-green spade from his backpack and plunged it into the ground, feeling for a hollow wooden thunk. Construction workers rebuilding a pagoda nearby took pictures on their phones, amused as he pockmarked the landscape with holes.

Dahai ignored them. He was almost thirty now, married, and dug for his early years.

XIAOXIAO

The fruit came from all over China. Apples from Xinjiang, pears from Hebei, tangerines from Zhejiang and Fujian. Every so often there might be dragon fruit from Hainan island in the far south, or clumps of baby bananas on the stem. They came by thirteen-metre-long truck, all the bounty of the land spreading its seeds, to the back door of the wholesale fruit shop which Xiaoxiao's parents ran, in the far north where no fruit grew.

Winter took the skin off your fingers here, north of the wall. The blanket of hard land above Beijing, previously known as Manchuria but simply called 'the north-east' in Chinese, is the head of the rooster which is supposed to be China's map. From its crest, you can see the Aurora Borealis and the midnight sun. Temperatures get down to minus forty, and snowfall comes up to your waist. There are still a few lonely Siberian tigers, who stray over from Russia without proper visas.

Heilongjiang province is named for the 'black dragon river' which snakes along its border with Russia. Four hours by train from the provincial capital, tucked between Inner Mongolia to the west and Siberia to the north, is Nehe.

Rows of identical apartment blocks are still under construction, as if the city had bloomed spontaneously from the tundra-like earth. But for a frozen river that you can drive a truck over in winter, it could be any other small Chinese city of just half a million people. Here, on 4 September 1985, Liu Xiao was born.

She was delivered by a midwife at home, on her parents' bed. For the first hour she didn't cry, and everyone was beside themselves. Then she began bawling to the gods and they tearfully wished she would shut up. At the age of seven days her ears were pierced with a needle and red thread, an old tradition to bring a child good luck and health. Seven days was also how long it took for her mother and father to name her, leafing through a fat dictionary to find a character they liked. In the end they settled on *xiao*, which means 'sky' or 'clouds' and is part of an idiom about a loud sound resounding through the heavens – like her first ear-splitting cries. In another tone the word means 'small', and from an early age her pet name was Xiaoxiao, little Xiao.

Xiaoxiao was a girl, and if she married her own child wouldn't continue the family name of Liu. The one-child policy, implemented in 1980 not long after Deng Xiaoping ushered in China's reform era, meant that her parents couldn't legally have another. But families were still catching up with the idea, especially further out from the urban hubs, and the law was far from monolithic. Xiaoxiao's parents waited another four years until her father left his strictly supervised work unit, then had a second child anyway – a son – and got away without paying the hefty fine.

These 'post-80s' only children, bearing all of the hopes and wishes that their parents missed out on in the Mao years, are mollycoddled to comic extremes during infancy. They are helped up after every fall, and wrapped in more layers of protection than a porcelain vase in transit. Add the attentions of two sets of grandparents, and the pampering snowballs into a smothering excess. In her first winter months, Xiaoxiao was only occasionally visible underneath layers of baby thermals, her cheeks the same shade as her crimson padded jacket.

Until the age of seven, she lived with her maternal grandparents in a countryside hamlet two hours' drive out of Nehe. Their courtyard home had pigs, geese, ducks, chickens, a dog and a single bed: a platform of clumped earth above a coal-fired stove, called a *kang*, on which Grandma, Grandpa and Xiaoxiao all slept in a bundle of shared warmth. Layers of newspaper were pasted across the walls and ceiling; headlines about Deng Xiaoping's southern tour of China in the early nineties found better use as cheap insulation. The only entertainment was traditional folk storytelling on the radio, while Xiaoxiao sat on her grandmother's lap.

It is common in China for grandparents to raise a child while mum and dad work long hours in cramped city conditions, sending back money. Tens of millions of the post-80s generation grew up like this. Those in the countryside whose parents are migrant workers far away are called 'left-behind children'. Whatever the circumstances, to be separated from your parents leaves its mark. Xiaoxiao's mother remembers with pain one time when she visited her daughter after being half a year away in Nehe. She went in for a hug only to see that Xiaoxiao didn't recognise her, running to hide behind Grandma's skirts.

Xiaoxiao moved back in with her parents shortly after, into the flat where she was born. Close at hand, on the edge of town, was the family fruit wholesaler's. She liked to play in the warehouse, which smelt of apples. Cardboard boxes were stacked high to the ceiling, forming corridors that got narrower with each new delivery. At first she assumed the trucks that arrived were from nearby, or maybe from her grandparents' village. Then her father showed her on a map of China where some of the fruit came from, and she never looked at the trucks in the same way again.

In her first years of school, as she learnt to read and write the thousands of characters necessary to be literate in Chinese, Xiaoxiao matched up the place names on the fruit boxes to locations on the map. She asked her mother about these exotic locations, and Mum – who had never travelled further than Beijing – would rattle off the requisite stereotypes. Sweet Xinjiang pomegranates? That's where there were dates and desert. Bulbous Henan apples? People are cheats in Henan. Smelly durian from Guangdong? They eat anything that moves down there.

Lands far away were all the more appealing because there was nothing to do in Nehe. In the nineties the city was smaller, with few cars on the streets and a single set of traffic lights at the central intersection, which was called Central Street. A popular drink among teenagers was (and still is) boiled Coke to warm their insides, poured straight out of the kettle. Those a little older favoured strong *baijiu* liquor made from sorghum or rice, earning the reputation North-easterners pride themselves on as formidable drinkers with quick tempers. In a Heilongjiang winter the only entertainment is boozing and fighting.

Xiaoxiao ate sweets instead. There was a shop that sold them next to her primary school: peanut nougat, White Rabbit candy, penny sweets in rustly wrappers with a picture of a stern old man on them, *tiaotiaotang* powder that crackled sugary on her tongue. She had three plastic dolls and embroidered clothes for them herself – sequinned tops, beaded hats, wedding dresses – having learnt the skill from her two aunts, both dressmakers. One of the dolls had blonde hair and blue eyes, a cheap knock-off Barbie which she called Ocean Baby. The three dolls were best friends, of course, and went on holidays together – to the deserts of Xinjiang, to Henan where people are cheats, and to Guangdong where people eat anything that moves.

The Chinese New Year, also called Spring Festival, was her favourite time. It was a fortnight of feasting and treats that marked the first month of the lunar calendar, beginning with a big family meal on New Year's Eve. Days of eating leftovers followed, while visiting increasingly distant family relations. Along with the other children she was given decorated red envelopes that contained small-denomination 'lucky money' in them. In the city's central park people lit fireworks and firecrackers on the frozen ice, sliding back just in time before the bang and pop. On the final night of the celebrations, Lantern Festival, she loved to watch the wish lanterns fly up and away.

TV played a big role in the holidays too. She watched the Chinese cartoons *Little Dragon Club* and *Black Cat Police Chief*, as well as the Japanese anime *Doraemon* ('robot cat' in Chinese) and also *Tom and Jerry*. Her favourite show was *Journey to the West*, a live-action serial based on the Ming-dynasty novel about the adventures of a monk, a sand demon, a pig spirit and the Monkey King as they quested for the sacred diamond sutras in India. It had ridiculous costumes and cheesy special effects – flying Taoist masters with white eyebrows as long as beards, animated magical weapons flashing on screen – but was a huge hit. The show still plays on repeat every year.

When Xiaoxiao started middle school, everything changed. Her dolls were taken away, TV was restricted and the fruit storeroom she played in became off bounds. The shift was so sudden that Xiaoxiao remembers thinking she was being punished for an unknown crime. Overnight, the pampering she was used to transformed into the true legacy of the only-child generation: crippling study and work pressure. Early childhood is a protected time, but the fairy tale crumbles as soon as you are old enough to hit the books twelve hours a day. 'Knowledge changes destiny,' Xiaoxiao's mother used to tell her at dinner, a familiar saying.

Schooldays began at 7am. The ritual in the middle of morning lessons, shared by children across China, was group eye exercises. For twenty minutes, the class of thirty or more kids rubbed the outside edges of their thumbs over and around their eyes in unison, up and down the sides of their noses and the skull behind their ears before pressing their temples. These exercises were supposedly effective in staving off myopia from all the book reading to follow, while Xiaoxiao's teachers lectured her without expecting anything but silent attention in return.

Geography, maths, science, history, Chinese, music, art. The topography of the thirty-four provinces, municipalities, autonomous regions and special administrative zones of China (thirty-three if you don't count Taiwan). Chinese inventions, foreign invasions. Ancient history and legend. Knowledge changes destiny. In English class, national text-books used the same cartoon boy and girl, Li Lei and Han Meimei, to explain grammar points through clunking dia-logue. Along with their foreign friends Lucy and Lily, a bird called Polly and a monkey called Monkey, they are the reason why if you ask a Chinese child, 'How are you?' their reply will likely be, to the word, 'I'm fine, thank you, and you?'

During break, Xiaoxiao sat off to one side from the other kids with her head in the clouds. The day ended at 7pm, when teams of students scrubbed the school clean according to a rota before they could go home. Xiaoxiao liked to gaze out at the dark northern sky through her classroom windows while she scraped the muck off them, and fantasise about those far-away places where the tanger-ines and dragon fruit and bananas came from.

DAHAI

On the outskirts of Beijing, a boy played with bullets. Dahai's father had been a soldier, like his father before him who fought in the Korean War, and the family was no stranger to guns. They were originally from Suizhou in the north of inland Hubei province. But in 1986, when Dahai was one year old, his father was assigned to the capital.

Beijing nestles in between mountain ranges on three sides, showing an arched back to Mongolia while its open face looks south-east. By the late nineties the city had long since spilled out of its Ming-dynasty city walls, themselves torn down in the Mao era and replaced by a ring road. Inside that ring road, millions of bicycles choked the hutong alleyways of the old town, which were hurriedly being destroyed to make way for high-rises. Outside it, at the thinning edges of the expanding city, fields of hulking construction cranes sat like gallows for the Titans.

Dahai's family was further out still, in a military compound in Miyun township, ten kilometres north-east in the shadow of the northern mountains. The People's Liberation Army, over two million strong, is as self-sufficient as a small nation. Both combat forces and workers such as

Dahai's father – responsible for army-related construction projects – are housed in these closed compounds. Some of them are vast, cities within cities, with their own water supply, fire service and police. Many use food coupons instead of money at canteens. All have a guard on the gates, with no outsiders allowed in unaccompanied.

To Dahai, his compound was the world. It was at the end of an unmarked road at the far edge of Miyun, with a sloping cliff face to one side that formed a natural barrier. At the west gate, a single bored guard in a box waved residents through. In a courtyard between apartment blocks, six ping-pong tables were nailed into the concrete, as if calculated to be precisely the right amount of communal entertainment. A large low hall at one end of the compound served as canteen, cinema and dance hall. At the other end was a second cinema, along with a badminton court and a decorative pond in a roundabout. Two industrial chimneys rose high behind it all, chugging out smoke from the factory workshop where the army unit made military odds and ends.

There were plenty of playmates for Dahai – children of the other soldiers and workers – and almost all of them went to the same school just outside the gates. Out there was another universe, one of rules and regulations. Inside, paradoxically, they had little supervision and free run of the compound. They played a game similar to Pogs with bottle caps, where if you flipped yours onto someone else's you could claim it. Then there were the toys: guns, mechanical jumping frogs, and coloured balls that made a loud blast when you banged them together, handy for frightening girls from behind.

A short track of rails led from the factory workshop to a cavernous storeroom by the east gate. Heavy boxes of bullets and car parts trundled over in a rail carriage and were stacked high before army trucks arrived to take them away. Dahai and the other children were forbidden from going into either factory or storehouse, so sneaking in became their favourite game. They played hide and seek, and stole bullets fresh from the line – short ones, fat ones, long tapered rifle ones, pinging and shiny. They placed them on the rails so that when the carriage rolled over, it flattened them into spearheads, which they fixed onto sticks with string and used to play war.

Dahai was a scrawny boy, with round wire-frame glasses and a mischievous grin. As soon as puberty hit he shot up like bamboo, and pockmarks sprouted on his face. At all times he wore the knotted red neckerchief that is part of China's primary school uniform and mark of the Young Pioneers. His given name Hai meant 'the sea', but nicknames are common in China, where the full name is too formal and a single character alone sounds odd unless duplicated. The tallest among his friends, he became Dahai – Big Sea – while his baby brother was Xiaoyang, Little Ocean.

When they were old enough for his parents to take them on outings, Dahai discovered there was life beyond the compound. Every year they went to the reservoir which Miyun is famous for, a tourist spot with green hills and once clear water. There were weekend trips to the Great Wall and the Ming-dynasty tombs. A more adventurous family holiday was to a theme park called Minsk World in the southern city of Shenzhen, where a Soviet aircraft carrier, the USSR *Minsk*, was moored as a tourist attraction. His mother took photographs of Dahai posing in front of the carrier, as well as next to a missile launcher and a decommissioned tank, and collected them in a photo album to show any girls (or journalists) he might bring home years later.

By his teens Dahai had grown out of playing with bottle caps and bullets, and was old enough to join the gangs. There were two of them, each with fifty to a hundred school children: the Beggars gang and the Red Star gang. Dahai joined the Beggars, so named because they would beg for treats at local shops, distracting the owner while hidden agents pilfered sweets and cigarettes from the cabinets. When not in school, gang members bicycled around the compound in large groups, keeping an eye out for the enemy. Fights were common, and periodically the Beggars and the Red Stars met for arranged battles, using fists, sticks, rods and stones. Each gang called their leader *laoda*, 'old big', the word used for Mafia bosses.

Before he started high school, Dahai got to play with real weapons. Military training boot camp or *junxun* has been arranged for all Chinese students since 1985, and became a mandatory fixture after the Tiananmen protests of 1989 – a conscious effort to inculcate students with the virtue of compliance. It happens before both high school and university, sometimes at the start of middle school as well, a week or two each time. Thousands of teenagers march and drill in unison, kitted out in full camo, and attend jingoistic lectures when not on their feet. No long or dyed hair is allowed for the boys, or accessories for the girls.

Dahai, used to a military environment and army paraphernalia from childhood, fitted right in. Most of the strict regulations were flouted by the students anyway. There was one opportunity to fire rounds of live ammunition, but it was mostly endless discipline while instructors told them how to stand, how to walk, how to shout together so it sounded like one voice. The mornings were early, with 5am runs before breakfast. The canteen food was slushy slop. But boot camp also had its perks. It was a good way to bond with classmates in the same dorm over how much they all hated it, and an opportunity to flirt with girls.

High school, when it started, was just as regimented. Miyun Number One High School is built on the scale of a prison, and could have been made from the same blueprint. Like most schools in China, there is an imposing front gate with a traffic barrier. A spiked fence runs around the perimeter, and motivational red banners hang along it and inside. '*Achieve virtue, cultivate the young.*' '*Happily and healthily grow up.*' Each teaching and dorm building has another message in characters fixed at the top, '*Study diligently, improve the reputation of the school.*' Dahai barely noticed them – they were part of the background, like the anodyne sentiments they expressed. '*Follow the core of socialism.*' '*Fervently love the fatherland.*'

Every morning, students lined up neatly in the yard for

roll call and exercises, dressed in baggy blue and red track-suit uniforms. School children in China all wear variations of these study pyjamas, regardless of gender. Part of the aim is to hide any hint of a girl's budding sexuality. Inside the classrooms were posters of inspirational figures – the early modern writer Lu Xun, the Mao-era model worker Lei Feng – as role models for the students, next to laminated thirty-point instructions for the daily eye exercises. The centrepiece of campus was an asphalt courtyard with twenty basketball hoops.

Despite his gangly height, Dahai was no good at sport. Nor did he thrive on the study routine, shunted from class to class, corralled into a pen of his elders' expectations. Most of all he hated the culture of obedience where teacher's word was gospel. Just like in boot camp, he was told to accept what he was taught without thinking. If he talked back, he might get a hard smack around the back of the head. Worse still were the class monitors – generally those with the best marks or family connections – who thought they were better than you as soon as they had a smidgeon of power.

He had outgrown the Beggars gang by now, and used his free time to read outside the curriculum. Japanese comics and novels by Murakami were his favourite, but he also dis-covered two authors whose writings resonated personally. The first was Wang Shuo, born in a Beijing military com-pound just like Dahai was. Dubbed father of China's 'hooligan literature', his breakthrough novel *Fierce Beasts* was about a gang of compound brats running wild during the Cultural Revolution. The second was Han Han, a middle-school dropout and writing prodigy who mocked China's rigid education system in his first novel, *Triple Door*, published when he was eighteen. One of his images described Chinese schools as producing students like chopsticks of exactly the same length.

Dahai wanted to be a different-length chopstick. He wrote it all down in his diary: his hopes, his frustrations, the girl he had a crush on. And one morning in May 2004, two weeks before he sat the college entrance exams, he buried it at the peak of the mountain to the north of his compound. He packed the teak box into a hole underneath the tree roots, and swept the soil over with his hands to cover it. It was his time capsule; the earth was its reader. In ten years, he said to himself, he would dig it up.

FRED

She liked banyan trees the best. They weren't as common as coconut trees, but were more beautiful with twisted trunks and veils of dangling hair connecting to the roots. There were enough of them to enjoy on the tropical island of Hainan, in China's far south. Over water from the megalopolis of the Pearl River Delta, the island province is right at the bottom of the map, hanging underneath a peninsula west of Hong Kong as if China had dripped it out. Not counting a spray of contested rocks in the South China Sea, it is the southernmost part of the People's Republic – politically part of the mainland, geographically not.

The south of China can feel like a different country entirely from the north. Wheat fields give way to rice paddies cut into the hillside, and arid yellow land gradates to green. The people are often built smaller, and speak Cantonese or a variety of dialects that are incomprehensible to those in the north, who mostly speak Mandarin. Differences in personality can be summed up by their respective cuisines: Northerners quick-fry their meat and speak just as directly, with a toughness that is sometimes only skin deep;

Southerners braise, boil and stew, but a soft exterior can hide subtle and sharp flavours.

Hainan itself is the same latitude as the Caribbean. The temperature in mid-December averages twenty degrees Celsius, and summers get up to forty. There are sandy beaches, palm and lychee and banana trees, mangoes and passion fruit and mangosteens. In the resort town of Sanya there is snorkelling, surfing, banana-boating and jet-skiing, while tourists from all over China (especially the frigid north-east) paddle in the ocean wearing beach pyjamas and plastic facekinis. If you're lucky you'll see a golden monkey in the lush central mountains. If you're unlucky a snake will fall onto you off a tree.

Hugging the northern shore, a ferry ride away from the continent, is the island's capital, Haikou. The name literally means 'mouth of the sea', but its nickname is 'coconut city'. You can buy a coconut at any convenience store, to hack open and drink with a straw. Spindly coconut trees line the streets, and only occasionally someone is killed by a falling package. Inside a gated residential community to the east of town, one such tree juts out over the road at forty-five degrees, like a raised traffic barrier. Further in is a rock garden with a miniature waterfall and sandy park. The buildings have pillar-strutted balconies in the European style, an architectural import thanks to returned migrants from former British colonies in Malaysia.

The girl who grew up in this luxurious setting didn't lack for anything. A live-in maid cleaned her room, laundered her clothes and cooked her meals. When she needed to shuttle around town or go to school, the family driver took her in their Mitsubishi. An only child, no expense was spared on her comfort and education, and she enjoyed the best of everything. There is a name for these sons and daughters of rich Chinese who live gilded lives: *fu'erdai*, the 'rich second generation'. She was in a closely related tribe: *guan'erdai*, the 'Party second generation', offspring of government officials.

There are tens of millions of Communist Party officials in China, of various ranks, including those who make up its leviathan bureaucracy. Her father had been in the machine for decades, at first in a human resources department and later rising higher (his job title and family name are undisclosed here to protect his identity). Like all officials his salary was nominally small, but the position came with a flat, a car and other perks. Her mother, also a Communist Party member, was a professor in one of the Party schools where officials were versed in their ABCs of communist ideology and governance.

When she was nine, her father travelled to Guangzhou, the nearest metropolis, to buy her a Chinese-made grand piano. She practised one hour every day. On top of her homework, reading time and chess practice, it was just another routine in a childhood overscheduled by ambitious parents. (There may be no tigers in Hainan, but there are always Tiger Mothers.) Playing the piano was her favourite chore, especially Frederick Chopin and Franz Schubert. She combined their two first names to make her own English name – Frederanz – and shortened it to Fred.

Fred was that kind of a student. Top of her class, first with the answer, perfect essays in neat small characters hugging the line. In her spare time she read *Pride and Prejudice*, *Jane Eyre* and *A Tale of Two Cities* in translation, alongside the four Chinese classics. Of those she liked *Dream of the Red Chamber* best, especially the descriptions of intrigue and backstabbing within a noble family. Meanwhile, the library at home was lined with more stolid fare: *Quotations of Mao Zedong* in thick red volumes next to revolutionary biographies, but also foreign political philosophy in translation from her mother's collection, including Adam Smith and John Stuart Mill.

Politics class was the worst. Patriotic education – a campaign launched in 1991 in reaction to the Tiananmen protests – is compulsory for all Chinese students. From middle school to the end of university each student tots up almost a thousand hours of it. Fred sat through two classes a week, each of the fifty minutes dragging endlessly. Modules included 'Mao Zedong Political Thought', 'Deng Xiaoping Economic Theory' and 'Jiang Zemin's Three Represents'. The dominant historical narrative was that the Communists liberated China after a century of humiliation at the hands of foreign powers. Whether the purpose is to drill political consciousness deeper, or bore the class out of having one at all, is unsure. Fred preferred to stare out of the fifth-floor window at the coconuts dangling outside.

Hers was the best school in Haikou, with marble-floored halls and lofty buildings. There is a statue of Confucius inside the front gate, but the Party is everywhere else. Set onto plinths around campus are varnished stone busts of Marx, Engels and Lenin. Fred and her friends put jumpers and scarves on them as a prank, to the infuriation of the head teacher. Fred was asked to be a class monitor, over-seeing her fellow students, but felt it was a sham and abdicated power after a week to better focus on study. The one time she got 77 out of 100 on a politics test, her mum was livid.

Fred got her real political education at home – the inside story on how the Communist Party actually worked. While her father was in the human resources department he had seen how local officials won their positions. His favourite complaint over dinner was that top officials got the job through connections not merit. Networks of patronage and mutual back-scratching, cemented by gift-giving and male bonding over banquets, came with the territory. If you didn't have a liver of steel to cope with all of the hard-liquor toasts, you were in the wrong line of work.

He learnt to play that game himself as he rose higher in the ranks, hosting other officials in high-end restaurants and being hosted in turn. They ate birds' nest soup, sea cucumber and other delicacies, learning to love the expense account. Fred wasn't invited to those feasts but often accompanied her parents on house visits. There she saw large jade ornaments, marble interiors. A gold watch here, designer specs there. Mention of a child in a prestigious university overseas. All clues to a lifestyle that didn't match the official salary.

Businessmen constantly courted her father for favours.

Fred remembers one time when a local property developer angling after a contract dropped off a hamper of fruit at their home, then left. Later her father found a large jade bracelet buried in the bottom, the most expensive variety worth tens of thousands of yuan. He invited the developer back and returned the bracelet. At Spring Festival, Fred's red envelopes were always stuffed with extra lucky money, sometimes over a thousand yuan in each.

One of her father's duties after his promotion was touring local villages whenever they held an election. Village elections were introduced in China in the eighties on a small scale, but by the millennium they were widespread. The contested position was that of Village Chief, a separate – and arguably less important – role to that of Party Chief, who was appointed by a less participatory process. Elections gave the Village Chief legitimacy, fixing a thorny problem of rural governance, but they were also a fledgling experiment in democracy at the level with the lowest stakes.

By many measures it was a failed experiment. Villagers were less educated and elections often devolved into tribal affairs where groups voted for the candidate who shared their surname. Just as common was for a candidate to buy votes outright. Some looked to the Party Chief to tell them who to vote for, and at other times it was the Party Chief who ran for Village Chief as well. The result was regularly contested, sometimes involving riots. After the first kerfuffle Fred's father always went with two police officers, and his function was to anoint the winner with official Communist Party approval – which some might say defeats the purpose.

Fred had learnt all about democracy in school. It wasn't a dirty word. China's supreme leaders used it all the time in speeches, even held it up as a national value. But it was always democracy with a lower case 'd'. A vague sense of popular agency, 'serving the people', but nothing as specific or taboo as multi-party national elections. The very word in Chinese is barely more than a century old: *minzhu*, the characters for 'people' and 'rule' originally combined in Japanese and imported to China later. The literal translation is 'rule by the people', but official use makes it sound more like 'rule *for* the people'. Put into elective practice, Fred only heard from her father how it fell short of the mark.

History was another topic at the dinner table. Fred's parents were keen that she knew the true story of China, not the bowdlerised version she got in school. Secure in their official status, they told her about starvation and ideological madness during the Great Leap Forward and the Cultural Revolution. Tiananmen they glossed over, but even what they did say was exceptional. For most of the post-80s generation, their parents don't tell them about China's recent past: why burden your child with that knowledge, when it might not be safe for them to know it?

One family story that struck home was how her grandfather, an official in the Education Ministry in the sixties, was sent for six years of reform by labour on a dam in Hainan's mountains when the political tides turned against him. He was rehabilitated years later, after humiliations including '*yinyang* head' where half of his hair was shaved off, while Red Guard teenagers threw rocks at his son,

Fred's dad. Fred couldn't reconcile that story with the bent but smiling man she knew as Granddad, any more than she could the tales of people eating bark to survive back then with the life of plenty around her, or the fact that her father was working for the same Party that had stoned him. It felt more like fairy tale than history.

Those times were gone, and for Fred's parents what mattered was building a good life for the next generation. In that respect officialdom was the smart choice: the proverbial 'iron rice bowl' that guaranteed a good living, except this bowl was gilded. For all the Party's past crimes it still held China together, was the common line of thinking. It was possible to live with that cognitive dissonance while the centre of power was two thousand kilometres away in Beijing. 'The mountains are tall, the emperor is far away' went the old proverb – and mountainous Hainan was as distant as it got.

It was a pleasant corner of China to call home. Islanders like Fred's family, who were ethnically Han but had come to Hainan generations ago, prided themselves on a leisurely attitude to life. There were long afternoons filled by tea-drinking, mah-jong marathons and meals of dim sum or fresh seafood while shooting the ocean breeze. Building golf courses has been illegal in China since the early 2000s, a capitalist excess, but Hainan has over twenty (developers called them 'nature resorts').

At the weekend and on holidays Fred's parents took her into the central mountains, where they had a second home. She read, caught fish in the creeks and played with the indigenous minority kids. But she was always back in time for the family ritual of watching the national news at 7pm, a mind-numbing, state-controlled programme broadcast simultaneously into homes all over China. She knew she would leave Hainan eventually. There was a whole nation above her. But when she was hidden in those hills, she didn't want to know it.

SNAIL

The pond at the back of the village used to be clear and unpolluted. Miao Lin played in it as a kid, poking at snails and slugs and tiny crabs with a twig. He splashed in the shallows and cupped water in his hands to throw over other kids as they passed by. There was only one path into town and that led past the gully, so everyone got splashed sooner or later.

The farmlands of northern Anhui province, inland from Shanghai, are historic countryside near the cradle of Chinese civilisation. The Taoist sage Laozi was supposedly born nearby, as was the general Cao Cao, immortalised in the *Romance of the Three Kingdoms*. Pearl Buck set her classic novel *The Good Earth* here, a rags-to-riches-to-rags story of a farmer who tilled the same fields that still stand, unimpressed by her Nobel Prize. Northern Anhui is also one of the poorest regions of China, and in the nineties its men and women started to seek their own riches in the cities, as part of the largest rural to urban migration in human history.

Miao Lin's family had worked this land for centuries, but his father joined the exodus when Miao Lin, born in

1987, was six. He went to Jiangsu to be a construction worker, and from there to Henan and Hebei and back again, changing jobs like clothes and sending money home every month. Miao Lin's mother and paternal grandparents tended to their crops while he was gone. They planted wheat in the autumn, soya beans and sweetcorn in the summer, as well as cabbage and chilli pepper and pak choi for the dinner table in garden plots around their home. Not an inch of land was wasted.

Even as a half-left-behind child, Miao Lin wasn't lonely. China's only-child generation never lack for company, surrounded as they are by kids their age. Miao Lin's three male cousins were like his brothers, and all of them were roughly the same age. The surname Miao – shared by most people in the village – combines two ideograms, 'grass' above 'field'. His given name Lin means 'forest', and is two ideograms for 'tree' side by side. His cousins Miao Sen, Miao Guodong and Miao Mei all share the same tree ideogram in their given names – an in-joke by their respective fathers, because trees grow in grassy fields.

Along with the other children in the village, the four of them played a version of cops and robbers with a single water gun (whoever had it was called King of the Kids). If they found a bird's nest in a clearing of reeds, they looked inside and sometimes stole the eggs. Hide and seek was another favourite game, and there were plenty of places to hide: nooks and crannies in between the brick and clay houses, pig pens and cow sheds, streams and groves. Miao Lin's craftiest hiding spot was in the outdoor toilets behind each home, clay and earth privies with a hole over a pit, vegetables growing in the fertile soil next to it.

The village, Tangzhangcun in Sixian county, was a two-hour bus journey from the nearest city. There were a hundred-odd households, and Miao Lin's bungalow was at the far western end, closest to Sixian town. Conditions were simple. There was a well pump outside, and an outer wall around two earth courtyards. In the first courtyard, their dog Little Yellow kept guard over chickens, ducks and geese. In the second courtyard, three pigs and a cow conspired around a trough. The house had one room for eating and another for sleeping. The kitchen was a separate shack off to one side in the first courtyard, little more than a giant wok over a hay-fired stove. Another side room was for storing the harvest, where a giant vat held up to ten tonnes of freshly chopped wheat.

They had twenty *mu* of land to grow it all on (one *mu* is 666 square metres) – a good amount – scattered piecemeal around the western fields, a legacy of communal farming in the fifties. Great mounds of earth rose up out of the crops every hundred metres or so, four or five to a field. They were the graves of their ancestors, buried in the soil they had lived off. In the moonlight they looked like silhouetted beasts, crouching to pounce. To think that some distant grandfather's bones still lay in the mound closest to his house gave Miao Lin the shivers.

His family had lived there for centuries. A major battle of the civil war between the Communists and the Nationalists had been fought nearby, at Huaihaizhanying. One well-flogged family story was that Miao Lin's great-grandfather had hidden his son, Miao Lin's grandfather, in a stack of hay when the troops came around recruiting young men – though no one remembers which of the two armies it was. During the Great Leap Forward, another of his uncles starved to death. In the Cultural Revolution they were, as peasants, of the right background to escape more or less unharmed. Now the times had changed all over again, and they were back at the bottom of the pile.

Before first light, Miao Lin walked thirty minutes through the fields to his primary school, at the cross-roads on the way into town. One day in class, his teacher said that each child should choose an English name for themselves, and wrote a list of popular, if old-fashioned, names on the board from a book. Miao Lin's cousin Guodong picked Gordon – a good fit. Other children got creative and chose random words because they were cool (Dragon, Sky, Rain), aspirational (Lucky, Clever) or just plain descriptive (Fatty). Miao Lin thought of the pond where he liked to play, and the animal who carried its home with it wherever it went, like he would when he left Anhui. He looked up the word in his dictionary: Snail.

*

There was an unspoken understanding between Snail and his parents that whatever he did in this life, he would never be a farmer. The most crucial goal was for him to settle in a city, as a resident and not a migrant worker like his father was. In the countryside his family had prospered some and suffered some more, but now there was only stigma and poverty for them there, while the rest of the nation was transforming into an urban society. If their son didn't get out, he would miss out.

Snail was a diligent student, and his parents put all their energy and savings into supporting him. When he got into one of the best high schools in the area, in Sixian, they were thrilled. Less than half of rural children attend high school in China (education is only compulsory up to the end of middle school at fifteen) and even then access is far from equal, as the best teachers are poached by urban schools with higher fees. Those who drop out find work in factories and on construction sites, or as building security guards, chefs, drivers and hairdressers. Those who get a college degree have a chance at a better life. Knowledge changes destiny.

More accurately, as Snail came to realise, the *gaokao* changes destiny. China's college entrance exams are over in two days, but that single mark out of 700 decides which university a student will go to, and by extension their job prospects. From day one of middle school, students are drilled that preparing for those two days six Junes later is the sole purpose of their existence. The tradition of using a single examination result to separate the wheat from the chaff dates back to the seventh century, with the old exam for the imperial civil service. It can feel like little has changed. When the pace picks up in high school, students cram fourteen-hour days, and those with the highest marks are fêted in the national press.

'*Supervision through scientific attitude*', blasts the facade of Snail's high school in golden embossed letters. '*Walk the road of inner development.*' In the first quad, a Soviet socialist-realist statue shows a student holding a football in one hand and a rocket in the other. The silver sphere of a planetarium, a feature of better Chinese high schools, perches on top of one building like a Death Star. At the back is a football pitch with spectator stands. Yet for all the pomp and circumstance of the campus, the classrooms themselves are threadbare: concrete floor, blackboard and roughly forty cramped desk-chairs. Students board in bunk beds, twelve to a room.

Each boulevard that crossed through the school is named after a top-tier Chinese university, and street signs displayed potted histories. At 6am Snail would rise, and walk along Tsinghua University Road ('founded in 1911, home to China's top-level science and technology students') to the main building for first class at 7am. At lunchtime he would take Renmin University Street ('founded in 1937, for the cultivation of China's outstanding talent') to the canteen, and wolf down sweet and sour pork or fish-flavoured aubergine with a bowl of rice. After class he would jog up Fudan University Road ('founded in 1905, Shanghai's top tier place of learning') to the sports ground for football practice, before dinner and homework until lights out at 10pm.

There was strictly no dating under the prudish eyes of the teachers. In the first three years of middle school Snail sat directly behind the same girl, whom everyone called

Xiaoli, Little Beautiful. Her best female friend sat to Snail's right, and Xiaoli would turn around to chat with her while Snail gawked. Sometimes he scrunched paper into balls and threw them at her back. But at the start of high school Snail chose sciences, Xiaoli chose humanities and the star-crossed lovers parted. Ever the romantic, when Snail saw her walking down one of the boulevards he would creep up behind and hit her on the head with his books.

Before he knew it, the day of judgement loomed: the *gaokao* was upon him. Most of his knowledge was crammed by rote memorisation. For the compulsory language and culture exam, critical-thinking skills were frowned upon. Imaginative answers were wrong answers. The essay question that carried a frightening percentage of the final mark was infamous for its ambiguous prompts, but examiners weren't afraid to give essays zero marks if a student got too creative – for instance mocking an aspect of Chinese politics or society.

Snail sat his exams on 6 and 7 June 2005 at another school down the road (schools swapped exam halls to prevent scrolls being hidden in the chair legs). He took four three-hour papers – Science, Maths, English, Language and Culture – each a stack of sheets crammed with diagrams and questions in small printed characters. That year in Anhui there were two titles to choose between for the dreaded essay: 'Grasping the journey of life' and 'The bright and dark side of the moon'. Snail scribbled in spidery characters for an hour about grasping the journey of life, but can't remember a single word of what he wrote. Those two days went by in a haze.

Leading up to and during the exams, his mother moved into a hotel in town to be near him. She cooked all his meals, did his laundry, and made sure he had nothing to worry about except study. At 5pm on the last afternoon, she waited with hundreds of other parents outside the school gates for him to come out of his final paper. When he stumbled out, she drove him back home in the family tuktuk, cooked a large meal and tried her best not to ask how it went until later.

Snail thought it went fine, but as soon as he left the examination hall he got the creeping sensation that all of what he had learnt was useless in the real world – begging to be forgotten. He could plot complicated mathematical graphs and solve university-level physics questions, but that wouldn't help him beyond his exam score. After two agonising weeks he rang a number to find out his mark, a breakdown of which was then posted to his school. When the envelope arrived he took out a thin slip of paper with the results of each of his four exams, and scanned to the right to find the combined three-digit number that would define the rest of his life.

LUCIFER

Li Yan always knew he was going to fail his college entrance exams. But marks aren't important when at the age of fifteen you decide you're going to be an international superstar.

He was born on 16 June 1989, less than two weeks after the bloody end of the Tiananmen Square student protests. His own coming of age was not one of political awakening – as it had been for the generation of young Chinese before him – but was set to the tune of South Korean pop music, Japanese porn and the rise of Chinese celebrity culture. He was a millennial to the bone.

Li is the second most common surname in the world (Wang is the first), shared by almost a hundred million Chinese. Li Yan wanted to stand out. His given name – suitably for the brand of superstardom he had his eye on – means 'rock'. From boyhood, he had the feeling he was special. He remembers the moment in his early teens when he looked into the mirror after his growth spurt and realised he was handsome, a 'smart brother'. From that day he had his sights set on stage mirrors and fame. The first step was to get to the capital.

It wasn't far away. Hebei is a populous northern province that encircles both the Beijing municipality and the port of Tianjin to its east. It has a reputation for choking smog, donkey meat, and being the province that isn't Beijing. Li Yan grew up in Gaocheng, a suburb an hour by bus from the provincial capital of Shijiazhuang. Gaocheng is a backwater's backwater: rows upon rows of street grid, filled with apartment blocks, hair salons, plastic-table-top restaurants, massage parlours, hand-job shacks, and the occasional school, hospital or government building. It is as ordinary as China gets, and to Li Yan it was the most boring place on the planet.

His father, a short red man with a crushed nose and no visible neck, had been a soldier stationed in Qinghai province to the far west. When he returned to his native Hebei he worked the land for a while, then moved his family into town where he opened a shop selling tractor parts. Now the farmers came to him, to repair their machinery before harvest season, and he made a good living. Li Yan's mother, a kind and doting woman with a mop of frizzy hair, taught maths in the local primary school where she embarrassed her son to death.

School just wasn't for him. Li Yan was the chatty kid who sat at the back, always late for roll call. His geography teacher slapped him around the back of the head whenever his attention drifted. Another teacher told a female student not to sit next to him or it would drag her marks down. Li Yan has a vague memory of making that teacher cry in grade six, though he never quite understood why. The best experience he had in middle school was a mock fashion show in art class where he was one of six to swagger up a makeshift catwalk. He got a new haircut for the occasion, an artfully swept fringe that he kept for ten years.

Instead of doing homework he goofed around with his friends. They scaled a factory wall nearby, stole scrap metal and sold it to scrap merchants who trundled by on three-wheeled carts. The ill-gotten proceeds funded Japanese porn DVDs from bootleg sellers on street corners or the kind of shop with a curtained door at the back. They climbed through the windows of each other's flats to watch them when their parents were out. Li Yan couldn't name the members of China's politburo standing committee but he could rattle off other names without a second's thought: Sola Aoi, Hitomi Tanaka, Maria Ozawa, Saori Hara, Sakura Sena, Akiho Yoshizawa.

And he listened to music. Most of the stuff on Chinese radio was sugary Mandopop, although he liked the Hong Kong band Beyond and the Taiwanese singer Jay Chou. Instead, he bought Western pop and rock from stores that sold discarded-CD imports. All the CDs had a hole punched near the edge of the disc by the record label when they were thrown out, but entrepreneurial Chinese scrappers bought them up in bulk and shipped them home. They were dirt cheap and you could still listen to all the tracks except the last couple, where the music skipped. They were called *dakou* or 'holed' CDs and introduced a whole generation to what their peers in America and Europe were banging heads to.

Li Yan sang along in pidgin English to Green Day, Blink-182, Rancid, Sum 41. When his best friend Li Fan, a skinny boy who wore skinny jeans, said that he wanted to learn guitar, the two of them loitered outside a music shop where a sales-clerk-cum-hippy taught guitar for beer money. All the other shops on the street were 'hair salons' in which young women sat in the window display like mannequins. Even the kids knew they were brothels, but they were more entranced by their teacher, who riffed on his Gibson while his Jesus-like hair swayed, his disciples sitting cross-legged on the shop floor.

The first time Li Yan plugged in an electric guitar he fell in love. It was loud, cool, and came right out of the songs he was listening to. He went to the shop for lessons every day after school, and most lunch breaks too, until his teacher got annoyed and asked him not to. His parents were permissive at first but at the first sign of dropping marks they balked. Li Yan had a brother, eight years older, who had just landed a stable job as a prison guard and was engaged. (His parents had paid a fine of 2,000 yuan to get away with the second birth, and his mother's salary was cut.) As the younger sibling, Li Yan had less pressure on his shoulders, but his father started to prod and probe. Why couldn't he study hard like his brother did? Then he could get into a good university, find a stable job, get married. It didn't cross his father's mind that to his son there were other standards of success.

When the end of middle school was in sight, the topic came up again over dinner. Instead of brushing it off as usual, Li Yan said he didn't want to go to university – he wanted to play music. His father leapt to his feet, and told him flat out to give up the guitar. It was a brain-dead hobby, he said, a Western game. Li Yan was taller than his father now, but skinny and awkward and he despaired at what to do. Before, he had punched walls and slapped himself in empty protest. This time he grabbed a glass from the tabletop and smashed it hard against his own head, dropping the shards as blood trickled down from under his fringe.

Guitar wasn't a game to Li Yan. He knew what his life would be like if he went to a good university, found a stable job, got married. He wouldn't be a farmer or a soldier, but he would be a worker ant and that was all the same to him. He felt he had something unique to say. He could either follow that feeling, or he could work nine to five. The family got back from the emergency department in the early hours of morning. When they sat down for dinner the next day his parents told him guitar was too 'low', but if he really wanted to play music they would find him a violin teacher and he could take the vocational exam for entry into music college. It was good enough for him.

*

Shijiazhuang is a concrete dustbowl of a city, but one step closer to Beijing. Its nickname among residents is *shiji-azang*, switching the characters to mean 'shit plus dirt'. At high school here, Li Yan had to take the *gaokao* as well as a special music exam – he rejected the violin in favour of the clarinet – but he needed a lower mark to pass. The pressure was off. Li Fan went to the same school, and after class broke they shredded guitar together or watched music videos online to discover new influences. Li Yan's favourite was the Toy Dolls' staccato punk. He loved the lead singer's oversized white sunglasses.

All of those bands sang in English, which for Li Yan became the language of escape. The problem was that for all the hours spent slogging vocab and grammar at school, his spoken English was atrocious. Chinese schools teach English like it's an equation to crack. Example sentences are uninspiring, about exchange students who would like (future conditional) to find the library, or how reform and opening up (gerund) developed China's economy. Most students find that by the end of a twelve-year education in English they can parse a technical essay but can't string together two sentences when talking to a native speaker.

Instead Li Yan joined a new craze sweeping China, an English-language group course that felt more like a cult. The leader was a charismatic man called Li Yang, who stood on stage with a microphone and roared out set phrases for the crowd to bellow back as loud as they could. The reasoning went: if you could scream English, you could talk it. Bigger events were held in stadiums to throngs of thousands, something between metal concerts and megachurch evangelism, with a healthy dose of self-help. Li Yan loved the positive message that anyone could succeed, if they only shouted hard enough. Appropriately enough, it was called Crazy English.

Both times Crazy English passed through Shijiazhuang while he was there, Li Yan stood as close to the front as he could in the crowd, and bawled back loud motivational sentences. 'GETTING DAILY EXERCISE IS IMPORTANT.' 'SHOUTING ENGLISH IS VERY HELPFUL [sic] CONQUERING YOUR SHYNESS.' 'MAKING MONEY IS EVERYBODY'S DREAM.' He bought an accompanying textbook and practised in the corridors of his school dorm, howling sentences at random until he drove his dorm mates up the wall. 'YOU ARE SPECIAL.' 'YOU ARE CRAZY.' 'YOU ARE GOING TO WIN.' His favourite passage was from Li Yang's own self-introduction, and he learnt it by heart: 'I WAS ONCE A POOR STUDENT OF ENGLISH AND IT WAS MY BIG HEADACHE AND TROUBLE MAKER.'

The louder the better was a mantra that fitted the rest of his life too. Scrimping and sponging money off his parents, he bought a pair of tight red trousers, flowery shirts, a polka-dotted jacket. Knock-off Converse shoes, flat-cap hats and colourful cravats. He experimented with two buttons undone on his shirt, then three, then four, then back to three when people started laughing. A pair of wrap-around white sunglasses – like the ones the singer in the Toy Dolls wore – completed the new look. Everyone in his dorms thought he looked like a clown.

In Shijiazhuang, as in other second-tier Chinese cities in the mid-2000s, there was a burgeoning alternative music scene where Li Yan could fit in by sticking out. At the weekend he went with Li Fan to gigs at a basement dive bar called Velvet Underground (the words 'Fuck School' are etched into the wooden bar). There was even a summer rock festival, and it was here in his second year of high school that Li Yan star-spotted a white guy. He was a red-bearded, scraggly-haired twenty-something, sitting on the kerb with a cigarette in one hand, a beer in the other and a guitar on his lap. To Li Yan he was the epitome of cool. He skipped up close and started shouting frantic half-sentences in Crazy English. To the best of both of their recollections, this was Li Yan's self-introduction:

'HELLO MY NAME IS LI YAN! I WAS ONCE A POOR STUDENT OF ENGLISH AND IT WAS MY BIG HEADACHE AND TROUBLE MAKER! I WANT TO PLAY MY PUNK MUSIC FOR YOU!!'

The foreigner was called Brian Walker. He was an American teaching English in Shijiazhuang on a self-described four-year alcoholic binge, and he let Li Yan play his punk music for him. In their way, they became friends. Li Yan went to Brian's flat, uninvited most of the time, to practise English at a more normal volume and talk about music. Brian was a musician too – he played flute, guitar, hand drums and bagpipes – and introduced Li Yan to The Pogues, The Dubliners, Tom Waits, Leonard Cohen. Li Yan drank it all in, while Brian drank spirits.

One day, Li Yan asked Brian to give him an English name. It was quite a responsibility, albeit one that English teachers in China are well used to. Brian racked his brains for male names beginning with L: Leo, Leonard, Liam, Lewis, Logan, Luke, Luther. Li Yan didn't like any of them.

'There's one more name which everyone knows that

begins with L,' Brian joked. 'But it's very unusual. It means the devil.'

Later, Li Yan looked up the word and found that it had another, literal meaning – bringer of light. Failing that, the devil worked. 'I am the light side of the darkness,' he would say later when he introduced himself to foreigners. It was something different, at least.

'I want that one,' he said, and Lucifer was born.

MIA

Mia got her first tattoo at seventeen: an AK-47 rifle across the small of her back, with the words *Bang of Youth* underneath in stencilled English. When her mother saw it she tried to scour it off with soap for two hours, tearfully repeating that men didn't like girls like that. Her father didn't speak to her for a week. That hurt even more, but Mia brushed it off and reminded herself why she got the tattoo in the first place – a symbol of independence.

She could understand why they couldn't understand. Mum was a PE teacher, and Dad worked in a city planning office. Like almost everyone else, they lived modestly in a two-bedroom high-rise apartment, with an interior balcony to hang laundry in and an air-con unit strapped outside. Born in the mid-sixties, they had missed the maddest years of the Mao era but were still old enough to come from a fundamentally conservative age. Their daughter was born in 1990, and they could scarcely believe that teenage girls now inked their bodies.

The 'post-90s' generation were leaving not only their parents behind, but the post-80s. One phrase used by young Chinese is 'a generation gap every five years' (some have it as every three), and the two digits of your birth year is essential information, often the first thing out of your mouth after your name and home province. A child born in '80 grew up in a China emerging from chaos and poverty; another born in '85 won't remember anything of or before the Tiananmen protests; a third born in '90 is a net native surrounded by international influences. That was Mia.

The English name was foisted on her by a teacher at school. She hated it with a passion until at the age of eighteen she saw a bootleg DVD of *Pulp Fiction*, and fell in love with the drug-dealer's wife Mia. Her Chinese name, Xiaorui, used two rare characters that meant 'deep water' and 'far-sighted', while the family name Kong was the same as that of Confucius, Kongzi. Some members of the family tenuously claimed a direct bloodline – along with thousands of other Chinese with the same surname.

It was her paternal grandfather who had first come out to Xinjiang in the fifties, as a car mechanic for the People's Liberation Army. The far western province is one sixth of China's landmass, the size of Alaska, but has just 1.5 per cent of China's population. It is homeland to the Uighurs, a Turkic and Muslim people, and a melting pot of other ethnic groups with high Scrabble scores (Kazakh, Kyrgyz, Tajik, Xibe, Uzbek). But it is also home to millions of Han Chinese, like Mia and her parents, who had lived there all their lives.

As a place to grow up, Xinjiang had its peculiarities. It is home to the Taklamakan desert, the flaming mountains and miles upon miles of nothing. In the south there are spices, dates and scorpions, where it can feel more like Persia than China. The young play football in the dust, the old smoke tobacco from long metal pipes. The sun sets at eleven in the summer and rises at eleven in the winter. Xinjiang should be two or three hours behind Beijing, but the powers that be decree China is one country, one time zone. Uighurs use local time; everything else runs on Beijing time. Some residents wear two watches to keep track.

Parts of Xinjiang have been brought into the folds of – and declared independence from – China several times over the centuries. The name Xinjiang itself dates from the Qing dynasty and literally means 'the new territories'. In 1949 the region was reclaimed by Mao's armies and declared an 'inseparable part of the unitary multi-ethnic Chinese nation'. Since then the osmosis of immigration – encouraged by the state's promise of good jobs – has changed the status quo of Xinjiang to Chinese as much as Uighur. Its capital of Urumqi, where Mia was born, is already well over half Han, and those figures don't include unregistered migrant workers.

Outside the Uighur quarters, mostly in the south of the city, Urumqi is generically Chinese. Office and apartment blocks – a new one every week – trace a skyline that could belong to any other provincial capital. At the canopy, familiar signs blast the names of companies and property development groups in metre-high neon characters. There are government buildings emblazoned with red stars, schools, hospitals and parks built by official investment to develop the west of the nation, and the morass of humanity pushing and shoving at the railway station. In short, all the interchangeable sights of urban China. To see them well into central Asia is enough to remind anyone that China is an empire.

The sun beat harder out here, and by her teens Mia had a deep suntan that other Chinese girls might shun as unfashionable. Her obsidian hair and eyes were from her genes, but her tattoos and baggy clothes were entirely her own style. Her school was joint Uighur and Han, just up the road from the Grand Bazaar in the city's south: a domed jungle of dyed silks, ornate daggers, scented soaps and iPhone cases. Next to the bazaar is the city's largest minareted mosque, heart of the Uighur community. Several times a day while Mia was in class, she could hear a faint 'Allahu Akbar' reverberate through the walls.

Teenage life was less pious. Scraps were a regular feature of break time and Uighur kids are good fighters. But Mia was tall, with a long reach and a fearlessness to commit. She won all her fights against the girls, and some against the boys. It was no coincidence that her favourite Disney character was the warrior princess Mulan. She smoked, drank beer and experimented with dating. The first boy she had a crush on was a Kazakh from the year above, with pale skin and soft eyes. After school, while the sun was still high, they bought sweet nutty cake from the backs of street carts, which Uighur men carved from a giant block with terrifyingly huge cleavers.

At home there were fewer distractions. During term Mia lived with her aunt at the foot of Red Mountain, Urumqi's central hillock, as it was closer to school. Her aunt was a warm woman who constantly ate black seeds – the sort that aunts across China crack open in their teeth – and she had two chips in her incisors to show for it. She was a Chinese-medicine doctor, and admonished Mia for blotches on her skin that signalled bad *qi*, an imbalance of *yin* and *yang*. Sometimes she gave a treatment on the house: acupuncture, cupping, herbs, moxibustion. Her philosophy was laminated in signs on the walls of her clinic: 'tranquillity, balance, quiet'.

Never a fan of the tranquil, Mia plugged in instead. She had a large collection of *dakou* CDs (Korn, Def Leppard, Nirvana, Kiss, Ozzy Osbourne, Iron Maiden) and streamed TV dramas and sitcoms online. YouTube wasn't blocked yet, although it was slower across the Pacific, but China had its own clone, Youku (the main difference is brightly colourful adverts that pop up every two seconds). She watched all of *I Love My Home*, one of China's first and most beloved nineties soaps, and later *Struggle* about college graduates in Beijing, mostly rich second-generation eye-candy with lifestyles she could only envy.

Her favourite shows were the American ones. She loved *Sex and the City* but above all *Friends*, which is hugely popular in China. Following the romantic entanglements of the six characters (she liked Chandler best), Mia was keenly curious about their lives. She assumed their high-ceilinged, artfully sofa-ed loft apartments were the norm in New York, where there must be so much living space. That they asked strangers out on dates, or that Joey kept condoms in his wallet, were revelations. Life must be pretty good in the US, she decided, if twenty-somethings could lounge around in a cafe all day.

There was a Chinese spinoff called *Love Apartment* but it wasn't the same, full of canned laughter and boinging sound effects. Another advantage of *Friends* was that she learnt English from watching it. On Youku the show had Chinese subtitles, but every time there was juicy slang or a biting Chandler one-liner, she paused, clicked back and listened to the English. Abandoning the useless grammar she was taught at school, the show became her main teaching aid. 'How *you* doin'?' she mimicked along with Joey. 'I'm *totally* not into that.' 'What*ever*.'

It was fashion that inspired Mia the most. The news kiosks opposite her school spread out state media papers – *People's Daily*, *China Daily*, *Beijing Daily*, *Global Times* – but also displayed lifestyle and fashion magazines, drowning out the propaganda with splashes of colour. Some were domestic glossies: chaste, milky-white cover girls and articles about how to bag a husband. Instead Mia took home the Chinese editions of *Cosmo* and *Vogue*, stacking them high at the foot of her bed. She cut out photos and plastered them on her wall. Naomi Campbell was her favourite model. The sheer boldness of editorial shoots seemed unreal to her, or transcendentally real, totally unafraid of convention.

Now Mia had something to fight for, instead of schoolyard scrapping. She was bright and worked hard, and applied to art and design school at Tsinghua University, one of the most competitive colleges in China. She burnt the candle at both ends to produce the marks and the portfolio she needed to get in. Her parents supported her study – she was their only child after all – but weren't able to influence her decisions any more. The news of her acceptance came while she was on a trip to 'Heaven Lake', a hundred kilometres from Urumqi, with her mother.

Before she left for Beijing, Mia got a second tattoo, on her upper left arm of a sea swallow clutching two cherries on the stem in its beak. Like the bird, she would be flying towards the ocean.

SNAIL

Snail's *gaokao* score was 584. It was just shy of the 600 out of 700 he was aiming for – a shortfall which still pains him like a mouth ulcer. The anxiety dreams that he was back at the exam desk, unprepared, took years to go away.

After a student takes the college entrance exam but before the score comes back, they predict how well they think they did. Then they select universities and courses accordingly, in order of preference. Snail's mark was lower than he predicted but still good enough to get into his first choice, China Mining and Technology University, to study automated electronics. It wasn't prestigious but had a decent reputation, and he was the first in his family to go to college. What's more, it was in the capital.

Snail took the fifteen-hour overnight train from Anhui to Beijing, hard-seat class (the cheapest ticket, with no space to recline in a carriage that smelled like cigarettes and burnt noodles). It was his first time out of his home province, and he carried most of his possessions with him. He spent much of the journey worrying that his classmates would look down on him as a yokel. But Mao Zedong's words, had he known them, might have been appropriate:

'Beijing is like a crucible in which one cannot but be transformed.'

By 2005, the nation's capital was a gridded monster, as if Hieronymus Bosch and Lenin had joined forces as urban planners. Millions of bicycles had given way to millions more cars. It took twenty minutes to walk the length of a single giant block, and further out from the centre overpasses were the only way across wide streets with high fencing to prevent jaywalking. The soundtrack of the city was a percussion of honks and electric scooter beeps, with a stray cymbal clash as someone hocked and spat.

The first thing Snail did when he arrived was to go to Tiananmen Square. It's a rite of passage for any new visitor: a photo opportunity at the middle of the middle kingdom. Next he took the subway all the way out to his university. Beijing is designed in a series of concentric ring roads that emanate like ripples from the Forbidden City next to the square. The first used to loop around the historic old town; the second traces where the city walls used to be; the third, fourth and fifth are progressively far away, each one less traffic-clogged. The joke among Beijing drivers goes that on the second ring road you're in second gear, on the third you're in third, and so on.

The university district is in the north-west between the third and the fourth ring roads. Here are the colleges that gave the boulevards their names in Snail's high school: Renmin University, Peking University, Tsinghua. Along with Fudan in Shanghai they are the most famous in China. The railway junction to their east is called Wudaokou: a bustle of student bars, bookshops and a dingy club called Propaganda familiar to legions of foreign-exchange students. Every fifteen minutes or so the barriers go down and a train rushes through. Snail's college was beyond it – quite literally on the wrong side of the tracks.

China Mining and Technology University is a typical campus, with wide paved avenues and even the occasional tree. Each dorm housed six students, and Snail's fears were allayed when he found out his roommates were all from the provinces too and just as out of place as he was. He also discovered that the study pressure he had lived under for the past decade had ended as suddenly as it had begun. He had climbed the granite face of the *gaokao*, been accepted into a good college, and provided that he didn't make a complete hash of things he would get through these four years and come out the other end with a university degree and the prospect of respectable employment in the city that it afforded.

With time to kill, he spent it doing nothing in particular. There were lectures in the morning but few and simple assignments, and the afternoons were his own. He took up rollerblading, looping in circuits around the basketball court in a group. At night a fierce woman guarded the front gate of their dorm building, and she didn't approve of students going out after hours. Snail and his dorm mates took turns climbing out of their second-storey window, sneaking back with clinking bags of beer and junk food which they hoisted up on a stick to the window before climbing up a pipe back in. They drank the beer on the roof while looking into the girls' dorm windows opposite.

In his more solitary hours, Snail read sci-fi. His main go-to was the Chinese magazine *Science Fiction World*, founded in 1979 and with a peak circulation of 200,000, sold in every kiosk outside every school and university gate. Most of the stories were about robots and aliens, clones and space travel, but every so often they satirised contemporary society, slipped past censors who dismissed sci-fi as kids' stuff. One story published in Snail's first year, 'The City of Silence' by Ma Boyong, was set in 2015 in a nameless totalitarian state where citizens only communicate online using an approved, and ever-diminishing, list of 'healthy words'. When a splinter group escape surveillance and vent their frustrations in a weekly 'talking club', the book they read to each other is George Orwell's *Nineteen Eighty-Four*.

Most of his time he spent not in bars but Internet bars. By the mid-2000s there was one on every block, the neon character *wang* for net – XX inside a gate pictogram – blaring outside like a cut-rate sex-shop sign. Snail found one such cave outside the east gate of campus in his first week. Inside, rows upon rows of identical monitors stretched into the windowless distance. Cigarette smoke clung to the ceiling, and a pale face was glued to each station. Over three hundred computers were divided into zones according to plushness of seating, and it was cheap at two yuan an hour (five yuan for VIP thrones). At the counter you could buy crisps, soft drinks, cigarettes and instant noodles in cardboard pots, fillable at a water boiler in the corner.

When punters hit the glowing power button in front of them, and logged on by tapping out a long string of numbers from their receipt, the screen lit up with an array of icons promising connection or distraction. The Internet had been slower coming to China than the West, but when it did it boomed, with hundreds of millions of users, mostly young and in the cities. A few checked email or chatted on QQ, China's biggest instant-messaging service. A handful surfed news and gossip sites, basking in the information age, or streamed films while wearing headphones as large as Princess Leia's hairbuns. Everyone else was eyeball-deep in games.

*

The first Chinese computer games in the nineties were underwhelming: boardgames such as Chinese chess, Mahjong and Go. Console games were banned in 2000 out of lingering fears of spiritual pollution, but foreign gaming companies saw an opportunity in the Internet bars and negotiated with Chinese technology firms to preinstall their games on each station. First came *Diablo* in 2001, with its dimly lit dungeons and obstinately animate skeletons. Next *Starcraft* introduced gamers to real-time strategy in the outer Milky Way. Network gaming followed on its heels, and by 2005, when Snail started playing, *World of Warcraft* was the most popular game in China.

World of Warcraft – *WoW* to its disciples – is a Massively Multiplayer Online Role-Playing Game or MMORPG (not all acronyms are born catchy), and truly a world unto itself.

The planet Azeroth to be precise, although Argus, K'aresh and Xoroth are only a few light years away. This primordial universe is populated by an ecology of beasts and critters, flora and fauna – and by the avatars of millions of players exploring terrain, finding treasure, completing mini-quests, battling beasts and each other. They are part of one of two warring factions: the Alliance (humans, dwarves, elves and all things nice) and the Horde (orcs, goblins, ogres and various degrees of undead).

Snail created his avatar in the image of a well-muscled, scantily clad female elf mage. He started with next to no equipment or gold, but quest by quest he levelled up until he had a nice long health bar, a small arsenal and mana galore. Some players skipped the early phases and bought existing avatars off 'farmers', entrepreneurial gamers who hoarded in-game skills and gold in order to sell them off for real yuan. Snail did it the slow way, relishing every detail of the artificial world. In the villages he rampaged, he always stopped to trample the roses.

As the hours and weeks and months went by, Snail's elf mage got swept along with the plot. She was part of the assault on Blackwing Lair, where the black dragon Nefarian had created a mutant breed of warriors to battle with the firelord Ragnaros. She helped throw down the Blood God Hakkar the Soulflayer in the jungle fortress of Zul'Gurub. She stormed the ruined temple of Ahn'Qiraj to vanquish C'Thun and his insectoid qiraji, and she laid waste to the fell sorcerer Kel'Thuzad's flying citadel. By the climactic showdown with the war orc Thrall, she was a battle-scarred veteran.

Every minute Snail spent in elfskin was a minute of college lost. He was a *zhainan*, literally 'home boy', a term used to describe geeks who never went out. His lecturers were oblivious but the student supervisor in his dorm noticed Snail's dropping marks, the glaze in his eyes and the odd hours he came back from the east gate. He twice warned Snail to stop gaming but the message didn't get through. Instead his supervisor rang northern Anhui, and spoke to Snail's parents.

FRED

Fred was in the library, surrounded by treasure: rare scrolls, classical novels, early Republican-era first editions. The reading room thrummed with the silence of mass swotting. Some students fell asleep at their desks between piles of books as tall as themselves. But that was to be expected in China's most prestigious university.

Naturally bright and with access to the best education, Fred had sailed through her college entrance exams, which in Hainan are marked out of 900. She got 829, the fifth-best mark in her year on the island. That meant she could take her pick of colleges and subjects, and she chose to study International Politics at Peking University. It was the holy grail for elite students, firmly on the right side of the tracks in the university district. Tsinghua University was next door, and side by side they were China's Oxbridge.

Peking University – known to its students as Beida, a shortening of the Chinese name – is an oasis of charm in the urban desert of Beijing's outer ring roads. Past the library there are quiet groves, pagoda-roofed teaching buildings, hidden dumpling stalls and arching bridges over algae-green ponds. To the north is Nameless Lake, a curving expanse of water with lilies, lotus flowers and a rocky island with a decorative stone boat from the Qianlong emperor's reign moored next to it. A multi-storey pagoda, once used as a water tower, rises past the lakeside. To the south is a garden full of immensely fat and lazy cats, waiting for passing students to feed them. When one was spotted looking at a book, it was adopted as Beida's 'scholar cat'.

Fred's first impression was all the ordinary buzz of freshers' week as new arrivals milled about campus to sign up for extra-curriculars. It was difficult to adjust. At school Fred was used to being the brightest spark; now, irritatingly, all her classmates were just as clever. After a pampered childhood, she wasn't used to dorm life, sharing a room with five other girls and using a communal shower. Back home in Hainan there had been plenty of space for everyone, among the green hills and on the sandy coastline. The north was crowded and noisy, and it didn't even feel like there was enough air.

In her major she studied both Chinese and Western politics. The style of education was still PowerPoint-driven but the professors were among the best in the country. It was intellectually challenging and surprisingly uncensored, although any criticism of the Communist Party was taboo. Meanwhile, her compulsory political education classes continued in parallel, two hours every week. In the mornings, as part of her degree, she read Thomas Hobbes and Hans Morgenthau. In the afternoons, she zoned out while being told for the hundredth time about Mao Zedong Thought and Deng Xiaoping Theory.

Dotted around the winding paths of the campus were statues to inspire students by example, from Lu Xun to Cervantes. There were also busts of college presidents and historical figures from the university's own past, equally famous in their own right. These were the ones who Fred admired the most, for Beida has been at the vanguard of the last century of change in China, and long before reading rooms and scholarly cats its reputation was for political protest.

*

The genesis of student dissent was 4 May 1919. The Qing dynasty had been overthrown in the Xinhai revolution of 1911, ending some four millennia of dynastic history. But the fledgling Republic was weak, divided and bullied by the Treaty of Versailles at the end of the First World War, which granted concessions to Japan in German-controlled Chinese territory. In this uneasy new era students and intellectuals were among the loudest voices, especially on the campus of Beida – then a tall red-brick building at the north-eastern corner outside the Forbidden City.

On the afternoon of 4 May over three thousand Beida students marched the short distance to Tiananmen Square. 'Don't sign the Versailles Treaty!' they chanted, demanding a stronger central government and a boycott of Japanese goods, which they symbolically burnt. They accused three Chinese officials of collaborating with the Japanese, tramped to the house of one and burnt it to the ground, beating the official so badly that his skin, a doctor noted, 'looked like fish-scales'. Some protesters were arrested, others took up their patriotic cause across the nation, and the May Fourth Movement was born.

It wasn't the first student protest march – that was in 1895 after defeat in war with Japan – but it sounded the clarion call for a whole generation. The May Fourth Movement had a bookish elder sibling, the New Culture Movement, which from the mid-1910s had rejected sclerotic old Chinese culture in favour of more progressive notions. They held up the twin idols of 'Mr Science' and 'Mr Democracy' (as opposed to 'Mr Confucius') and argued that there was much to learn from the West. Lu Xun joined the fray, satirising traditional customs as cannibalism. China's very future was at stake.

The flagship magazine of the movement, founded in 1915 by the then dean of Beida, Chen Duxiu, was called *New Youth*. 'Youth are like early spring,' Chen wrote in his opening editorial, 'like the morning sun, like budding blooms and first shoots, like the sharp blade fresh from the whetstone; youth is the most precious time of life.' He called China's students 'fresh, vigorous cells inside the human body', and exhorted them to 'drive out the rotten, corrupted cells' of the old guard. Six years later, in 1921, he co-founded the Chinese Communist Party with Beida's librarian, Li Dazhao. The librarian's assistant was a young man with a mole on his upper lip who had written an essay for the magazine on the importance of exercise. The byline: Mao Zedong.

When Mao founded the People's Republic of China in

1949 he declared May Fourth a national holiday, 'Youth Day'. Years later, when he felt the Chinese revolution needed to be reignited, he tapped the same rebellious young blood by forming the Red Guards from the ranks of middle and high schoolers. Beida was closed along with the other universities, except for a handful of students from politically correct backgrounds. All the knowledge required was in Mao's little red book. 'You young people,' read one of his quotations from a 1957 speech to Chinese students in Moscow, 'are in the bloom of life, like the sun at eight or nine in the morning . . . The world belongs to you. China's future belongs to you.'

That future, thankfully, died with Mao in 1976. When Deng Xiaoping reopened the universities in 1978 and trumpeted 'four modernisations' to reform China, dissent resurfaced in what was later called a 'Beijing Spring'. On a strip of brick wall to the west of the leaders' complex of Zhongnanhai, public posters were permitted to criticise the Mao years. It was nicknamed Democracy Wall after one of the posters went further to demand the 'fifth modernisation' of democracy, declaring 'we do not want to serve as mere tools of dictators'. It earned the author, a twenty-eight year-old former Red Guard called Wei Jingsheng, a prison bunk for eighteen years.

The iconoclasm of the decade that followed was likened to coming out of the dark to be dazzled by the day. Throughout the eighties, Chinese students were exposed to fresh culture and ideas – free to experiment with long hair and listen to jazz – and with that came the hope that a new politics might also be born. In 1986 and 1987 small-scale student demonstrations called for faster political reform. And in April 1989, when Fred was three, Beida students marched again on Tiananmen Square, this time from their new campus in the north-east which had been relocated in the fifties.

At first they went to mourn the death of Hu Yaobang, a reformist official who had been purged in the wake of the 1986 protests. They were joined by students from other colleges, and before long the growing crowd was demanding official accountability, a free press, greater personal freedoms: not a new government, but a better one. Numbers swelled. Workers joined. Hunger strikes began. The Goddess of Democracy was unveiled, a ten-metre-high papier-mâché statue holding her flame aloft to face off the portrait of Mao above the gate of the Forbidden City. Students signed a 'New May Fourth Manifesto'. Seventy years on, China's elite youth had reconnected the thread of their legacy of protest. A month later, they died for it.

*

The anniversary of 4 June 1989 is a muted affair in the grounds of Peking University. The original 'triangle' of concrete near the library where the students first assembled has been built over, with another one paved nearby. Student supervisors warn student union leaders to keep an eye out for troublemakers, and the university assigns a couple of its regular security guards to roam the triangle, checking that no banners are unfurled. The guards have a boring job:

there is never any drama, just another quietly leafy summer day. The only new feature is the occasional foreign reporter, out fishing.

Although Fred would never have dreamt of marking the anniversary herself, she was surprised at the indifference of her peers. For many of them, accurate information about the protests was swallowed in the black hole of patriotic education. History textbooks either gloss over the Tiananmen protests entirely or throw in a few lines about a 'student upheaval', in which subversive Western forces tried to destabilise the country while protest leaders acted out of self-interest. The massacre itself is subject to strict state-sponsored amnesia, and 4 June is a date the Party would rather scrub from the calendar. Online, it's safer to call it 35 May.

More students knew full well what the day signified – they just had other priorities. Too young to remember the rebellious mood of 1989, they face intense competition for success in an environment where there is more to gain from silence and everything to lose from speech. Collective history is of less concern than individual futures. Besides, some of the hopes articulated by the Tiananmen generation had been achieved. 'What do we want?' said student leader Wu'er Kaixi. 'Nike shoes. Lots of free time to take our girl-friends to a bar. The freedom to discuss an issue with someone. And to get a little respect from society.' The post-Tiananmen generation already had most of that, went the argument, so why risk losing it?

It was only at Beida that Fred found out the full story

for herself. Outside the classroom, her professors – some of whom had participated in or supported the protests – were surprisingly keen to talk about it. She watched the American documentary *The Gate of Heavenly Peace* about the demonstration and killings, which a student had posted on a university bulletin-board thread (it didn't stay up long). Like others around her she skirted online censorship through proxies, 'climbing the wall' as it was called, to read accounts of the protests from the Western and Hong Kong presses. She saw the iconic picture of the tank man, and more graphic images too: dead students and soldiers, charred bodies on roads she had walked down.

Her first feeling was of betrayal. China's military was meant to protect its people, not kill them. For all the hours of education instilling love of country, why had none of her teachers mentioned this before, let alone her parents? She appreciated the irony that the June Fourthers were killed on orders from the same Communist government that emerged from the legacy of the May Fourthers. But another truth was just as apparent to her: China had changed all over again between 1989 and now.

Far from protesting against the Communist Party, Beida students were now clambering over each other to join it. The Party was 80 million strong and keen to swell its ranks further by co-opting elite students. Every primary school child is a member of the Young Pioneers, and many middle- and high-schoolers join the Communist Youth League (Fred did when she was fourteen), but it is only at college age that full Party membership becomes possible. Careerism, rather than politics, motivates most of the eligible candidates. Being a Party member is useful CV padding, a shiny red feather in your cap, especially when angling for competitive jobs in a state-owned enterprise or bank.

At other universities, only the best students are invited by their supervisors to apply. At Beida they are all the best. The application form is as long as the emperor's robes and includes an essay explaining your reasons for applying and political stance, as well as a backlog of termly 'thought reports'. No one bothers to write those reports during college but samples are easy to find online to copy and paste – it's all cookie cutter anyway, expressing patriotism, love of socialism and optimism for the future. It isn't uncommon for a student to knock out two years' worth of thought reports in a weekend.

In Fred's Politics department, to the best of her knowledge, every single one of her classmates applied. Everyone except her. It was less than a week into her first term before a senior student-union member invited her to give it a try – with her marks and an official in the family, she was the perfect candidate. But she had no interest in joining for joining's sake. Fred wanted to be an academic like her mother, she could take or leave the CV-booster, and she disliked empty political posturing. Precisely because she was a daughter of the Party, she was too close to the system to have any illusions about it.

Back home on Hainan, her father had been promoted again, and was now in the administration of an inland town. With new power came new false friends. Some developers offered direct bribes, which he turned down. The more cunning among them appealed to his fatherhood. Fred remembers one time in her first year at Beida when he called her to discuss a proposal from a well-connected businessman who said he could get her into college overseas for graduate study and would pay all her fees. That was a sweeter offer, but they rejected it too.

Cramming in the library, surrounded by the intellectual history of China's past, it was hard for Fred not to feel those revolutionary thinkers were just gathering dust. State presence was keenly felt on campus, where the Party secretary was more powerful than the college president. There might be busts of Beida's anti-establishment figures on display but their stone silence was contagious. Fred's professors knew where the red line was: not an overt diktat but a tacit understanding of what not to say.

She was at the birthplace of May Fourth and the Tiananmen protests, the origin of the New Culture Movement and Chinese communism. But her peers were a different kind of new youth, and a generation divorced from history. The tradition of student protest was broken. What new ideologies had replaced it, besides materialism and careerism, she was yet to discover. For now, after a century of dissent, no one seemed to care.

DAHAI

Dahai couldn't care less about his own degree, Computer Science at Wuhan University. It was his parents who had pressured him into choosing the subject for its employment prospects, regardless of whether he liked it or not. Distant tracks were laid early.

His four years at college were still the best of his life, twelve hours by train away from Beijing in the capital of Hubei, his birth province. Wuhan, where the first shots were fired in the Xinhai Revolution that brought down the Qing dynasty in 1911, is a sprawling metropolis that straddles the Yangtze. Locals call it 'river city', and when fog rolls over the waters past Yellow Crane Pagoda the scene can be ethereally beautiful. It's just far enough south to miss out on central heating in winter, which is only provided for cities above the Yangtze, but has an equally warming peppery cuisine. Dahai's college staple was 'dry hot noodles' mixed with thick peanut sauce and chilli paste.

His favourite haunt was Zebra cafe, named after an oddity of the local dialect in which a zebra – *ge banma* – sounds like the slang for 'fuck'. Dahai and his friends holed up there to chain-smoke and play board games set in ancient Chinese warring kingdoms. In his dorm after hours, they roleplayed at *Killers*, a talking-based group game popular in China at the time. He played computer games too, mostly the shoot-'em-up *Counter Strike*, in which he liked best to hide in tower windows and wait for the others to come out into the open below, before picking them off one by one. There was nothing more satisfying than a clean Player Kill.

On weekend nights he went to the web of interconnecting lakes, laced with long bridges, not far from Wuhan university in the south-east of the city. Here was Vox livehouse, which hosted alternative music gigs. Behind the stage, painted in cursive English, were the words '*Voice of Youth, Voice of Freedom*'. It took Dahai a few visits before he deciphered the meaning, but when he did he liked the sound of it. With friends he formed an amateur band – he played acoustic guitar – and in empty rooms on idle afternoons they butchered Coldplay covers. It was the first time he felt the space around him to sing.

As the workload was easier than in high school, he spent most of his time procrastinating online. Instead of gaming, he preferred to scroll through the university bulletin-board forums or BBS, where students discussed anything and everything. He chatted on QQ, the instant-messaging service, and he bookmarked Sina.com, a commercial news site filled with cramped articles in a tiny font. It was still subject to state censorship but Dahai trusted it more than the print newspapers, which with a few brave exceptions were mouthpieces written in Party-speak. His rule of thumb when it came to the news was: if it wasn't online, it wasn't true.

Best of all he liked the blogs. Blogging was still a relatively new form in China in the mid-2000s, embraced mostly by those with something different to say. The first Chinese blog to take off, in 2003, was the sex diary of a woman in her twenties, Muzi Mei. Sina provided the most popular platform and soon hosted millions of blogs, of which a handful skirted the political red line. The artist Ai Weiwei openly mocked the government in his, and years later was shut down for it. But Dahai's favourite was that of the dropout novelist he had read in school, Han Han.

After his early literary success, Han Han spent as much time race-car driving on the Shanghai circuit as he did writing, and his chiselled good looks didn't hurt the brand. He started blogging in 2006, posting a mix of personal and social commentary with a healthy dose of cynicism. Before long the sharpness of his wit as well as his jawline had made him the most-read blogger in the world, with over 300 million hits, and comments in the hundreds below each post. Born in 1982 he was just three years older than Dahai (their birthdays are three days apart), and his core audience were all post-80s too.

'This generation is really quite traditional,' reads one of Han Han's blog posts from Dahai's time at Wuhan. 'Society at large, however, gives them plenty of negative labels. They're "self-oriented," we're told, or they "don't care about politics." This is unfair. To be self-oriented is actually not a bad thing, and many expressions of this focus on the self are a direct consequence of the one-child policy.' Han Han continues: 'As for charging them with not caring about politics, that's a ridiculous claim. In the current environment, politics isn't something one can't afford to care about.' But he isn't all pessimism: 'On the other hand, we can happily note that this generation has improved general standards of conduct: basic things like not littering, spitting or cutting in line are good habits established by those born after the Cultural Revolution ended.'

In the spring of 2008, Dahai's final term at university, Han Han reacted coolly to a sequence of dramatic events. In March there were riots in Tibet, and protests during the Olympic torch rally in Paris inspired a boycott of French goods in China ('not patriotism but a game for losers,' chimed in Han Han). In May an earthquake killed tens of thousands in Sichuan, and Sharon Stone called it karmic retribution for Chinese oppression of Tibet ('if you look at her actual words, we have no reason to be angry'). Corruption scandals among officials continued to break apace ('if all of them could restrict themselves to eight hundred thousand yuan in bribes over thirteen years,' Han Han sarcastically wrote of a later scandal, 'this would be a heaven-sent blessing').

To Dahai, reading Han Han's posts and the comments was more than an Internet connection – it was a very real connection to the rest of his generation, across the nation. He had never felt engaged with his society until he went online and saw people his age talking about the same things as he was. Most of those topics were mundane: popular culture, personal lives. But social issues crept in at the edges, and commenters were angry about the same things too: inequality, pressure and unfair competition for limited resources, while those born rich took the lion's share of the spoils of China's development.

In June 2008, as the Beijing Olympics neared, Dahai graduated. He now held a bachelor's degree in a subject he despised, and found that there were no jobs in which to use it anyway. Competition for white-collar work was just too fierce, and tens of thousands of other graduates had picked computer science for the same reason he had. According to official statistics college graduate unemployment in China hovers around the ten per cent mark, but more realistic estimates put it at sixteen per cent, and others as high as twenty-five per cent. That was another reason why young people had time to post on blogs – and another reason why so many of their comments were bitter.

In the end Dahai's father scored him a job. The People's Liberation Army owned massive interests in construction, and had once overseen many of the engineering work units that built China's major infrastructure projects: its railways, roads and bridges. Those construction firms had technically split from the PLA in the mid-eighties, but they kept close links and were still state owned. Through his army connections, Dahai's dad found a team-leader position for his son at one of them. It was a stable job with good prospects, but once again in a field Dahai didn't enjoy. It also meant moving away from his new-found freedom in Wuhan, and back to the capital.

*

He started work on 1 August, one week before the Games began at 8pm on 8/8/08 ('eight' is a lucky number in China as it sounds like the word for 'make money'). Olympic fever was breaking, coverage blanketed all channels, and Beijing swarmed with tourists and volunteers. The streets had been scrubbed clean, while migrant workers and pancake sellers had been kicked off them. The Olympic torch above the Bird's Nest stadium waited to be lit. A dedicated subway line had been built connecting straight to the Olympic village – line eight – and further lines were planned. The city was more attractive than ever above ground, but below it was still being made.

Underground was where Dahai went. The China Railway —th Construction Bureau Ltd. (the number is redacted at Dahai's request) is one of several that made real on blueprints passed down from on high, mostly building railway and subway lines. Dahai's work unit was digging a tunnel from Beijing Station near the city centre to Beijing West Station 9.6 kilometres away. When it was finished there would be a dedicated rail link between the two, to help passengers make connecting trains. The project necessitated demolishing homes whose foundations were in the way, so it wasn't due for completion until 2014.

Digging teams had already set off, one from each end.

Dahai's team worked from a tunnel entrance two kilometres west of the central rail station, so as not to disturb traffic. The site was closed off with corrugated steel sheets, each emblazoned with the —th Construction Bureau's name. There was a gated front entrance, and also a loose panel that gave access from the back, if you knew where to look. Just inside was a full-length mirror, and a poster next to it checklisted the kit you should wear to go further: hard hat, thick boots, eyewear for the dust, a harness if necessary.

The mouth of the pit was roofed over by a tall metal hut, with a mechanised platform inside to bring a digging crane down and lift earth back out. Red banners hung next to it – just like those at Dahai's school – exhorting workers to 'actively outdo expectations' and 'carefully control standardisation'. To one side, a staircase zigzagged down eight flights into the pit. The tunnel itself was wide, straight and domed, as if built for a monstrous snake god. The way was lit by dots of electric light, tracing the way like tea lamps through dirt-choked air until their glow disappeared in the distance.

At the railing before the tunnel, hazard signs recited all the ways you could be injured, each with a helpful illustration inside a yellow-and-black triangle. Man falling down pit, rock falling on man, steel girder falling on man, work tool hitting man, man's arm being trapped in machinery, man being electrocuted, man being consumed by flames underground, earth collapsing under man's feet. Another two circles with red lines through them were reminders not to work while drunk or carry flammable goods. A safety officer was assigned to the team too, lest the signs be ignored.

There were roughly a dozen men in Dahai's team (out of a total of forty to fifty in the work unit) and most of them were migrants with less education than he had. Although many were older than him, as a university graduate he was directing their engineering work in the tunnel as a 'technician'. He was unclear quite how a degree in computer science qualified him for that. His monthly salary was 1,800 yuan – not much, but it was a job and that was more than some of his peers could hope for. The main downside was the hours: eight- to ten-hour day or night shifts, alternating weekly, seven days a week. The only days off were national holidays.

While his team slept, a second team took over for the other shift. To further maximise efficiency, the dorms for workers were on site, a J-shaped building above ground inside the same fence as the pit, each room bunking four. There was also a canteen, a small car park, an administrative office with a blueprint of the tunnel plan, a meeting room for official functions, and another private canteen for entertaining visiting bosses, off limits to the grunts. More slogans were hung around the length of the building. A theme emerged: '*Standardise management policy*' . . . '*Standardise work allocation*' . . . '*Standardise procedure*'.

The tunnel site was where Dahai lived, slept, ate and worked. His morning commute took thirty seconds. There were restaurants in the area if he felt like a good meal and a beer, but otherwise there was no reason to leave the perimeter. Everything he needed was provided for him by his employer. The whole arrangement was a throwback to the Mao era, when work units or *danwei* were assigned to you out of school or college. Back then your work unit controlled almost every aspect of your life, even giving permission for marriages. Those days were gone but the work units remained, and it was Dahai's habit to simply call his job 'the *danwei*'.

While the Olympics and Paralympics played out, Dahai watched a few events on TV with national pride but not much interest. When it was all over everyone breathed a sigh of relief that it had gone without hitch, and Beijing returned to normal. Only then did it sink in for Dahai that this was his life now. After his childhood in the military compound, his horizons had widened in college only to narrow dramatically again – once more he was fenced in. When he put on his hard hat and descended into the pit, he looked along the length of the tunnel and saw that for him too, there was only one direction.

XIAOXIAO

Xiaoxiao had made it out of her home town, if only by a little. Harbin is the provincial capital of Heilongjiang, and one step closer to those far-away places she fantasised about, but still the frigid north-east. The train journey from her birthplace of Nehe to her college in Harbin passed by the oil fields of Daqing, which provide a good portion of China's energy. Out of the window she gazed at the hundreds of small oil rigs flitting by, dipping their metal beaks to the ground as they levered the pump, like toy birds that dunk down to drink the liquid below them before bobbing back up. She called them kowtow machines.

At the end of the nineteenth century, Harbin was a low spread of mostly wooden houses, the main trading link with Siberia. The Russians who crossed the border over the next century (called the 'old hairy ones' by elderly Chinese) left their mark on its rising architecture, from the brightly coloured onion domes of St Sofia Church to the cobbled streets that vein the city centre. Orthodox steeples shot up like bamboo. Thousands of Jews fled east to escape the pogroms and they too settled in Harbin, building synagogues next to the churches.

In twenty-first-century Harbin, the familiar refrains of urban China coexist with its frontier eccentricities. The Songhua River that runs through the city is frozen solid for half of the year, used by ice-fishers, tourist sleighers and death-wish swimmers. North of the river is a Siberian Tiger Park where visitors can feed live goats to the tigers or ride out into the enclosure with a squawking chicken tied to the roof of their jeep. Every winter the streets are lined with swans and horses carved out of ice, and a ticketed park fills with tourists for the Ice Sculpture Festival, which has everything from thirty-metre-high recreations of the Empire State Building to a Goliath Father Christmas.

At Harbin Normal University ('Normal' is a common English prefix for Chinese teaching colleges) Xiaoxiao spent five happy years studying art. She was fast friends with her dorm mates, in particular a girl from the far north called Wen Jing, from whom she was inseparable. During the day they ate yoghurt ice lollies next to the Songhua, and watched the mail train chundling across the iron bridge that the Russians built. At night they ate on a street of cheap restaurants outside campus. Their favourite was a local-style barbecue joint that grilled anything that could fit on a skewer, from cabbage to caterpillar pupa to sliced bread (almost, but not quite, bringing toast to China).

On idle afternoons they sat on the edge of the basketball court next to their dorms, and watched the boys show off. North-eastern men have a reputation for being tall and tough, and the college boys took pains to live up to it. Some of them wore bling – gold chains and rings – and bantered in heavily accented local slang. Women are often taller in the north-east too, but Xiaoxiao had settled at exactly five foot – living up to her pet name 'little Xiao' – with a wide face, delicate features and soft smile. She didn't like the bragging and posturing of the boys around her, which she called restless. She had a boyfriend in college, but they split up on graduation day.

That same day, her mother told her she should find two things as soon as possible: a stable job, and a husband. Like most Chinese mothers, she had disapproved of Xiaoxiao dating while still a student, but at graduation expected her daughter to immediately find a life partner. Xiaoxiao thought that was unfair, but understood it was the mindset of her parents' generation: many of them had been virgins before marriage, and felt that a woman's life was only secure with a husband. Society had changed too quickly for them to keep up. She brushed her mother off, and focused on what to do with her new-found independence.

One of Xiaoxiao's favourite pastimes was going to the movies. The year after she graduated a Chinese blockbuster called *The Promotion Diaries of Du Lala* was released, based on a novel. The story follows a pretty female protagonist who lands an entry-level position at an international company and rises in the ranks (facilitated, depressingly, by a relationship with a senior male co-worker) until she is a high-flying sales executive with designer handbags to match. Each time Du Lala gets promoted, the figure of her new salary tallies up on screen, next to a shot of her putting on a more expensive pair of shoes: 3,000 yuan a month –

3,500 – 6,000 – 25,000! The film ends when she gets back together with her boss.

It was a model many of Xiaoxiao's classmates emulated, applying for starting positions in big companies and banks – not iron rice bowls, but sleek silver ones. This was the next stage of the path laid out for the post-80s, which starts with the *gaokao* and ends with having kids of your own. But a survey showed that over half of post-80s college graduates were dissatisfied with their job. Xiaoxiao had something different in mind: small-business entrepreneurship, an appealing alternative for those among her peers who wanted to escape the rat race. Du Lala be damned, she would be her own boss.

*

She had discussed the idea with her best friend Wen Jing a few months before they left university. There was a place they knew in an alley behind the street of cheap restaurants: a half-abandoned *dakou* CD shop, between a dry cleaner's and a primary school, that was closing down. It thrust out from the street front, and was misbuilt so the front door hovered a half-metre above ground level, with steps leading up. The walls were chipped brick, the interior spartan. Their plan was to transform it into an artistic clothes shop for the college crowd. That summer they put their heads and their savings together, and rented it for 1,750 yuan a month.

The shop was in pitiful condition when they were handed the keys, but Xiaoxiao and Wen Jing got creative on a budget. They trawled second-hand markets for cheap furniture, and hung a chandelier from the ceiling through the middle of a mirror inside a picture frame. They strung fairy lights across the walls, and suspended pot plants inside empty medicine bottles on strings. With the help of friends they knocked up a roofed conservatory outside the elevated front door, as a chill-out space, and placed a tattered sofa inside. There was a counter and clothing racks, hemp curtains and handmade art everywhere.

They spent hours customising retro women's clothes – embroidering designs, artfully ripping jeans, threading beaded accessories – and slowly filled the racks. All the shop needed was a name. Wen Jing had adopted three kittens that lived inside: Tigress, the fiercest; Jiong, named for a Chinese character (囧) that looks like a surprised face; and Lowly, the runt of the litter. They thought of calling the place Three Cats Home, but in the end decided that an English word would be more fashionable. There was one that Xiaoxiao liked in particular, for the roundness of its sound as much as its elegaic meaning. They painted it on the front of the store in careful white cursive: *Remember*.

The vibe was something between hippie and hipster, best described by a trending Chinese phrase at the time, 'artistic youth'. One online meme was to illustrate the three types of post-80s youth with variations on a theme. The *putong qingnian* or 'ordinary youth' were office drones, indistinguishable in a crowd: they wore their watch normally. The *wenyi qingnian* or 'artistic youth' put on airs to be seen as cool and different: they twisted their watchface to the underside of the wrist. The *erbi qingnian* or 'dumbass youth' were the punch line of the visual joke: they strapped the watch around their ankle.

The clientele at Remember was artistic youth too, students seeking beaded bracelets or thick-rimmed lenseless specs to set them apart on campus. Xiaoxiao and Wen Jing's old university classmates dropped by from time to time to sit on the conservatory sofa, play with the cats and chat. It became a hideaway for their friends and regulars, even if few of them bought anything. Xiaoxiao had a Polaroid camera, another badge of the artistic youth, and took pictures of everything. A group meal – click. A new decoration – click. Tigress trying her best to tear the sofa apart – click, click, click. The whitewashed Polaroids whirred out of the camera, and she shook them into life.

Xiaoxiao had a string of hobbies, and went through a phase where she was obsessed with the Western zodiac. Chinese astrology was passé but the West was exotic, and her birth year of the ox didn't mean as much to her as her star sign, Virgo ('maiden' in Chinese). Her ideal match was Taurus ('golden bull') or Cancer ('giant crab'), and the least compatible was Libra ('sky scales'). She believed blood type was a personality indicator too – another fashion among post-80s, this time an import from Japan. Type Bs like her were honest and creative, a good fit for a more conservative type A. ABs were picky and demanding, Os were stubborn and impulsive.

Next she developed an interest in Buddhism, which was newly resurgent in China. Once-destroyed temples were renovated and fitted with turnstiles. Souvenir stalls were set up outside them, selling religious trinkets to enlighten your wallet. Businessmen bought good karma by donating to a Buddhist master, who prayed on their behalf for success in their deals. Xiaoxiao felt disdain for the commercialisation of urban Buddhism, but hers was more a vague spiritualism still. She liked the accoutrements best, the dangling prayer beads, and the faith itself was just another accessory.

Her search was for meaning beyond the material. Idolatry of money was everywhere around her: the Du Lalas of the world, the *baijinnü* ('money-worshipping girls') who window-shopped Harbin's famously expensive animal furs. Xiaoxiao wanted something beyond money to give her life a sense of purpose. She read about Tibet, and dreamt of travelling to Lhasa – projecting the same spiritual ideals onto the Tibetan plateau that the West does. *On the Road* was one of her favourite books.

The shop was making a small profit by the end of its first year, but neither she nor Wen Jing put their minds to expanding the business. Remember was Xiaoxiao's respite from a high-pressure society and the mark of her independence. It was somewhere to call her own, even if she fantasised of going further. She knew it would be years before she might make good on those daydreams of travel. But for now, she was content not to be chasing promotions when there were sweeter memories to be made.

LUCIFER

Half a kilometre east of Peking University, in between a porridge stall and a restaurant specialising in duck head, a high wooden door guarded a dull grey-black building front. Idle during the day, at night the paving outside filled with students smoking cheap cigarettes and chugging Tsingtao beer out of dark green bottles. Most were in scruffy jeans and T-shirts, a few were in leather jackets with spiky Mohicans. When the letters 'D-22' stencilled across the top of the building lit up, the doors opened.

Inside, past the bar and a table football table that sloped to the right, a corridor of floor space ended in a raised stage, with a drum kit, lonely microphone stands and stray leads. Behind it were the graffiti-covered toilets and a backstage room, the walls an iconic deep crimson. From a balcony along one side, a punter could look down on the stage like Caesar surveying his gladiators. Photo portraits of bands, with the dressing-room red wall as background, hung around the smoke-veiled performance area – musicians contorting their faces in rock grimaces, showing off sleeve tattoos and piercings, staring down the camera lens or giving it the finger.

In the summer of 2007, when Lucifer made it to Beijing, D-22 was just hitting its stride as a rock-music venue. Rock had only come to China in the eighties, with giants like He Yong and Cui Jian, whose tune 'Nothing To My Name' became a theme song for the Tiananmen protesters. The hair waterfalls of metal band Tang Dynasty followed in the late nineties, and the punk of Brain Failure with its lead singer's leopard-print buzzcut. Each new generation brought a new sensibility and set of influences, cramming into a decade what the West had in half a century. The scene was underground only in the sense of being unnoticed by most young Chinese, who listened to sickly sweet pop from Hong Kong, Korea and Taiwan, as well as Avril Lavigne and Britney Spears.

That was true of Lucifer's classmates at Peking Opera and Art University, where he had scraped through his college entrance exams to get a place to study music (his score was 276 out of 700; the pass grade for vocational courses was 260). As at school, he didn't take his studies seriously. After three days of the compulsory military boot camp, he faked haemorrhoids to get excused and slept in until noon for the remainder. He left his dorm room to live with a friend. He skipped lectures and chased girls. By day, he learnt the five eras of classical music history, perfected his clarinet embouchure, and sang Do, Re, Mi, Fa, Sol, La, Ti, Do on loop with a singing instructor. By night, he made his own music.

Li Fan, his childhood friend, was in Beijing too, and they formed a band they had first cobbled together in high school. Li Fan learnt the drums, and Lucifer strummed chord progressions while improvising a melody over the top, singing meaningless Chinglish until a song gelled. All their favourite bands were foreign, and they wanted an English name for theirs too. Lucifer got his English dictionary out and paged through it. When he got into the Rs, the word *rustic* leapt out as it reminded him of the American band Rancid. He looked at the Chinese definition: *nongcunde*, of or relating to the countryside. He thought of his early childhood on the farms of Hebei province, and the name was settled. When he was world famous, he told himself, it would remind him of his roots.

Every weekend, Lucifer rode the bus for an hour and a half to D-22, at the opposite compass point of the city from his college. At one gig, while dancing madly in his loudest peacock outfit, he saw a middle-aged foreigner standing off to one side of the crowd, watching the musicians closely, always the first to clap at the end of a song. Lucifer bounced up and launched into his Crazy English self-introduction. The man was friendly and bought him a cheap beer, which won Lucifer over unconditionally. Only then did he discover he was talking to Michael Pettis, the owner.

Pettis is a former Wall Street bond trader and financial scholar at Peking University who founded and funded D-22 in 2006, hoping to kick-start a nascent music scene of the kind he had witnessed in New York in the seventies. While it existed the club was a creative crucible, a magnet for students, dropouts, hooligans and hipsters from all over China, united by their disaffection with mainstream culture. Their anthem was a song by the band Carsick Cars, 'Zhongh-nanhai' – the compound from which China's leaders rule, although the song is ostensibly about the cigarette brand of the same name. Pettis coined terms for the progression of Chinese rock from Cui Jian, 'generation one', to today. Lucifer's peers were 'generation six'.

Upstairs in his office, Pettis welcomed Rustic to gig at D-22. At first they played the Wednesday student band nights, and struggled to find their sound. When they needed a new bassist, Lucifer knew just who he wanted to ask. Wang Heyong had been in the year above at his high school in Shijiazhuang, although they didn't get along after Lucifer borrowed and broke one of his amplifiers. He was lanky and pale, with a bush of glam-metal hair and a rose tattoo on his upper arm. His on-stage style was all tight leather trousers, studded collars and buckets of mascara. For his stage name he chose Ricky Sixx, which he tattooed under the rose along with two Chinese characters for fire.

With Ricky, Lucifer wrote a dozen punk pop rock songs with titles such as 'Poison Beauty', 'Wild Woman' and 'Erotic Films'. The pair worked on stage routines too: a matching crouched stride timed to the bass line, synchronised flying kicks, leaning back to back and dipping low like guitar heroes. Green Day was a big influence for the music, Toy Dolls for the style. Lucifer rented a basement flat in the southern suburbs of Fengtai district for 200 yuan a month, but mostly he loitered on the curb of Drum Tower East Street, a strip of guitar shops and cafes that is a hub for hipsters and home to another livehouse, MAO.

After warming the stage for a bigger band called Joyside, Rustic developed their own fanbase. In December 2009 they performed their biggest gig yet at D-22, as the headline act. Lucifer took the stage in leopard-print trousers, a black-and-white polka-dotted shirt and a checked orange jacket, his trademark white-framed sunglasses covering his baby-cheeked face. Ricky Sixx had on matching leopard-skins, four different belts wrapped around his midriff, a short leather jacket with cowboy tassels open on his bare hairless chest, a black stocking up one arm to the elbow, metal-studded leather gloves, a neck choker and a spangly bandana holding back his unruly mop.

'*I have not seen your face for a long time*,' Lucifer croaked into the mic while picking out a guitar riff like a metronome. '*I wanna be dancing in your head*,' he breathed, plucking a distorted higher note like a bird call. '*I wanna hear your voice in my bed*,' while scanning the crowd for pretty girls. '*Now I am the king of your paradise*,' as Ricky pounded a wall of bass out of nowhere, Li Fan attacked his drums, and the speakers to either side of them trembled with the sudden volume.

'WILD WOMAN!' Lucifer and Ricky screamed the chorus together.

'WILD WOMAN!' Ricky stuck out his tongue and held the long head of his bass guitar straight up from his crotch, leaving no room for imagination.

'WILD WOMAN!' They caught each other's eye and timed an air-kick together.

'HEY YOU ASSHOLE.' The final line propelled

Lucifer into his guitar solo, part of which he performed while convulsing on his back on the floor.

The crowd below was mostly T-shirted students in glasses quietly bobbing their heads, but a few at the front moshed like madmen. As the last song of the set ended, one of them climbed up on stage, faced the audience Jesus-like and torqued his body off the platform onto a bed of raised hands. They carried him back while Lucifer and Ricky dragged out the wailing feedback – until the music cut out and the surfer was unceremoniously dumped, thudding to the dirty floor among the cigarette butts.

*

Rustic had achieved some fame among Beijing's counter-culture denizens, but Lucifer wanted more. When a Canadian expat mentioned a competition called Global Battle of the Bands, Lucifer's ears pricked up. He thought twice when he saw registration cost fifty yuan for each band member, but still signed Rustic up the next day.

Global Battle of the Bands or GBoB – Lucifer pronounced it as 'gbob', in one sound – was a live music competition with local qualifying heats and a grand final in London. The winner got ten thousand dollars in cash, a record deal for a single, and a golden statuette declaring them 'Best New Band in the World'. Lucifer knew it was inconceivable they would get that far. To even get to the London final, Rustic would first have to triumph in three separate rounds to be crowned China's representative.

The first heats were in Beijing, at a rock venue called

Yugong Yishan – 'The Old Fool Who Moved the Mountain', after Chairman Mao's favourite ancient proverb, of a
man who moves a mountain out of sheer stubbornness
when the gods take pity on him. '*I've got no bell end,*'
Lucifer sang in slurred English while wearing a school uniform. '*I am totally borastic. I never do the business. They call
me stupid Lucifer.*' He got close up behind Ricky, grinding
into him while the panel of judges took notes.

At the Beijing final, in front of an audience, the duo
pulled off all their stage antics. Halfway through the first
song, Lucifer took out his clarinet and played it instead of
the guitar solo, while Ricky reached across and strummed
his dangling guitar for him, until by the end they were both
stroking each other's guitar strings in a feedback-loop orgy.
The judges conferred, and announced to cheers that Rustic
was the winner. It may have helped that one of them was
the expat who had encouraged Lucifer to sign up to the
competition in the first place.

The China final was held in Hong Kong. It was Lucifer's
first time outside of the mainland, and his first plane ride.
He was taken aback by how hot and humid Hong Kong
was; even in December, the city felt like a jungle. Rustic's
show the next day would be at a venue called The Cavern,
in the jelly-shot-fuelled bar district of Lan Kwai Fong.
There were five bands competing, from Beijing, Shanghai,
Guangzhou and Macau as well as the Hong Kong home
team. This was Lucifer's biggest chance to make good on
his dream. The grand final in London was within reach.

The night before the performance, Lucifer had a powerful dream. He dreamt he was walking by the side of a river, with a fresh moist smell in the air and green trees all around him. On the other bank of the river was a flight of stone stairs, ascending too high into the sky to see their end. All of a sudden he was *on* the stairs, climbing up and up and up. At the top, beyond geography, was a house. Inside the house were an old woman and a little girl. He told the woman he didn't know where to go next. She smiled at him, took out two needles and jabbed them into the acupuncture points of his left hand, in the fleshy gap between his thumb and forefinger. Lucifer felt a surge of energy – and jumped straight out of the window.

He woke up in a sweat, and knew he was going to win.

MIA

Mia liked to stand at the back of the crowd. She came to D-22 once or twice a week, to nurse a beer, pull on a lipstick-coated cigarette and watch the gig at a safe distance from the moshpit. Across a concrete overpass from the club, on the other side of the honking main road, was her college, Tsinghua University.

Tsinghua is just as prestigious as Peking University next door, but has a reputation for science and engineering rather than the humanities, and lacks its rival's romantic charm. Each department building is a beached steel-and-concrete whale, and the canteens and sports facilities are built on just as industrial a scale. A grid of boulevards dissects the two square kilometres of campus, which flows with ten thousand rickety bikes as students weave their way to and from class. At those moments it can seem as if every Tsinghua student has the same buzz cut and wears the same thin-frame glasses – a sea of indistinguishable male nerds.

In that crowd, Mia immediately stood out. She was studying at the fashion school to the east of campus, a bohemian bubble among all the engineering majors. In her first year, reading about British fashion subcultures, she stumbled on pictures of sixties skinheads and decided to become one. For a woman that meant a skinhead feather cut – shaved crown with fringe, long sides and mullet at the back – but Mia went for a version of the bob instead, something between skinhead and punk inspired by her namesake, the character in *Pulp Fiction*. She was tall, with a beauty spot over her upper left lip and a pierced septum, and had swagger. On nights out she wore a leather jacket, fishnet stockings and denim skirt with knock-off Doc Martens.

It was only later that she discovered skinheads had a bad name abroad as violent or neo-Nazi. The milder culture of the original skinheads that she first learnt about came out of Jamaican music and working-class rebellion. There were fewer than ten other ersatz skinheads in Beijing by her estimate. They all went to the same gigs, and stayed up late after to eat Xinjiang-style kebabs on the kerbside before stumbling back to their beds, or sometimes to someone else's. The first nights Mia returned to her dorm in the small hours, the doorman on shift looked her up and down and refused to believe she was a Tsinghua student until she got her ID out (once not even then).

The next morning it was class as usual. Tsinghua Academy of Arts and Design is as self-consciously modern as the squiggly sculpture on the lawn outside it. Paintings and calligraphies line the corridors, which lead to workshops filled with a mess of half-finished student projects like art landfills. Upstairs is room C318: the 'Fashion Design Lab'.

Wooden workspaces as long as the trees they came from are dotted with sewing machines, fabric samples, rulers and supersized scissors. Rows of mannequins stand guard along the walls like headless Terracotta Warriors, with amputated arms and a conical ceiling lamp above each neck stump, as if it had sucked the noggin up.

This was where Mia learnt the tricks of her trade. In the lecture halls she was taught the history of fashion in China and the West, from Elizabethan ruffs to the Asian cheongsam dress. In the fashion lab she experimented for herself. One of her portfolio projects was recreating dresses from the Song dynasty that showed more leg than in a red-light district. Her classmates were for the most part rich-princess sorts, used to chintz and marble. At every step she was reminded of the conventions of feminine beauty in China that she so disdained.

In beauty magazines the models and celebrities were all pale and delicate, with a kittenish air. Adverts reminded women that their skin should be as white as possible. Pale skin was originally a status marker – those from higher rungs of society spent less time in the sun – but has since got mixed up with notions of innocence, purity and virginity. Chinese girls don't go to the tanning salon, they buy skin-whitening products. Photoshop is so widespread that the shorthand 'PS-ed' suffices to mock a touched-up photograph, and plastic surgery is common. The most popular cosmetic operation is to add the 'double eyelids' which most Asians are born without. Cheekbones are raised, noses thinned and chins sharpened to look like a snake or fox spirit – the vixen demons of Chinese legend that took the form of beautiful women to tempt men before quite literally eating their hearts.

On dating sites or on Renren, a clone of Facebook, Chinese girls all seem to go for the same look in their profile picture selfies. Camera angle from above, pouting lips, eyes as large as possible (often made larger by special contact lenses or photo editing tools). Their cutesy expressions are straight out of Japanese and Korean TV, often accompanied by a hand gesture: two fingers in Vs below bow-tied hair, or hands scrunched up next to rouged cheeks as if whiskers. The infantilisation seeps into dating culture too. Girlfriends throw coquettish fits like spoiled children, with much flailing of arms, playful slapping and foot stamping. Boyfriends supposedly find it endearing, and it even has a name: *sajiao*, 'lovable tantrums'. Beds overflowing with cuddly toy animals aren't unusual for girls well into their twenties. Dependence is confused with desirability.

Mia thought the fox-spirit girls looked factory-produced: made in China. She called them 'babies', mocking their dress sense – gaudy sequined T-shirts with random English words on them – and their habit of saying 'very *fashion*' in English to show off. Some Chinese boys were too effeminate for her tastes also, especially if they agreed to carry their girlfriend's handbag or to wear matching outfits in public. (If they didn't agree, the persuasive power of the lovable tantrum would be unleashed.) Her own boyfriend worked as a stage-hand at the livehouse Yugong Yishan, rigging set lights. His English name, appropriately, was Setlight. He was Han

Chinese from Xinjiang just like her, and made from tougher stock.

Mia enjoyed being different. Her skin was darker, a gift from the beating sun of her childhood, and she sunbathed whenever she had the chance. She wouldn't have thrown a lovable tantrum if her life depended on it. Although her get-up was skinhead, she listened to everything from punk to hip hop. One song by the rap crew she liked the best, Yinsan'r, is called 'Beijing hoodlums'. It opens to bestial growls and fades out to gunfire, while the lyrics idolise drinking and guns. But underneath the derivative machismo is a real anger at the machine. 'Which child hasn't been forced to endure education,' goes one lyric, 'only to come out with a degree and become a stupid cunt cut from the same mould?'

Instead, Mia indulged in her own private rebellion. Each punk night out was an act of resistance against the milky-white Lolitas around her. After gigs at D-22 and Yugong, she stayed up with Setlight until the sun rose – at a more reasonable hour in Beijing than what they were used to in their childhoods in the far west.

*

By the next time Mia visited home in Urumqi, the mood had changed dramatically. That summer of 2009, riots shocked Xinjiang's capital. The catalyst was three thousand miles away in a Guangdong factory, where six Uighur workers were wrongly accused of raping two Han Chinese girls. Two Uighurs died in the ensuing brawl, and repressed grievances back in Xianjiang bubbled out from under the lid. On 5 July, street protests outside Urumqi's Grand Bazaar turned violent. Rioters threw stones, burnt Han-owned shops and cars, attacked civilians. Over a hundred people died – both Han killed by Uighurs, and Uighurs killed by the police – before order was restored.

For the Uighurs, there was ample cause to be angry. Investment in the region was seen to benefit Chinese immigrants, like Mia's family, while Uighurs felt they were second-class citizens in their ancestral homeland. Rules forbade religious head coverings and prevented schoolchildren from going to the mosque. Fasting customs during Ramadan were discouraged by local authorities. Uighur language and culture were diluted by a patronising colonial-rule mindset. A handful of radicals wanted to split as an independent nation, East Turkestan. The overwhelming majority wanted more simple, everyday freedoms and rights.

From the Han Chinese perspective, Uighurs were biting the hand that fed them. For some, the violence confirmed their stereotype that Uighurs were crude and barbarous. Two days after the riots thousands of Han migrants gathered for a counter-demonstration, and tensions simmered while the city divided into uneasy de facto segregation. Where before the two worlds ran parallel, now they faced off. Han families were afraid to go to Uighur quarters in the south of the city, and told their children not to play with Uighur kids. They spoke of 7/5 in the same way that Americans talk of 9/11, with a before and an after.

When Mia was in Urumqi later that summer for the

holidays, the Internet had been switched off in reaction to the riots. It would remain so for the next ten months, all but completely shut off across Xinjiang while mobile-phone service was also restricted. The area around the Grand Bazaar was watched over by truckfuls of People's Armed Police soldiers. Mia's mother didn't mince her words about the Uighurs, calling them uncivilised and savage. She had exactly the same opinion about her daughter's skinhead look and clothes. Mia nodded along blankly to it all, like she had learnt to as a child. To her, it was as if her parents preferred her to be docile than happy.

In that respect she identified with the Uighurs. They had become like skinheads in society's eyes – threatening, even violent – but no one took the effort to understand their culture or the reasons for their rebellion. Like them, she wanted to be apart from the rest of China. But her mindfulness of Xinjiang's status ended there. It would always be the home she wanted to leave behind. She didn't follow its politics, or politics at all. The only Zhongnanhai she cared about were the cigarettes she smoked. And if 5 July was a failed independence day for radical Uighurs, Mia was concerned only with her own independence.

She turned twenty that same summer, and knew she wanted to make a career in the fashion world. Every day she felt excited – at times smug – to be a Tsinghua student, cream of the crop. And every night she escaped to those places where she could be unique and not be judged for it. All she wanted was to decide her own future, independently. It wasn't easy, but it was worth rebelling for.

SNAIL

Snail flew on dragon-back across the Great Sea of Azeroth. He soared over the islands of Kezan and Zandalar, and above the candy swirl of the Maelstrom vortex which hides the aquatic city of Nazjatar, to land on the western continent of Kalimdor. To the south were the Caverns of Time, where the dread wyrm Nozdormu lay undisturbed since the War of the Ancients. Snail let him lie a few aeons more, and set off across the Abyssal Sands to where his true foe lurked.

Meanwhile, in the flesh-and-blood realm of the Internet bar outside the east gate of China Mining and Technology University, Snail stared at pixels on a screen. His lunch breaks in *World of Warcraft* had turned into afternoons, the afternoons into mornings, the mornings into days. He skipped lectures, blagged assignments, and designed a rota with his classmates who took turns covering for each other at roll call. Soon he was spending ten hours a day in Azeroth. All-night sessions were a regular habit. His longest marathon was sixty hours straight – three days and two nights – eating hot meals for five yuan out of boxes trolleyed by, washing them down with sugary drinks to keep his energy high. His mouse hand darted purposefully as his fingers tapped and clicked like gunfire. His eyes never left his avatar, a scantily clad female elf mage.

Un'Goro Crater steamed to the west. The air was humid and the devilsaurs were wild. Passing out of the sands, he skirted the Lakkari Tar Pits to the foot of Fire Plume Ridge, a looming mountain of volcanic rock. It's a good spot for mining essence of fire, if you can withstand the temperatures of up to 428,000 degrees Kraklenheit. At the peak lived Blazerunner, a powerful fire elemental best snuffed out with the Silver Totem of Aquementas. Snail began the long climb.

It was more than an escape: the game offered a sense of accomplishment that three-dimensional life lacked. On campus he was just another country boy in the city, and when he graduated he would be just another worker ant. In *World of Warcraft* he was *someone*, with experience and gold and war gear that commanded the respect of other players. But at the back of his mind he recognised his compulsion. It was the brain buzz, the dopamine rush when he hit that glowing power-on button or heard the sound of the game firing up, promising hours of oblivion. Just thinking about it triggered a cycle of desire and response he could no longer fight. His right brain compelled him to play even as his left brain told him not to. He knew he was wasting time, that his elf's achievements meant nothing outside the fantasy world. He tried to quit again and again. But he always came back.

The summit was in sight. Green smoke hung in the air

and lava veined the mountainside. The heat was unbearable, and Snail was losing health as fast as he could replenish it with spells. Blazerunner would be nearby now, poised for the ambush. Snail climbed a craggy ridge and charged his mana, steeling himself for the battle ahead – oblivious to a new danger in the south-east.

At the entrance to the Internet bar, two humanoids walked in. They were older than the usual clientele, wearing shabby clothing and with a rough look to them. Prowling the aisles they scanned the hundreds-strong sea of gamers, each face buried in its monitor. Sighting their unsuspecting target, they honed in on him with terrifying speed and accuracy.

Snail pulled out the Silver Totem of Aquementas, holding it high to shine forth in righteous light. But raising his eyes he faced the surprise attack from a more fearsome enemy still. It reared out of nowhere above his screen, with fiery eyes that sent an icy chill through his bones, the two-headed dread demon – his mum and dad.

'MIAO LIN!!'

Snail was so fixated on the game that he hadn't conceived of peril from outside it. His monitor was tucked away in the dark at the back of the bar, next to the VIP seating. Of all interruptions the last he expected was his parents, whom he had left behind in his village in Anhui. Ever since his supervisor first rang to tell them about his gaming habit, his mum had urged him to stop. Now she had recruited his father, and together they had orchestrated the intervention.

The next minute was a blur, but Snail remembers his father yanking him by his ear clear out of his seat, dragging him down the aisle and bundling him out of the Internet bar before he could even log out of his account. While his elf floundered in the lava, rudderless, Snail was pulled out of *World of Warcraft* to face something he hadn't seen in a long time: sunlight.

*

The Chinese Health Ministry first declared Internet addiction a clinical disorder in 2008, but the media had diagnosed it long before. The definition (alarmingly) was spending six or more hours online a day. Network games were dubbed 'electronic heroin' by state experts, rotting the brains of the nation's youth, and the number of Internet addicts was estimated in the tens of millions. Cartoon policemen popped up on screens, telling gamers to take a break. In 2005, a South Korean played for fifty hours without eating or sleeping, and died at his keyboard. Another picture that did the rounds later was of a Taiwanese gamer found dead in an Internet bar, with rigor mortis so that one arm still stretched towards the keyboard, the other reaching for the mouse.

For Snail, the game didn't feel like an addiction – it felt like home. His perspective was like that of the film *War of Internet Addiction*, uploaded to Chinese video sites in early 2010 by the user 'sexy corn'. A feature-length machinima film, made using screengrabs of live-action play from within World of Warcraft, it starts as a pastiche of the *Terminator* films and goes on to criticise government censorship of gaming. 'We are the generation that grew up playing games,' one digital troll (of the literal, green kind) says in an impassioned speech to his censor. 'Our love of the game and the vulnerable position of its players in this society has not changed . . . What sucked us in was not the game but the sense of belonging the game gave to us. We dutifully go to work in crowded buses. We consume our food despite the unknown chemicals inside. We don't complain about our pitiful salaries . . . Why can't we have one yuan per hour of cheap fun?'

The censor is impassive. 'Nice speech,' he says, 'but it's useless. You have a voice, so what? The power behind me can easily overwhelm all of your voices.'

'How can we not speak out just because our voices are small,' the troll replies. 'Everyone in front of their screen, raise your hand and send your power to me. When they killed YouTube, you didn't raise your hand. When they blocked Twitter, you didn't raise your hand. Now we may lose *WoW* too. I know we're just "fart people" . . . but at least you can raise your hand in front of your screen, and pass your voice and power to me through the web. For our only emotional home, let's shout together: We are *WoW* gamers!'

For Snail's mother and father, it was all a bit hard to grasp. In rural Anhui, the notion of elf mages vanquishing fire demons was remote to say the least. But they knew what slacking off was. Snail's father reminded him of the opportunities he had by going to university, and of the whole family's sacrifice to get him there. With a degree, his could be the first generation of the Miao family to settle in a city. Snail had always told himself that the consequences of his time-wasting were reparable, that he could catch up on work. But when they talked with his student supervisor it became clear that he was too far behind, and the unthinkable happened. There was no choice but for him to drop out.

When it came to getting his head right, Snail's parents weren't taking any chances. With the supervisor's help, the first time his mother used the Internet was to look up the website for an Internet-addiction rehab centre. '*Internet Addiction!*' blared a prominent warning on the site, over an image of a skeleton sitting at a keyboard with headphones on. '*The heartache of so many parents! The "poison" of so many children!*' There was an equation to drive the point home: '*Quitting Internet Addiction = Helping our Youth to Mature their Spirit + Improving Family Education.*' Below was an address.

From the outside, the detox camp looked like a school. There were no barred windows or barbed-wire fences, just a gated entrance and a receptionist. Even still, these institutions have a reputation. They are in essence private boot camps with military discipline and Internet-addiction therapy, and there is no way to get online once inside. There are also persistent rumours of rough physical treatment, and at some facilities electro-shock treatment is part of the cure. Among roughly three hundred such centres in China, there have been seven reported deaths.

At the camp which Snail's father took him to, on the outskirts of West Beijing, their approach seemed to be to bore patients into mental health. One of the managers gave them a brisk tour of the premises. There was little to see: spartan dorm rooms, offices, lecture rooms and an exercise yard. Enrollees stayed for two or three months before being released as productive members of society. They slept in bunk beds and rose at the crack of dawn, wearing army fatigues just like in school military training. Each day was scheduled tightly with drills, chores and agonisingly dull group therapy sessions about the perils of the Internet. When a new inmate entered the camp any electronic device beyond a digital watch was confiscated, and there were regular sweeps for stashed mobiles. The only computers were in the administrative offices, under lock and key.

No one was forced to enrol, in theory. Every new arrival signed themselves over to the camp's tender loving care. But in practice it was the parents who made the decision, and the child who for better or worse had no choice but to comply. The pot-bellied manager talked only to Snail's parents, speechifying about the troubled post-80s kids as if Snail wasn't there. Only at the end of the tour did the manager look at him, to say just four words.

'We can cure you.'

FRED

The vacuum of belief Fred felt on the campus of Peking University or 'Beida' was one reason why she didn't brush off the stranger who stopped her to tell her about Jesus. It was springtime by the banks of Nameless Lake, near the grave of Edgar Snow, the American journalist who interviewed Mao in the thirties. The stranger was a Korean girl a touch older than she was, friendly and respectful. Yes, Fred had heard about Jesus. No, she didn't know that he had died to save humanity. Sure, she would join a gathering later to find out how and why.

China has even more Christians than it has Communist Party members. Estimates vary wildly but most put the number around the hundred million mark. Many Christians are in the countryside, where faith has spread quickly among the rural poor, but a larger proportion still are urban and young. For some it's an escape; for a few it's a trendy experiment with a Western religion; for others it's a calling. Now that cities are richer and living conditions more stable, many of their generation look for a purpose and meaning to life beyond the pursuit of material success.

It was the politeness of the group that attracted Fred,

when she went to the Korean girl's apartment. These informal congregations in private flats are known as 'house churches', where Christianity and the Bible are discussed over green tea and assorted fruit. In a nominally atheistic state, faith is permitted but not encouraged and unregistered religious organisations are technically illegal. So too was the campus evangelism of the Korean, who wasn't a Beida student.

There were registered churches as well, approved by the authorities. The closest to Beida was two blocks south of campus, past the multi-storey electronics superstores that dominated the tech quarter of Zhongguancun. It was a giant building modelled on American megachurches, with the acoustics of an opera hall. Services were held all day, every day with microphone-clutching preachers and crowds of thousands – walk-in redemption. But the sanctioned message was subtly different and downplayed acceptance of Jesus as the only route to personal salvation. The state reserved that privilege.

Fred preferred the house church. She went every Saturday afternoon and the group – mostly students and young professionals – varied from two or three to a dozen, like a book club. The flat was in a high-rise complex not far from the megachurch, and looked the same as any other apartment next to it. There was no sign on the door save the number (out of fear the neighbours would report them to the police) nor any religious decoration inside as best as Fred can remember. Just a stack of Bibles on the table next to orange squash, Coca-Cola, fruit and cakes. No font but a sofa, no communion but the snack bowl.

The Bibles were in Chinese translation, and the group discussed parables from the gospels of Matai, Make, Lujia and Yuehan. Fred liked best the golden rule of Matai 7.12: 'How you wish for others to treat you, you should also treat them the same.' It seemed a good principle for a culture that often ignored the needs of strangers, and reminded her of something Confucius had said, although he formulated it as the silver rule: 'Whatever you don't want done to you, don't do to others.' Most of all she respected the steadfastness of her new friends' belief, their honesty in speaking of personal struggles and the sense of belonging to a community with shared ideals.

She liked the evangelism less. Only a week after joining the house church, the Korean girl asked Fred to help spread the word to her classmates at Beida – like the Party, they wanted to recruit the brightest students. The dogma was hard to swallow too, an unchallengeable Truth to be taken on faith alone. That rang a bell too. Fred went to the weekly meetings for most of her first year at Beida, but in the end she didn't want to convert her fellow students and resented it when the group pushed her to. After the summer holiday, her fervour waned. She stopped going to the church, then stopped taking their calls.

*

Impressionable, idealistic, bored by both the Party and the dissenting line, Fred was still looking for something to believe in. In the spring term of her second year at Beida, she joined a comparative politics class and encountered a new creed: nationalism and the left wing.

The political spectrum is reversed in China: the left is conservative, the right is liberal. Most of Fred's professors were on the right wing, which held up the free market as their gospel and talked about deepening economic reform, perhaps liberalising China's politics along with it. Her peers were largely sympathetic to the right too – the same ones who had rushed to join the Party for career reasons. But Fred was unconvinced. Instead she drifted towards the other pole of a more statist model on the left, which reclaimed socialist tenets for twenty-first-century China.

Pan Wei, who taught the politics class, was a charismatic man. He was a Beijinger but got his Ph.D. at Berkeley University, and published widely about Chinese politics. He had made an impression on Fred the year before, when he gave a pep talk to her department after a classmate jumped to his death from a dorm-building roof. A short man in his late forties, he had a high forehead and an even higher, reedy voice. He was Manchu, of the ethnicity native to China's north-east that had formed the Qing empire, and claimed a direct bloodline to the old imperial court. It was an air of royalty that he carried into the lecture hall.

One of the most provocative thinkers of the 'New Left', Pan Wei made much of China's exceptionalism. The West, he argued, was historically a nomadic society which by nature favoured individualism, while China was by tradition agrarian and better suited to collectivism. In short: the

European and American model simply wouldn't work here. Arguing against democracy, he considered elections and other forms of direct civil participation unsuitable for China, coining the term 'consultative rule of law' as an alternative middle path. He was no Party hack – his position was too far left even for the Communist Politburo – but he supported the principle of a strong central state with ultimate control over China's economy and society.

For Fred it was a compelling sermon. She felt the same misgivings as Pan Wei did when her other professors talked about Western political models – very well and fine, but would it work in an Asian civilisation that had evolved independently on a completely separate track? She thought about the village elections on Hainan, and how candidates bought or bullied villagers who didn't have enough education to make 'one person, one vote' work. China's only democratic election, in December 1912, ended when the winning candidate was assassinated. Some form of authoritarianism, meanwhile, had kept China functioning for millennia. It wasn't perfect, she knew, but it held the country together.

Outside class Pan Wei nurtured a clique of admiring students, mostly his own postgrads and the occasional undergrad spark like Fred. He was often seen about campus with one of these disciples in tow, and regularly invited his favourites to his office for tea. Two plush sofas squared off each other under a spacious window, with fruit and seeds on the table in between them. Pan Wei served the tea 'kung fu' style as they talked, into thumbsized porcelain cups over latticed wood with a tray underneath to catch spillage. They discussed history, literature, philosophy, politics. Current affairs, old historical wounds. Fred listened, and fell under his spell.

Her political compass swung sharply left but the core foundation of her new beliefs was an entirely mainstream patriotism, shared by many of her generation. A fear of China slipping back into chaos, without a muscular central government that continued to develop the country steadily. An acceptance of certain sacrifices to maintain stability, including limits on free speech and personal liberty. A muted mistrust of other countries that seemed to want to contain China, once the 'sick man of Asia', just as it was getting healthy again. Above all, a loyalty to her nation – the word for which in Chinese, *guojia*, doesn't differentiate 'country' from 'state' and includes the character for 'home'. Those beliefs were partly a product of her education and environment, but also came from a simple desire to see China strong.

Nationalism has a long history as a siren song for young Chinese. Its outlet is often anti-foreign sentiment, carrying forward the torch of the Boxer Rebellion of 1899–1901 in which many Westerners in China were killed. A century later, in 1999, when NATO bombed the Chinese Embassy in Belgrade, furious protestors refused to believe it was an accident. In 2008, after the Olympic torch rally was disrupted in Paris, they flung insults at France and boycotted the supermarket chain Carrefour. But the most dramatic form of nationalism has always been against Japan.

The same season that Fred started taking Pan Wei's class, the spring of 2005, her peers picked up the baton again. The flashpoint this time was a Japanese school textbook that was seen as glossing over Japan's war crimes against China (and Japan's support of an independent Taiwan didn't help either). In March, youth in dozens of Chinese cities took to the streets. In April, when a Beida student was beaten by Japanese foreign-exchange students in retaliation, demonstrations flared more violently. Numbers swelled to thousands. Many of the chants were xenophobic. Among the slogans was 'patriotism is not a sin'.

The state allowed the protests – even tacitly condoned them – but knew the venom could just as easily turn on them if they were seen as weak against Japan, as it had on 4 May 1919 during the Republican era. In many respects the protesters, who were generally less educated than Fred's classmates, were just venting steam. There was a word for them: *fenqing*, the 'angry youth'. By switching the first character to another with the same pronunciation, it became the 'shitty youth'.

The angry or shitty youth were only the loud minority. Fred knew it was ironic that Japanese textbooks had sparked the trouble while Chinese schoolbooks were just as guilty of massaging history: anti-Japanese sentiment was years of patriotic education coming home to roost. Her own breed of nationalism was more thoughtful and rooted in ideology. Many educated young Chinese who identified with the left gathered online at a website called 'Utopia', where editors praised Maoism and criticised social inequality. Their loyalty was to the cause not the Party, and later the site was shut down. But while Fred wasn't unquestioningly behind her government, she increasingly defended it. An apt analogy was from Confucian thought: the state as parents, with filial piety expected.

Along with her political sea-change, Fred's views about the Tiananmen protests also shifted. Before she had felt betrayed, but now she saw them as if through a wider lens. Hadn't China's growth since the crackdown, she thought, depended on the stability that followed? Would her country be as prosperous today had the movement led to a power vacuum, itself no guarantee of reform? Wasn't it better that China hadn't gone the way of the Soviet Union? Even the censorship she smarted at before seemed an almost justifiable measure to prevent disorder. By the time Tiananmen turned eighteen in 2007 – an adult in its own right – Fred wished the Western media would stop harping on about it and let China move on.

She was moving on too. She graduated that summer, and continued her studies at Beida for a master's in comparative politics. She was there throughout the next round of nationalist demonstrations in the wake of the 2008 Tibet riots, which were covered with a perceived bias by the Western media that led to the creation of www.anti-CNN.com by a post-80s 'angry youth', Rao Jin. The Olympics followed, with its surge of national pride. The following autumn, America and Europe were hit by a financial crisis that the Chinese media talked about with more than a hint of *schadenfreude*. The democratic West's free market was faltering, the New Left preached, while Leninist China was stronger than ever.

In October 2009 the People's Republic turned sixty with jingoistic fanfare on Tiananmen Square, over twenty years since the Tiananmen movement. Fred had been at Beida for six years, and her internal calendar was adjusted to the academic year: September her January, June her December. She spent Spring Festival and the long summers among the coconuts in Hainan, but each time she returned to campus it felt a little more like home. When Fred started her politics Ph.D. that autumn, it was still at Beida. She had been converted to Beijing.

LUCIFER

Lucifer's premonition came true, and Rustic sailed through the China finals of Global Battle of the Bands. The grand final in London was pushed back to April 2010, delayed by snowstorms and the eruption in Iceland of Eyjafjallajökull. Even then Rustic very nearly didn't make it, as volcanic ash was clogging their flight options. They landed at midnight the day before the competition – the first time in a foreign country for them all – and missed the meeting for the bands explaining how the contest would work. The show the following night was at the Scala, near King's Cross railway station.

There were nineteen other bands competing for the title of Best New Band in the World, from Japan, Norway, Kazakhstan, Israel, Montenegro, Italy, Belgium, Ukraine, Romania, England, Scotland, Serbia, Nepal, Malaysia, Canada, Australia, Iceland, Germany and the Netherlands. Each had twelve minutes and two songs to impress the judges. Lucifer had no auspicious dreams this time, only jetlag, and didn't expect anything more than a good time. Rustic was just a Chinese band after all, he thought, mimicking their favourite Western music but very much the underdogs.

Ricky Sixx had grown out his mane to truly rock-god proportions, and dyed it blond. For the gig he wore leg-crushing leathers and draped a glittering black scarf over his bare chest. Lucifer switched his signature white sunglasses for orange frames, with a polka-dotted cravat for good measure. They started their set with a song from their early days, 'Girls Are Not Yours'.

'*Sexy girls flit before my sleeping eyes,*' Lucifer sang. '*I can look but I can never catch.*' His guitar line ebbed and soared. '*But when the daark is comiing,*' he slurred as the drum beat slowed like a dying heart, '*girls in my braiin, girls. in. my. braiiin . . .*' The melody faded into silence, for one second, then another, before Li Fan smashed his cymbals and shouted, '*1! 2! 3! 4! –*'

'GIRLS ARE NOT YOURS!!' Ricky screamed the chorus in a falsetto. '*Any good boys but never like you Ricky,*' Lucifer answered him.

'GIRLS ARE NOT YOURS!!' Ricky hollered louder. '*Who wants to travel by bus or by subway?*' came back the reply.

'GIRLS ARE NOT YOURS!!' Ricky's voice was beginning to crack. '*You waste your life, you waste your body.*'

'GIRLS ARE NOT YOURS!!' He gave it one last wail. '*They said, please stay away from us.*'

The crowd held up their fists with thumb and little finger raised in the gesture of rock solidarity – throwing the horns. Lucifer played his guitar solo in between Ricky's legs. It was loud, fun and confusing. Then, just as the show started to make sense, Lucifer brought out his clarinet.

Rustic had been sixth in the line-up (Lucifer's lucky number) and watched the rest of the night from the sidelines. Pumped with adrenalin, they drank in the atmosphere and drank dry the bar at the Scala, which reminded them of some of the venues back in Beijing except that the beers were five times as expensive. It finally sunk home that they were in London, home of the Sex Pistols and the Clash.

When all the bands had played, the four judges took the stage. One of them clutched a golden trophy in the shape of the competition's logo, a fireball with a mischievous face.

'Before, I would say a couple of words about the band that won,' said the organiser. 'The jury thought the winning band had a fantastic energy on stage. It was totally original. It was really entertaining. They brought new instruments that no one else had. It was raw, it was energetic, it had fantastic songs and guitar riffs – what more do you need?' He passed the mic to the woman next to him.

'OK,' she said. 'So our big winner' . . . pausing like a pro as whoops of anticipation floated up from the floor . . . 'is' . . . the man with the trophy raised it high . . . '*China!*'

In the quickest ten seconds of his life, Lucifer jumped on stage, karate-kicked at Li Fan, pushed Ricky aside boisterously, hugged the organiser, kissed the female judge and took a bow with his bandmates. Each took turns to hold the trophy aloft, and Lucifer grabbed the mic.

'There are a lot of beautiful girls tonight,' he told the crowd. They knew where to find him.

*

After the initial euphoria, there was no red carpet. Rustic had won a ten-day UK tour the following year and ten thousand dollars, more than a starting annual salary in China. But that night it struck them that nothing fundamental had changed. The rest of the prize money, read the small print, went towards their single release, and the cash in hand wasn't so huge a sum when split three ways. The name of the competition sounded grand but it didn't have much clout outside Britain. They even had to pay for their own beers at the after-party.

By the time Lucifer flew home as a triumphant returning hero, Beijing had flipped the switch to summer. Balls of white fluff floated in the air like there had been an explosion at the pillow factory: willow catkin pollen, which descends on the city every late April like clockwork. Pineapple chunks on sticks appeared for sale on three-wheeled carts. Street-food stalls sold sugary yoghurt drinks, and cold noodles in cardboard pots. Residents planted watermelon and chilli peppers in troughs of earth on their balconies.

After sell-out homecoming gigs at D-22, MAO and Yugong Yishan, life settled back to normal for Rustic. The buzz died down after the first month; the first tranche of their prize money was spent by the second. Lucifer graduated from music college but didn't look for a job. Instead he spent his days loitering on Drum Tower East Road, waiting for night to fall. He didn't drink hard or smoke cigarettes and weed like other musicians. Chasing girls was his drug of choice.

The China outside his social circle could just as well have not existed. Lucifer couldn't name any of China's serving politicians besides the president and premier, and his country's past was meaningless to him compared to his own present. He didn't find out about the Tiananmen protests until he was in college. He barely knew what the Cultural Revolution referred to – he hadn't been listening in class when it came up – and the only seventies history he was interested in was the development of British punk.

There was a word coined for young Chinese from outside who floated through the capital: *beipiao*, 'Beijing drifters'. Lucifer was a *beipiao*. On the Drum Tower strip he might be at the very heart of the city, yet his sense of belonging to it was withheld. He had some notoriety from the competition win and his dream of fame was closer. But when it came down to it, he was struggling just like anyone else – wafting on the wind through Beijing with the willow catkin pollen.

In the summer of 2011, Rustic went on a China tour to coincide with their first album, released by the record label attached to D-22. Over three weeks in May they travelled to nine cities: Changsha, Guangzhou, Chengdu, Xi'an, Lanzhou, Nanchang, Wuhan, Zhengzhou and back to Beijing. Some of the gigs were at deserted downtown dives. Others were in bars with a stage for karaoke, where the crowds were more used to Mandopop than Chinese rock. In cheap hotels the three of them shared a double room (one got the floor). Several shows bombed. In short, it was glorious.

The album itself had a blood-red cover, with pairs of sexy stockinged legs jutting out like bicycle-wheel spokes from the hub hole of the disc. The title was *City of Heartbreak 'n' Horror* – named for the way they felt about Beijing and because they thought it sounded cool. On the back of the sleeve Lucifer wrote a few words in English, with polishing help from the studio:

> Maybe society thinks of rock music as harmful and unhealthy, but has anyone ever thought this through? It's like Marxist-Leninist Thought: conflict exists inside everything. Good and bad exist in any living thing or phenomenon. They are mutually restrictive and in constant contact. Rock should be inspiration for the young, hopeful, dreamy, and the future.

He wasn't being glib. Despite the lacklustre response to Rustic's China tour, Lucifer's ambitions were already running ahead of him. He saw himself as a poster boy for the new generation in China: the young, hopeful and dreamy. He fantasised about stadium gigs and movie deals, legions of fans chanting his name. The only cause for doubt was hairline cracks in his friendship with Ricky.

In September Rustic finally returned to the UK for their victory tour. The first trip had been rushed, but now they had the time and space to enjoy London. They made a pilgrimage to Abbey Road studios and posed for the obligatory photo-op at the zebra crossing. They were disappointed to discover that Oxford Circus was just an intersection – and a small one by Chinese standards. At Stables Market and Camden Town they recorded videos while Lucifer talked to strangers in (now slightly less Crazy) English. He befriended a drunk street busker and borrowed his guitar to strum a tune. And he went to Amy Winehouse's house to pay his respects two months after she died. 'We love you Amy,' he said to the empty white facade, then flirted with a group of Italian girls who were passing by.

Next, Rustic went on the road. In Birmingham they were mistaken for Koreans. In Manchester they walked the curry mile. In Liverpool they had a pint at the Cavern Club, where the Beatles used to gig. In Newcastle Lucifer shot an arty music video while walking the piers, his fringe swept by the sea wind. None of them remembers what happened in Glasgow. Later that year Rustic secured sponsorship from Converse in China, and later still they played at South by Southwest, the music festival in Austin, Texas. From there Lucifer flew to New York to see Brian Walker, his old friend from Shijiazhuang. Everywhere he played, he could see his face on posters and felt like he had made it.

The band had come a long way since its awkward teens. By some measures Lucifer had achieved his ambitions. But soon the invites dried up and it became clear that they weren't going to break through to the foreign circuit. The domestic market didn't want rock but saccharine pop. Crowds in the alternative music scene were rarely larger than a few score. Rustic flogged their CD at the merch table with every show, for fifty yuan a pop, but it never amounted to much. Some gigs paid as little as a couple of hundred yuan between them. The unwelcome thought crept into Lucifer's mind that he wasn't living *the* dream but living *a* dream. His life was like his lyrics:

> *We have nothing new*
> *Our job is to lose*
> *No bed no girls*
> *No home no condoms*
> *Rock 'n' roll for money 'n' sex*

Ricky and Lucifer had been fighting since the UK tour. Lucifer wanted to guide the band into the poppier end of punk, and sing in Chinese not English in the hope of selling domestically. To Ricky that was selling out on the cultural iconoclasm that the rock community stood for. He wanted the band to move towards the Axl Rose, Led Zeppelin end of the spectrum. Their extrovert egos produced sparks on stage but now their magnetism was misaligned. To Ricky music was rebellion; to Lucifer it was his career. After one clash and false exit too many, at the end of 2011 Ricky left Rustic for good.

Without him, the band was a tricycle missing a wheel. Lucifer found a new bassist and taught him their songs, but it just didn't feel the same when he played guitar in between the new guy's legs. Lucifer had lost his Beelzebub. After a few months, with no new inspiration and fading zeal, Rustic split up. Lucifer had to come up with a new plan.

DAHAI

Three years had gone by since the Olympics, and the tunnel was growing longer. Every day – or night if that was the shift – Dahai was down there, under twenty metres of earth and concrete. It was eerily beautiful at times, when the other workers were silhouetted through the swirling dust against the arm light of a digging crane. But mostly it was a slog.

Now twenty-five, Dahai wasn't earning nearly enough money and was feeling the full weight of work pressure particular to his generation. Where in early years there are four grandparents and two parents to shower attention on one child (the rule of 4-2-1), in adult life this reverses so that an only child has to provide for two ageing parents and four retired grandparents (1-2-4). If the expectation for women is to marry, for men it is more bluntly economic, an uphill struggle to be a high earner in a system rigged against the less privileged. One punning expression for it is *yalishanda*, 'pressure as great as a mountain' – a homophone for Alexander the Great.

Dahai disliked his work unit, especially the bosses who talked about targets, quotas and socialist working spirit, but he had no choice but to play along in order to be promoted. He was still living in the worksite dorms, sleeping in a bunk bed as he had been ever since his first year at university. He was painfully skinny, and experimented with greasy shoulder-length hair to offset his pockmarks. His love life was a wasteland. At times he imagined he was a superhero, in an idle and unspecific way. Sometimes the villains were his bosses, other times the leaders of the country. At the end of his shifts, when he was the only one left in the tunnel, he had a habit of talking to himself.

'Dahai, you're looking very smart today,' he would say.

'That's right, Dahai, you *are* looking smart today,' came back his reply.

Already he felt like the life he had imagined for himself in college was closed to him. Back then he had fantasised of being in a band, writing edgy rebellious songs. When he went to one of Rustic's gigs at D-22, he suffered a pang of envy at Lucifer's footloose life, and realised that he would never follow it. Instead he was a wage slave, obeying his superiors like he had obeyed his parents, teachers and military drill instructors before them. 'Obey' was the motif that stalked his life. He was a numbered and collared worker now – even his private email address was a string of digits. Instead, as before, he found his escape online.

*

Of the more than half a billion people who had an Internet connection in China, many self-identified as *wangmin*: 'citizens of the net'. They were an oppressed population.

Initially loose restrictions, a result of censors underestimating the power of the Internet, had tightened. The Education Department tried to roll out pre-installed software called Green Dam Youth Escort which would block porn and other 'unhealthy' websites, but gave up in 2009. Google pulled out of China in 2010, and the Great Firewall grew higher. But for each attempt the government made to create a safe and healthy web, the netizens only resisted more creatively.

Dahai still logged onto bulletin boards and followed blogs, but by 2011 social media was king and the main forum was Weibo. Literally 'microblog', the most popular Weibo was owned by Sina, the tech company that also hosted news and blogs. It was something between Twitter and Facebook, both of which were blocked in 2009, the same year Weibo launched. Underneath a pale blue navigation bar you could post, repost, 'like' and comment, as well as receiving private messages. As on Twitter, text is limited to a hundred and forty characters, but it only takes two characters to form most Chinese words so they stretch a lot further. ('In the Chinese language,' Ai Weiwei said, 'a hundred and forty characters is a novella.')

Dahai signed up in May 2010. His self-description line was 'In a universe this big every coincidence is inevitable' – playing on the character for his surname, Yu, which in another tone meant universe. His profile picture was a sepia sketch of his face in profile, and his first post was a picture of his college band with the words 'commemorating our already passed youth'. He followed old university buddies, made new Internet friends and reposted links and commentary from the 'Big Vs', the verified accounts of celebrity microbloggers. Even as he was stuck inside his work unit's corrugated-steel perimeter, his worldview was expanding.

To understand netizens he first had to decode online slang – a 'parallel language system' in the phrase of one Chinese blogger, full of puns and knowing winks. An extreme version of it, adopted from Taiwan and Hong Kong, was called 'Martian script', fusing constantly changing symbols, abbreviations, foreign words and intentional typos into a shibboleth script that none but the initiated could understand:

喜欢ωǒ尐吖头 脾气拽ご绿★城浪子 让我☆ve嗳伱.
乖乖▄潴 冰炫Girl★ 少铼伤ωǒ★弃婴. 小☆珥δ躲
ωǒ彐b坏のωǒ鉟懂LoVe.

More widespread was an expanding glossary of punning homophones (the narrow range of Chinese phonology means that many characters share the same or a similar pronunciation) to create a unique glossary.

Dahai took a crash course, incorporating each new slang into his own posts. Some played on English pronunciation: 3Q (*san-q*) for 'thank you', 88 (*baba*) for 'bye bye', *haipi* for 'happy'. Others used numbers: 517 when read aloud in Chinese sounds like 'I want to eat' (McDonald's use it in their delivery number) and 520 sounds like 'I love you' (5201314 is 'I love you for a lifetime and a world'). 'What?' (*shenme*) became 'mystical horse' (*shenma*). 'Venerable country' changed a character into 'expensive country'.

Caonima, in fourth-third-first tones, means 'fuck your mother', but the same three syllables in third-second-third tones are 'grass mud horse', a less NSFW way to express the same sentiment.

Webspeak was mostly creative fun, but the homophones were also coined as alternatives to sensitive words blocked by the Propaganda Department (the 'Ministry of Truth' to netizens who read Orwell). Charter '08 – *lingbaxianzhang*, the democratic manifesto that landed Liu Xiaobo in jail – became 'county magistrate lymph' through a similar pronunciation. Even the word for 'harmony', *hexie*, took on new meaning when President Hu Jintao's call for a 'harmonious society' led to undesirable posts being 'harmonised'. When the word 'harmonised' was in a Kafkaesque twist itself censored, netizens used another soundalike, 'river crab'.

Before long a living ecosystem emerged. Joining the river crab of censorship was the 'elephant of truth' (*zhenxiang*, from the officialese for 'real situation'). The 'poison jackal' (*ducai*, 'dictatorship') shared a watering hole with the 'monkey-snake' (*houshe*, 'state mouthpiece'). 'Valley doves' (*guge*, 'Google') flew above 'watered weasel-apes' (*guanliyuan*, 'administrators') and 'horses of deception' (*qishima*) roamed the plains of the Mahler Gobi (*malegebi*, 'your mother's cunt'). Each creature was illustrated, and when netizens found images of the South American alpaca they adopted it as the long-lost grass mud horse, symbol of their resistance.

Every so often, one of Dahai's posts which included a

sensitive word would be deleted. There was never any explanation or notice. It was just gone – flagged by software, then harmonised by a foot soldier in China's small army of human censors. Some of the blacklisted words (or numbers, like 6/4) were obvious. Others were part of a bizarre game of cat and mouse. The word 'carrot' was briefly blocked as it shared a character with Hu Jintao's surname. Netizens started posting screengrabs of text to avoid the bots, and if a post or account was deleted it wasn't difficult to reincarnate it elsewhere. But the censors' strategy was as much to guide online discussion as to shut it down. Pro-government commenters, mostly Dahai's own age, were reportedly paid fifty cents per post. Netizens mockingly dubbed them the 'fifty cent party'.

As he dived deeper into the web, the influence of the half-serious, half-jokey resistance rubbed off. Dahai's views became even more implicitly anti-state. But he doubted whether the netizens had real power. They played the vigilante in 'human flesh search engines' to track down wrongdoers, such as a woman caught on video crushing a kitten to death with her stilletos – but that was just a mob, exposing and humiliating whoever they wanted. Weibo played its role in organising street protests too, using the euphemism 'let's go for a stroll' – yet the marches were only ever parochial, mostly about environmental pollution or local official corruption.

There was one area where connectivity was genuinely transformative: news spread fast. Before the Internet an embarrassing event for the government could be buried, and Dahai had never trusted TV or newspaper news. Weibo changed the rules. In July 2011 a train on the high-speed rail network going at 300 kph collided into the back of another train which had stopped outside the city of Wenzhou. It derailed and flew off the viaduct, killing forty. The railway ministry sent teams to dig a hole, presumably in which to hide the crashed carriage, and the Ministry of Truth tried to stifle the news. But by then pictures were all over the net. Thanks to Weibo, it was one story that couldn't be buried.

Dahai reposted all the news that made the authorities look bad. Corrupt officials, sex scandals, local protests – each click of the share button was a small act of mutiny. It was a modicum of rebellion that he couldn't afford outside his digital other life. By adding his voice to those of others online, he thought he could put pressure on the government to fix the nation's problems and make society fairer to those on its lowest rungs. As a citizen he couldn't change a thing; as a netizen he might change China. One web slogan summed it up: 'Reposting is power'.

Yet for all his righteousness Dahai acknowledged he was also just blowing off steam. In particular he like to poke fun at the second-generation rich kids who used Weibo to show off their luxury lifestyle. When a twenty-year-old called Guo Meimei posted photos of her Maserati sports car and Hermès handbags, netizens spotted that she claimed to work for Red Cross in China (in fact her sugar daddy did). When the son of a deputy police chief ran over and killed a college girl, his protest while resisting arrest – 'My dad is Li

Gang!' – became a catchphrase. The bratty and privileged became hate figures online, outlets for the bitterness of the less fortunate.

More still of Dahai's posts were about nothing more sensational than trending gossip or his favourite music. The rule held as true in China as elsewhere that the most shared photo on social media at any given moment is a kitten gif. And none of the posts that ridiculed national scandals translated into street protests. For all of the indignation on Weibo in the wake of the Wenzhou train crash, not a single netizen put their feet where their fingertips were. When China's so-called 'Jasmine Revolution' followed the Arab Spring, there were as many journalists as demonstrators.

Behind each Weibo account indulging in vaguely anti-authoritarian posts was a youth like Dahai: reclusive, holding down a job, nonconfrontational. What Dahai could say online he wouldn't dream of telling his work-unit bosses to their faces. He knew that netizens were ordinary and powerless alone – the 'fart people' or 'shitizens' in one official's phrase that they self-deprecatingly embraced. But it still felt good to vent. The web was his release from the other nets that trapped him.

SNAIL

Snail escaped Internet-addiction boot camp before he was even enrolled. Having dropped out of college, he persuaded his parents it wouldn't do him any good to be locked away – and the treatment had its price tag, which would cut into his father's earnings as a migrant worker. Instead his parents insisted he come back to the village in Anhui, where his mother could keep a weather eye on him. At least, like rehab, there was no Internet connection.

It was spring when Snail returned to his childhood home of Tangzhuangcun. When he stepped into his family court-yard he felt like he had walked in a wide circle, only to discover the line led back to the start. Since boyhood the single most important goal set up for him had been to get out of the countryside. What had all his efforts to go to college been for if he was back in the fields again, his hands empty of any harvest of his own?

On the face of things little had changed in the village, but the small differences added up. The pond where Snail used to play as a child was half dried-up and filthy with pollution, a frothy green pit used as the village rubbish dump. His old primary school had been converted into a medical clinic, and the playground was being used to grow cotton. His grandmother had switched her insecticide hand pump for an electric upgrade. The most noticeable change was how quiet it was: the village was emptier than ever. Snail was the only person there who wasn't a child or over forty. Everyone else his age was working in the towns and cities, where he had failed.

His mother cooked his meals and hung his laundry out for him. She had converted to Christianity a few years back – as many people her age had in the countryside – and she kept a calendar on the wall with Jesus in different poses for each month, like a holy calendar girl. There was nothing for Snail to do except watch reruns of *Journey to the West* on daytime TV. In his childhood home it was all too easy to regress. He pushed to the back of his mind the dread that he might have to learn to work the land for a living.

Here where all possibility of gaming was removed, Snail found it surprisingly easy not to crave it. Almost as soon as he was waking up to a world where there were trees outside instead of Internet bars, he felt restored. His first feeling was anger and shame that the urge faded this quickly, after he had wrestled with it through more broken resolutions than he could remember. That soon gave way to a wash of relief tinged with longing regret as he accepted *World of Warcraft* was behind him. It was a part of his story that he couldn't scrub out, and he understood how he had come to be addicted. At the root, it wasn't who he was.

Life was dull in the village, and Snail grew restless. Worse still, all of his neighbours gossiped about him, saying that he had failed in Beijing. After two months of lying about, he finally moved on. His father found him a job at a karaoke parlour across the provincial border in Jiangsu, where his uncle was a manager. Snail was overqualified but there was always room for one more hand on deck. After fourteen years of fruitless education he needed to begin working, and the bottom was the only place left to look.

*

Karaoke is more than a pastime in China, it's a way of life. Originally an import from Japan, karaoke parlours stand in for any real bar culture. In every town centre, you can see the same three English letters in enticing neon: K. T. V. All roads lead to Karaoke TV, and with enough alcohol most group dinners end up there too. Gathering with friends to drink and sing in a private room with a TV screen and microphones is the closest equivalent of going down the pub – an important part of bonding and courtship, and a necessary means to cultivate business connections.

The KTV where Snail started work that summer was in Changshu, two hours inland from Shanghai. Changshu has the feel of an outpost town, filled with businesses that want cheaper rents than in the city while still being close enough to trade. At times it seems like most of its residents are migrants from the provinces who were aiming for Shanghai but didn't quite make it. There is little to see beside office buildings and residential blocks, and a single crossroads near the centre is the hub for all entertainment when the businessmen knock off. Dotted around the edges of the crossroads, next to the hotels and twenty-four-hour restaurants, are the bright lights of not one but five KTVs.

Snail's employers were the sixth, tucked up a side road with dimmer street lighting, and the most opulent of them all. The building stood alone and apart, box-shaped and lit up with bright blue LED panels. The entire ground floor was an abandoned dance hall – its dusty balconies derelict, its front doors permanently locked. The karaoke parlour was in the floors above it, and the only entrance was a golden lift door set into one side of the building. Next to it was a small sign in red characters: 'No minors allowed inside'. When the lift doors opened on the third floor, two receptionists greeted customers with pearly grins and the name of the establishment.

'Welcome to Bali Island International Pleasure Hall!'

There was no Bali island theme inside, only the luxury that the words implied. While Snail's uncle was a manager behind the scenes, the true proprietress was a middle-aged lady with orange-dyed hair and a penchant for leather boots called Mrs Money (her surname is the same character). When Mrs Money smiled, she showed four golden teeth. When Mrs Money frowned, her brow was a mountain range. If new arrivals looked like their pockets were well-lined, she smiled.

The interior, as with all KTVs, was a maze of private rooms. There were a few score of them spread over three floors, each with a soundproofed door. The walls and floors of the corridors were a creamy marble, lined by full-length gilt mirrors and chandeliers. Even the dustbins were gold and shiny: Mrs Money liked her bling. On the top floor was an alcove with a shrine to an angry Taoist God (red face, bulging eyes, neatly trimmed goatee). Offerings of nuts and fruit were laid out below his withering gaze, next to a collection box where revellers could mollify him with small change.

The rooms themselves were decorated with plush red sofas, marble-topped tables, drooping chandeliers and fake European-style paintings of naked people eating fruit. One wall had a wide-screen TV, with a touch-screen control panel by the sofa-side where revellers could choose songs from Cantopop to Christina Aguilera. The rooms ranged in price from 666 yuan to 999 yuan to occupy for an evening. Platters of cherry tomatoes and sliced watermelon were laid on, and watery beers lined up by the dozen. Some groups preferred to buy a bottle of whisky, generally Black Label, then pour it into mixing jugs along with iced tea and crushed ice, a karaoke staple. 'K powder' or ketamine was a popular party drug if that was your thing, a sedative high also used as horse tranquilliser. For other thrills, 300 yuan extra bought you a girl.

The KTV girls waited in a locker room at the back of the establishment, around a bend behind the lift entrance and out of sight. While they were on shift Mrs Money kept their ID cards (eighty-two of them) behind a glass display cabinet. The room was guarded idly by a friendly old man at a small wooden desk, with a thermos of tea and a drawer full of instant noodles. The girls on call sat on a long black sofa in short skirts and low blouses, flipping through their phones until Mrs Money dispatched them to whichever of the rooms had asked for one (or two, or four).

Karaoke girls are expected to provide 'three accompaniments' for the group they are nested into: drinking, dancing and singing. The 'fourth accompaniment' is illegal but widespread in China, and negotiable for a fee. For many of the men who came to this kind of upper-end karaoke parlour, prostitution was the logical end to a good night, all part of the male bonding that built camaraderie and sealed business deals. The girls were young: mostly in their early twenties, although Snail remembers one being just sixteen. The boys on staff were waiters, replenishing fruit platters and taking orders for more whisky and iced tea.

Snail wasn't among them. His uncle wanted to shelter him from what went on behind those closed doors, fearful that it might corrupt him. Instead he assigned his nephew to watch over the car park, for which Snail was paid 600 yuan a month. It was a meaningless job, like many others created for employment's sake in China. He greeted customers, ushered them to an available parking space, then walked them to the lift entrance. Hours later when they stumbled out again, he guided them back to their car in case their memory had been clouded. Sometimes a man came out with a KTV girl on his arm, who got into the car with him. No one asked any questions, not least about drinking and driving.

Snail wasn't immune to his female colleagues. Once, one of the girls came down unaccompanied at the end of the night and asked him to walk her home. She was from Anhui as well – many of the staff came from the countryside or anonymous provincial towns, inching closer to Shanghai. When she and Snail arrived at her door in the early hours of morning, she turned the back of her strappy dress to him and asked him to adjust the zip. Oblivious until then, Snail suddenly felt the atmosphere was strange. He mumbled something about having to get home and left the girl fumbling with her key.

Snail was living with his aunt and uncle in town. They were under strict instructions from his parents not to let him play computer games, but in practice left him to his own devices. His shift at Bali Island started at 6pm and ended any time between 2am and 4am. By the time he stumbled out of bed late the next morning, his uncle was already gone and he had time to kill. There were several Internet bars in the area and he entered one within his first week. But when he tried logging into his *World of Warcraft* account he found he was locked out: another gamer had stolen his elf mage avatar, with all her hard-won treasure and experience, and changed the password. He guessed it had happened after his parents pulled him out of his old Internet bar before he had time to switch his console off. He created new avatars – an orc, a human, an even bigger orc, a gnome – but it didn't feel the same and soon he gave up for good.

As summer wore on, Snail spent most of his time bicycling around town, but Changshu had little to offer. On the eastern periphery of the entertainment crossroads was a Western-style bar called Free Man. (Its slogan was in English: 'Free man, Free time.') Bars are still an oddity outside of big cities in China, sign of a budding nightlife culture for twenty-somethings who are too cash-strapped for a private room at KTV but still want to go out. The bar served luminescent cocktails and fake brand whisky, while a few brave dancers bobbed awkwardly on a dance floor with two stripper poles. At the weekend the place was overrun with the kind of effortfully trendy provincial youth whose over-the-top hairstyles (and the fact that many work in hair salons) give them a mocking nickname: *xijianchui*, the 'wash-cut-blowdrys'.

Changshu was the graveyard of their ambition, as it was for Snail's colleagues at the KTV. Most had dropped out of education after middle school and their current careers were the best they could hope for – the end of the line. Here was the true reality for the majority of young Chinese: karaoke staff, hair-salon assistants, building guards, lift attendants, delivery boys, waiters. If he had graduated from university Snail would have had a shot at something better, or at least better paid. Now there was every possibility that this kind of work was as high as he could go. For the first time, he panicked.

When he dropped out of college, his student supervisor had said that they could take him back if he wanted a second chance. He would have to take remedial classes to catch up on all the work he had missed, but he could still graduate only a year late and get his life back on track. By the first bite of winter in November, after six months at Bali Island International Pleasure Hall, Snail made his mind up. He said goodbye to Mrs Money, and prepared to go back to school after the Chinese new year.

XIAOXIAO

Xiaoxiao's mother was calling every day now. Sure enough, after the usual chatter it came – the nudge, the hint, the outright warning. You're twenty-six. When are you going to get married?

Every Chinese woman in her twenties knows the nudge. It starts as early as college graduation and increases in intensity with each birthday, rising to panic pitch by thirty. It might be a sly aside in a text or an emotionally manipulative tone, but the message is clear: don't focus on your career, it's more important to find a husband. If he's conventionally successful and lives close to home, all the better. Xiaoxiao's mother only wished her well, but was born into conservative times and couldn't understand why her daughter was delaying. Xiaoxiao had brushed the nudge off skilfully until now, but the war of attrition was getting harder to bear.

After three years of memories she had closed her clothes shop, Remember. Rents had risen and the trickle of money from selling hand-embroidered dresses in a back alley didn't make for a sustainable business. More distressingly, she had fallen out with her best friend and co-owner Wen Jing. It was such a trivial disagreement that Xiaoxiao couldn't place what triggered the fight, but heated exchanges on text message only made things worse, and before she knew it they weren't on speaking terms. When the time came to renew their lease, they let the shop go and someone else took it over.

Xiaoxiao pursued another passion: coffee. Cafe culture was still pretty new to China – most people drank tea – but students had developed a taste for instant coffee after Nescafé-fuelled late-night cramming sessions, and ground-bean artisanal brews followed. Xiaoxiao loved the rituals of coffee and found work as a barista at a cafe inside a converted synagogue in central Harbin. It had high stained-glass windows, chipped walls and a cavernous ceiling. The star of David still hung outside. It was called Aoguya, after a remote edge of the north-east where the Ewenki minority lived in mountain forests. The Chinese owner of the cafe had spent some time there and thought the name was evocative.

As the Songhua river froze and ice sculptures appeared on Harbin's cobbled tourist streets, Xiaoxiao spent her days steaming espressos while the windows misted with condensation. The wooden beams of the original interior had been preserved, and smelt ancient. It was an enchanting place to work, and she was happy there. When they peeled off the yellowed wallpaper while renovating they found a slogan from the Cultural Revolution underneath, blaring in large red characters: 'Smash the Four Olds'. They pasted new wallpaper over and left the words underneath for the next generation of archaeologists to discover.

She had no burning career ambitions and was content simply to live independently in her own style. She was as much an 'artistic youth' as ever, and a gentle soul at heart. She had been single since graduating from college, and didn't like the men around her – macho North-easterner types who wore bling. Besides, she was in no rush to settle down. Waiting until her thirties would be just fine, if only her family would leave her alone.

They wouldn't. After Xiaoxiao's twenty-sixth birthday in September 2011 her mother warned her about becoming a 'leftover woman', *shengnü*. The term was first coined by no less than the Women's Federation, China's official women's rights organisation with close ties to the Communist Party, and referred to highly educated women who didn't settle. 'Pretty girls don't need a lot of education to marry into a rich and powerful family,' read a post on the Women's Federation website just after International Women's Day in March 2011, 'but girls with an average or ugly appearance will find it difficult. These kinds of girls hope to further their education in order to increase their competitiveness. The tragedy is they don't realise that as women age they are worth less and less, so by the time they get their MA or Ph.D., they are already old, like yellowed pearls.'

The media picked up the term and ran with it. One article divided leftover women into four categories, with cutesy cartoons. Those between twenty-five and twenty-seven were 'leftover warriors' and still had a fighting chance. Women aged twenty-eight to thirty were 'the ones who must triumph'. After thirty the diagnosis went downhill fast; at thirty-five your situation was declared hopeless. The American scholar Leta Hong Fincher argued it was a deliberate campaign to match educated women with the millions of surplus bachelors in China, a product of gender-selective abortion within the one-child policy. Without wives those men were a potentially restive threat to social order, and the true demographic leftovers.

A bigger problem was society itself, where sexist norms were deeply entrenched. Gender equality had slipped backwards from the days when women held up half the sky as equal partners in the Chinese Revolution. One of few positive legacies of Mao's rule was a greater acceptance of women in the workplace and as business leaders. But familiar problems were resurgent: a widening pay gap, systemic sexual harassment at work, cultural chauvinism. Property deeds were routinely signed in the man's name as a matter of convention, and there was no explicit law punishing domestic violence. A woman's worth was still judged in relation to men.

There was progress with each new generation. From Xiaoxiao's perspective, unmarried women in their late twenties and thirties were the vanguard. As always the post-80s were challenging the blinkered thinking of older generations, slowly transforming their society by sheer force of numbers. And so when one month after her birthday there was a special festival for single people, while her mother needled her Xiaoxiao was secretly pleased.

*

The festival was originally invented for the leftover men. In 1993, the story goes, four Nanjing University students were slouching on their dorm bunkbeds, slurping instant noodles, drinking beer, chain-smoking and complaining that the ladies weren't falling over each other to get at them. They were 'bare branches', they grumbled, using a word for single men, *guanggun*, that still carried stigma. 'From today,' one of them said, pleased by the recurring bare branch of the number one in that day's date, 'November 11th will be called Singles Day.'

Whether there's any truth to this origin myth or not, the idea stuck. What started as an in-joke became a self-mocking campus tradition, embraced by girlfriendless students who were fed up with sleeping alone while couples had not one but two Valentine's days – a traditional Chinese day for lovers in the summer as well as the newly popular Western import. When those students graduated and found work, Singles Day spread. Soon it became an excuse for old friends to get together once a year to talk about jobs, property prices and why the women still weren't biting.

Little by little, people came to see the mock-festival as an opportunity to either celebrate or shed their single status. Speed-dating events sprouted in cities. Bars and clubs advertised special deals for the night. Singles Day became the chance to tell a girl you had a crush on that you liked her, or to propose to your partner. The number of couples registering to be married leapt every 11 November. It was called *tuoguang*, 'shedding your bare branchness', but the phrase had a double entendre of 'strip naked' – which only partially explains why some singles marked the day with the more eccentric tradition of going for a group run, bark naked.

One year flashmobs emerged on a Beijing city bus route marked number 11, organised on bulletin boards online. Participants were instructed to wear a turban and carry a stick, say, 'The weather is really nice,' to anyone else in a turban and stay on until the end of the line, to the bewilderment of regular passengers. Fans of Japanese manga, adopting a more sinister joke from a comic book, called it 'barbecue day' and suggested that all couples should be burnt. Singles Day even had its own special food: four deep-fried crullers, a breakfast snack, to represent the four number ones in the date, with a single dumpling in the middle for the dot.

The celebration of singlehood struck a chord with young Chinese, both men and women, who resented the pressure to find a partner. It was *their* festival – invented by the young and for the young, not a traditional Chinese holiday or a Western import. But in the late 2000s Internet retail companies started to take an interest in Singles Day. November was a seasonal slump in sales between mid-autumn festival and Chinese New Year, and offline business had proved that the day was a useful sales gimmick. In 2009 Taobao, the eBay-like online store comprised of individual sellers, trialled a mass discount with participating retailers. The next year they marketed it hard, selling almost a billion yuan's worth of goods in twenty-four hours.

This year the festival fell on a triple eleven – 11.11.11 – and was promoted by Taobao as 'Super Singles Day'. Tens of millions of shoppers, single or not, waited for the stroke of midnight when sales began to snap up the best deals. There were teddy bears, sexy underwear, wedding gowns, 'bare branch' IDs mocked up to look like marriage documents. But there were also discounts on everything else that had nothing to do with dating: mobile phone cases, winter thermals, rice cookers, gloves and scarves. Every time 'double eleven' day came around, Taobao shifted more total value: three billion yuan, nine billion, fifty billion, ninety billion. Soon the origins of the day were completely lost in the shopping frenzy. November 11th was associated only with online sales.

Xiaoxiao joined the shopping spree on Super Singles Day, but her single status was being assaulted on all sides. Behind her was the family pressure to marry. In front was a consumer culture that fetishised weddings, with a bride on every billboard. Her old classmates were getting hitched in a domino tumble of marriages and it was no longer easy to mollify her mother, whose anxiety was overwhelming. The rest of her extended family started to worry her about it too, and all of society seemed to join in. Years later, an advert for a dating website would show a young woman at her grandmother's sickbed, getting married just to please grandma because 'I can't take my time being picky any more'.

*

Xiaoxiao saw her own grandma over Spring Festival the year after, back in her home town of Nehe. On the second day of the new year celebrations the tradition was for married women to visit their parents, having spent New Year's Eve itself with their husband's family. As with most traditions it wasn't taken too seriously but carried more weight with the elderly. Xiaoxiao had seen in the new year with her mother and father, and instead went that afternoon to visit her maternal grandparents, who had raised her until the age of seven out in the countryside.

In their old age they had moved to the city, and were settled into a two-bedroom apartment just like everybody else. The courtyard of the residential block was slippery with black ice when Xiaoxiao arrived. On the fourth floor, a green metal door guarded a spartan interior where her grandparents were watching melodramatic soaps and anti-Japanese war dramas on TV. Grandma poured tea and laid out seeds to snack on while they made small talk. Grandpa put on his century-old spectacles – passed down through the generations – to look at Xiaoxiao's photos on her phone, and struggled with the concept of swiping left.

They were both well into their seventies, and suddenly it struck Xiaoxiao that they didn't have many more years left. Grandma, who used to cuddle her on the heated *kang* bed of her childhood, was white-haired and frail. She hobbled slightly when she walked but still insisted on walking down the stairs to see Xiaoxiao off. The stairwell was cold, with stickers advertising home services plastered on the walls and insulated piping. On the third floor Xiaoxiao told her grandmother to stay, and went down another flight before she heard Grandma call out to her. She turned and looked back up. What Grandma said next is etched into her memory.

'While I am still alive, will I see you married?'

That cut Xiaoxiao to the bone. She had a sensitive disposition and it genuinely hurt to see her family in distress about her future. She may have rolled her eyes whenever her mother brought it up, but filial piety is still deeply ingrained in China. Xiaoxiao knew Grandma could never understand her reasons for wanting to be single. How to bridge that gulf between them? How to explain that she thought late twenties wasn't 'left over', that she didn't want to just settle?

'Of course!' Xiaoxiao replied in a thin voice with a forced smile. She spun around and bounded down the steps before Grandma could see her eyes water. By the time she got to the bottom, and on the train all the way back to Harbin, she couldn't stop crying.

MIA

For a generation as diverse as Mia's there are various tribes to identify with. The 'working grunt tribe' (*shangbanzu*) or 'urged tribe' (*beicuizu*) are the nine-to-fivers pressured into conformity. The 'strawberry tribe' (*caomeizu*) are nice to look at but soft inside, flitting from job to job and avoiding responsibility. The 'moonlight tribe' (*yueguangzu*) spend their monthly wages shopping – a punning double meaning of 'moonlight' and 'spend it all' – while the 'bite the old tribe' (*kenlaozu*) still live off mum and dad. Almost everyone's in the 'rush-rush tribe' (*benbenzu*) but those who can't hack it might join the 'crush-crush tribe' (*nieniezu*), named for a brief craze where stressed young workers took out their frustrations by crushing packets of instant noodles in supermarket aisles.

If the post-80s were on a conveyor belt from exams to college to work to marriage, the post-90s wanted to get off the track. Their tribes were as often subcultures that marked them as nonconformists – making up for the lost youth of those who came before them. They were the punks, skaters, cosplayers, graffiti artists. The *shamate* youth (named for the English word 'smart') whose over-the-top hairstyles and outfits were somewhere between goth and Japan's counter-culture Harajuku street. The metalheads and the skinheads, Mia's own tribe. Their elders were quick to grumble that they were 'brain dead' or 'too open', but in the cities young attitudes to everything from work to sex challenged convention. Tattoos were no longer taboo but trendy, with a tattoo parlour on every bar-district street corner.

Mia had two new tattoos herself. One was a buxom girl on her left arm – based on her Virgo star sign – with the words 'Pretty Vacant' after the Sex Pistols song. The second was a cobweb on her elbow, an old-school prison tattoo. Both were her own designs. But if Mia was a rebel, she was also ambitious. In her fourth and final year at Tsinghua University she interned part-time at the Chinese edition of the fashion glossy *Harper's Bazaar*. (She turned up to the interview in her full skinhead regalia.) After graduating in June 2012 she stayed on as a full-time intern with a small stipend.

Bazaar's China office is in a sparkling high-rise called Trends Tower at the centre of Beijing's commercial and business district. Next door is the World Trade Commercial Building, and a short taxi ride away is the CCTV Tower – both modernist glass monsters. The plaza next door, known in English as 'The Place', is a shiny trap of Starbucks and burger joints canopied high overhead by LED panels that stretch for a hundred metres. Light shows run at night, and there was a rumour that a rich second-generation kid once rented the entire display to play video games. If a visitor to Beijing doesn't venture outside a square kilometre from the hotels near here (as sometimes happens) he or she might get the false impression that China is just like the West, or years ahead.

Every weekday morning Mia swivelled into the palatial lobby of Trends Tower, took a touch-screen lift directly to the eighteenth floor, then switched to another regular lift up to the twenty-first. *Bazaar* took up the whole floor in an open-plan mess of Apple Macs and magazine stacks. Staff bustled about between mannequins, while delivery boys arrived every other minute with parcels to sign for. Movie posters covered the walls and open suitcases overflowed with clothing samples. The tiled floor was kept sparkling white by a cleaner who moved through the middle of it all, sticking out like Liberace's sore thumb.

Mia's boss was a Chinese Anna Wintour type with a daunting reputation in the industry. She took a shine to Mia, amused that while everyone else wore high heels and designer brands, Mia still showed up in Doc Martens and a leather jacket. Mia's duties were an intern's cliché – that Starbucks was just downstairs – but she worked tirelessly. Later she would watch the movie *The Devil Wears Prada* and identify with the main character, a fresh young graduate running errands for her ice-queen editor. She had come a long way: from the Grand Bazaar to *Harper's Bazaar*.

It was a consumerist temple, but Mia didn't blindly worship the gods of Gucci and Versace. A film called *Tiny Times* that came out in 2013 summed up everything Mia disdained about the material girl type. The plot was an excuse for pretty girls to swan about in designer brands talking about money and men. The young director of the film and author of the novels it was based on, Guo Jingming, was metrosexual to the point of androgyny and clearly spinning his creation for the money (two sequels came out within a year). The female lead worked at a fashion magazine called *Me*.

Mia counted a dozen other female interns at *Bazaar*. Most were from rich families and each of them seemed to come to work in a new outfit every day. Mia scorned it as *xuanfu*: 'showing off wealth'. She didn't have the money to match their expensive labels and instead adjusted high-street clothes to make them look new. But she was the one given more responsibility by her boss, taken along as an assistant for photo shoots that made the glossy central spreads. Mia watched and learnt while the other interns watched and got jealous.

Her real friends were the male interns, who were gay to the last man. The LGBT scene was thriving in Beijing, with the gay club Destination packed every weekend, a magazine called *Gay Spot* and an annual queer film festival. But it wasn't easy: pressure to conform meant that most gay men hadn't come out to their parents, and in all but the most liberal workplaces it was safer to stay in the closet. When one of Mia's gay male friends returned to his home town of Chongqing for Spring Festival, he asked Mia if he could show his parents a picture of her and pretend she was his girlfriend. It kept them off his back for another year.

Mia had started to get the nudge from her own mother, and resolutely ignored it. She was twenty-two and had just split up with her college boyfriend of the last four years,

Setlight. They had grown into different people from the young couple who had fallen in love, until one day they realised there was no deeper compatibility beyond the emotions that had first bonded them together. Mia moved on first, and the relationship matured her. As she had lived with Setlight for her first year out of college, she needed to find a new place to call home.

*

The hutongs at the heart of Beijing date back to the thirteenth century when the Mongols invaded China and established the Yuan dynasty. The alleyways that veined the city were rebuilt and named for the Mongolian word for well, with its throaty 'h'. Over the last decades many of these historic areas have been torn down and rebuilt by developers, the character for 'demolish' painted on doors like portent of a Biblical plague. But labyrinthine blocks of hutongs remain, preserved by city planners. Those around the Drum Tower, built by the Mongols in 1272 at the exact centre of the old city, are among them.

Fuxue hutong is one block east of the Drum tower. At one end is a barracks for the People's Armed Police, where two guards stand facing a faded stencil of Lei Feng, the Mao-era model worker. At the other end are a primary school and a pet shop. In between are a mah-jong parlour, a training school for blind masseurs and a brothel (less than fifty yards from the school). A street market cuts the block in half from north to south, where buckets of eggs, drums of spice, tin cylinders of steamed dumplings, hanging hunks of meat, whole cooked ducks and live fish flapping in shallow pans of water are all ready to be weighed and bagged for a clutch of notes and a tinkle of coins. This is where residents overlap to shop for groceries: the mah-jong players, the blind masseurs, the off-duty prostitutes and soldiers.

Mia's shoebox studio was at no. 21 Little Fuxue hutong, a narrow tributary of the main alleyway. Inside the street entrance, a series of connected courtyards extended deep in an intricate maze of unmarked doors. It was called a 'big mixed courtyard', with over thirty households squeezed into the same address. If a package arrived, the delivery boy would just yell the recipient's name until someone opened their window or pointed at a door. Some of the flats were renovated (and rented to foreigners at a mark up) but most of the apartments were spartan and cheap, and tenants tended to be in either their twenties or their sixties.

For the older residents of the hutongs, life started early. They rose before dawn to buy vegetables in the market, walk their dogs or fly their pigeons (an old Beijinger pastime for those with a rooftop aviary). Mia, meanwhile, only had to be in the office mid-morning and slept in. The old timers didn't leave the hutong block for days on end, but she commuted by subway to the commercial district. They had lived there for decades, while she was just passing through. They went to bed at 9 or 10pm with a glass of warm water, when she was getting ready to go out. The two generations lived in the same courtyard but occupied different universes.

Mia partied every weekend in those days, and some

week nights too. She went out with the same three female friends – her 'booze and meat mates', a phrase for lads on the lash which they appropriated. The first stop was generally Sanlitun 'dirty' bar street, a strip of watering holes tucked away near the coloured-glass Rubik's cube of the Uniqlo store. The night might lead on to the clubs to the west of the old Workers' Stadium, with names like Babyface, Angel, Coco Banana, Elements and Lantern. Or they would drum 'n' bass until dawn at Dada, a stone's throw from the Drum Tower.

Mia got plenty of attention from boys in clubs. One night in April a Chinese guy tried to pick her up by explaining how the date in English was pronounced 4-1-9, which sounded like 'for one night'. Mia just laughed. She had abandoned her skinhead look for club wear – one themed birthday outing with her booze-and-meat girls was brightly coloured leather catsuits. Whatever the outfit, she wore a silver necklace with a knuckle-duster pendant that spelled out the word '*Bitch*' in English. Her iPhone case had a plastic knuckle-dusters grip too, and she kept the real thing in her handbag.

Also in the clubs were the 'money-worshipping girls' dolled up in high heels, low hems and frilly lace. Mia thought they were all fakes, hoping to bag one of the rich second-generation brats who used the Workers' Stadium strip as their hunting grounds. Once, at Lantern, Mia got in a fight with one of them over some drunken slight which ended with a cigarette being stubbed out on Mia's thigh. The two disentangled before Mia got her knuckle-dusters out, and she dragged herself back to Little Fuxue hutong where her cat Naibao ('milk dumpling') was waiting for her.

She was friendly with her middle-aged landlord, Mr Li, whose family had owned property in the courtyard for generations (it was taken away during the Cultural Revolution but given back afterwards). Mr Li was short, plump and bald, with the piratic Beijing accent that adds an 'r' to the end of words. In the summer he rolled up his shirt to cool his beer belly while playing Chinese chess on the street corner with his neighbours – all of them showing more midriff than Britney Spears. Whenever he saw Mia in the courtyard he said, 'Going out, eh?' or 'Coming back, eh?' in greeting. Sometimes he ran into her on his way to the market before dawn, and commented approvingly on how early she rose. It was beyond his ken that she might only just be coming home.

Mia worked as hard as she played, and after over a year as an intern she was offered a fashion stylist job at *Bazaar*. It was what her false friends in the office would have given a gloved arm and stockinged leg for. She celebrated by going out the following Halloween in a sexy nurse costume. Any foreign holiday in China is an excuse for young Chinese to party, even if it is just to eat 'Western' food: pizza for Thanksgiving, spaghetti for Easter. That Christmas Mia went club-hopping instead, decked out in a red felt skirt with white trimming and a sprig of holly.

She got back to the hutong in the first light of Boxing Day, just in time for Mr Li, groceries in hand, to say, 'Going out, eh?'

LUCIFER

When rock didn't make him famous, Lucifer tried TV. Rustic had burnt bright but short. D-22 club had closed in early 2012, and the scene had moved on. But talent and dating shows were booming, and here he looked for a new adoring audience.

The first big hit was *If You Are The One*, an equivalent of the British show *Take Me Out*. In the show a single male suitor tries to impress a line-up of twenty-four women standing behind podiums, who accept or reject him by keeping their light on or switching it off. If more than one light is left on at the end, he gets to choose. It was a refreshing change from the usual fare on Chinese TV, soppy Qing-dynasty soaps and variety-show style galas. The ratings soared and every channel wanted a piece of the pie, producing copies of copycats.

The media wrung their hands about materialistic dating attitudes in *If You Are The One*, and took them as a sign of the times. In 2010 attention focused on Ma Nuo, a twenty-three-year-old woman who, when asked by a young graduate if she would go for a bike ride with him, retorted, 'I would rather cry in the back of a BMW than laugh on the back of a bicycle.' Two months later a rich second-generation contestant called Liu Yunchao boasted of having six million yuan in the bank – the figure tallied up on the big screen while the audience oohed and aahed. Netizens found bitter truth in the implication that a guy's chances were linked to the size of his wallet.

The ever-prudish SAPPRFT – the State Administration of Press, Publication, Radio, Film and Television – didn't approve either. In the wake of the Ma Nuo controversy they issued a notice that 'rich young people' and the 'morally suspect' should not be allowed on dating shows. Instead contenders found more indirect ways to show off wealth, ensuring good airtime for their flats and cars in the self-introductory videos that came between question rounds. Eventually SAPPRFT restricted the number of dating shows and banned them from prime time, arguing that they were damaging to the spiritual health of the nation. But by then they were everywhere.

Be Mr Right was one of the provincial copycats, made by a smaller channel called South-East TV and recorded in a shared Beijing studio. The set-up was the same as *If You Are The One*, with a gallery of single women judging nervous suitors by turns. It didn't have the biggest budget but made up for it in post-production: boingy noises and words flashing up on screen in a bulbous font with multiple exclamation marks. Lucifer's friend B Ge, 'Brother B', had introduced Lucifer to the show's producer, having been on it himself.

Brother B was a twig-skinny Beijinger whose shtick was

playing the loser in comic videos online. A self-consciously 'dumbass youth', *erbiqingnian*, the term also gave him his stage name: to call anything *er*, second rate or B, was to mock it, and *bi* was also a swear word. His speciality was performing stupid antics in public places – blowing up condoms in supermarket aisles, doing chin-ups in the subway – while shouting into the camera. His goofball persona won him over a hundred thousand fans on Weibo and a sponsorship deal with a video site, income he supplemented as a comedy wedding host.

Lucifer was taking supplementary music classes at China Minorities University, where he learnt to play the piano, but was living in an eastern suburb of Beijing so far out it was part of Hebei, his home province. Called Yanjiao or 'swallow district' for the capital's ancient name, Yanjing, it took almost two hours by bus to travel the thirty-five kilometres into the centre of Beijing. But housing was cheap and plentiful and the commute was shared with tens of thousands of other young Chinese priced out by rents in the city. Lucifer lived hand to mouth, relying on an allowance from his parents – a classic 'bite the old tribe'. The irony was not lost on him that after dreaming so long of making it to Beijing, he was technically back in Hebei.

He approached *Be Mr Right* with the same spirit of opportunism in which the show itself had been conceived. He wasn't in it to find a date, but wanted the exposure of TV to replicate Brother B's viral fame. Even if he made a fool of himself, that was still a kind of fame. He overslept on the February morning his segment was due to shoot, and tumbled into a taxi driven by an acquaintance who took him to the studio off meter (friends in low places). Once there he was rushed through make-up and given a briefing by the producer, who prepped him for how the skit would go and what was expected of him, even feeding him lines. Lucifer's fifteen minutes of fame beckoned.

*

On stage, a domed wormhole of blue and yellow lights started to flash. Above it an LCD screen blazed the show's title in pink cursive characters – *Be Mr Right: Challenge of the Happy 100* – next to the provocative curves of a cartoon sex bomb. Lucifer burst onto set through the tunnel in a stripy jacket, black polo neck and his favourite red trousers, with an acoustic guitar slung around his shoulder. He grinned and waved at the live audience, who applauded dutifully.

The host, Zhao Yi'ou, was a thickset middle-aged man with a cigarette-stained voice. A panel of two commentators sat behind a raised desk to one side: former singer Dong Lu, and resident 'psychology expert' Wang Jianyi, although she offered no credentials. In front of them all, staggered on rising steps, thirty young women with numbered badges perched on high stools, long legs artfully crossed. They were a parade of high heels, higher hems, fake eyelashes and straps galore, more colourful than a set of drawing crayons. The first question Zhao had asked them was 'Who here likes shopping?' Every hand went up.

Lucifer introduced himself. 'I'm called Li Yan, I'm

studying at Central Minorities University, and I have my own rock 'n' roll band. I'm the lead singer. Thank you.'

'Eh, a rock 'n' roll band?' prompted the host. 'Why don't you play a song for us then?'

'Now?' Lucifer asked, feigning surprise. What good luck he had his guitar with him. He swung the instrument down and with fast, cheery chords launched into one of his own songs, 'I Love You Girl'. As he sang he climbed the steps among the ladies, to cheers from the audience.

'*I lost my pizza in the backpackers,*' he sang, a reference to a youth hostel in England where Rustic had ordered a pizza only to find other guests had eaten it. '*Can you find it?*'

He stopped next to number 4, a knockout in cut-offs and a tank top, and dipped his guitar low to get close and personal. She pulled back, bringing her hands up to protect her space before laughing awkwardly at herself.

'*I lost myself on the highway,*' he moved on to his next target, '*don't know where to go. Can you help me?*' Everyone was clapping along by the chorus. '*I love you giiirl. You're in the miracles. I want to be your boy when you're blue, when you're sad and blue.*'

'Very *hot!*' the host complimented, affectedly saying the word in English. 'That number 4 you sang to,' he joked, 'there's two ways you could describe that moment: one is interacting, another is harassing.' The audience laughed. 'Number 4, which did you feel it was?'

'I think he's very passionate,' number 4 blushed. 'I didn't

know he would get so close. But his eyes are very attractive, I got an electric shock from them.'

Lucifer flushed red and couldn't stop grinning. Next the host set him up to boast about Global Battle of the Bands, Rustic's victory and the prize money. Then his introductory video came up on the big screen, in which he talked about his romantic troubles. 'I've dated Chinese girls,' he said, 'but their material expectations were too high. I really hate materialistic girls. But all the girls around me are like that. What can I do?'

The women had a chance to react, and number 17 seized the chance. 'You're generalising, you're being self-centred,' she said. 'It's not that all Chinese girls are materialistic, it's that you only look at the materialistic girls. On the subway, you're looking at the pretty girls batting their eyelashes, but you don't see the ones reading books.'

'I've been heartbroken a couple of times,' Lucifer went on, ignoring her. 'Now I have a different idea about love. I want to be a gold-digger.'

The audience gasped, the ladies sniggered. The phrase he had used, *dao chamen*, literally meant for a groom to move in with the bride's family after marriage, flipping tradition on its head. Now it meant any guy marrying for money. 'That doesn't mean I'm not willing to struggle,' Lucifer explained, 'I just want to find a way for me to get closer to success more easily. So I want to find a rich girl, who can buy a flat in Beijing for us.'

'She pays ninety-nine per cent, you pay one per cent?' Zhao Yi'ou asked.

'She can pay ninety-five per cent.'

Number 23 had her hand up. 'You say mainland girls are materialistic,' she said. 'I think you're more materialistic than we are. I think a real man wouldn't say that.'

'If girls can be materialistic,' Lucifer retorted, 'why can't I be materialistic too? Humanity is equal after all, men and women should be equal. When we find our other half, we might face lots of difficulties we hadn't considered before. So if we make sure those hardships at the beginning aren't so many, then we can overcome the new ones together.'

'Young fellow, let me ask you something,' cut in Wang Jianyi, the psychology expert, conservative in an all-pink outfit with scarf and bobcut. 'I wonder, do you have any requirements about age?' The audience guffawed. 'If a woman can provide for you, she might be of a certain age already. Or if she's a young lady it's probably her dad's money, and what's that got to do with you?'

'Teacher,' replied Lucifer, 'any age is OK.'

The host moved on to the next segment of the show, in which Lucifer chose six women from the line-up and they all answered multiple-choice questions about dating. If Lucifer's answers matched either theirs or the most popular 'female choice' according to a pre-show survey, he would win a cash prize.

The first question popped up on the screen: 'Your boy-friend is always speaking his home dialect with his family. What do you do?' Options ranged from 'Ask him not to' to 'So I can't understand him, no big deal'. Lucifer and his ladies scratched at touch screens, and their answers were revealed at the same time. All six women chose C: 'Secretly study the dialect yourself.' Lucifer chose E: 'A tooth for a tooth – start talking in your own dialect or a foreign language.' The girls were not impressed.

The second question rang a bell: 'In what conditions can a woman allow a man to be a gold-digger?' Lucifer plumped for A: 'If he's a good catch but comes from a poor family.' Three of the hopefuls had chosen the same answer, but it was far and away the least popular choice in the survey data, with only two per cent support.

Lucifer justified his choice. 'I think a sensible woman like that,' he said, 'will be able to find a great guy. My goal isn't an apartment and it isn't a car. It's to have good economic conditions and less trouble, so I can focus on my music and follow my dream.'

'*Standing on a giant's shoulders* –' the host prompted.

'– *to fly higher, to go further*,' Lucifer completed the cliché. 'Without money for good foundations, I can't build a skyscraper,' he continued excitedly. 'Let me tell you – I want to be a superstar, an international superstar.'

Number 17, who had challenged him earlier, piped up. 'Making music in a city or in a village,' she said, 'what's the difference? So long as you're talented you should be able to achieve anything if you work hard.'

Dong Lu, the other guest expert, answered for Lucifer. 'Do you know what the most important thing in music is? Money. Whether you're in a city or in a village, the place doesn't matter but the equipment does. Equipment is a musician's wok for cooking. Can you use a block of wood to fry eggs?'

'I believe if I'm a good chef,' number 17 shot back, 'someone will give me the wok, to let me show off my skills.'

'He wants to show he's a good chef too!' Dong Lu exclaimed. 'He just needs to find a good wok.'

'A wok,' Zhao Yi'ou summed up, 'that loves him.'

Bringing things to a close, he explained that Lucifer had won 900 yuan but faced a final choice. He could take the money and run, or he could ask one of the three women who had matched his answer to go out with him. If she said yes, they would share the cash on a date. If she turned him down he would leave empty handed.

Among the three prospectives was number 4, the beauty whom Lucifer had first serenaded. He asked her, and she accepted. Draping an arm over her shoulder like a conquering hero, Lucifer walked out through the flashing neon vortex and back into the cabled mundanity of the TV studio, with no bright lights and no one watching.

On the way to the exit, number 4 told him she already had boyfriend and was just doing this for fun. They never did meet for a date, but added each other on social media. When he flicked through her profile photos he saw her boyfriend had a Mercedes and wore expensive clothes. Lucifer might have won on reality TV, but in reality he could never compete.

DAHAI

Dahai wasn't having luck with the ladies either. He was over the hump of the mid-twenties, and the pressure to start a family is as real for men in China as it is for women. That is partly residue of the old Confucian notion that producing an heir is a son's most important filial duty – and expectations are higher for an only child. At Spring Festival if a son doesn't produce a girlfriend he will often be asked about it. The desperate few buy the services of a fake girlfriend on Taobao for just such a purpose. Above all men are choked with stress in a dating culture that, in their eyes at least, judges them by their financial success.

There were three 'haves' expected of a man: a flat, a car and savings. With those, it was implied, he could attract the fourth: someone to share them with. Dahai had none. That was called a *sanwunan*, a 'three withouts man'. Instead he faced the three 'highs': high property costs, high car prices, high medical fees. He had been promoted to 'assistant engineer' and his salary had gone up to 4,000–5,000 yuan a month depending on performance, even though his duties overseeing the tunnel work were the same. But it wasn't nearly enough, and housing prices in Beijing were so far out of his reach that the flats might as well be on the moon. He did a napkin calculation of how long he would have to work at this rate until he could buy one, and came up with the depressing figure of fifty years.

Dahai was a *guanggun*, one of the 'bare branches' after whom Singles Day was named. With an estimated 118 boys born to each 100 girls in his generation there were over twenty million of them already, graphed to rise to forty million by 2040. They were competing for a smaller pool of women in the knowledge that some of them would never find a wife, and many worried that they wouldn't make the cut. The phrase for the masculine ideal was *gaofushuai*: 'tall, rich, handsome'. (The equivalent for women was *baifumei*: 'white, rich, pretty'.) Dahai was tall and not bad looking, with strong features and a new buzz cut, but again he fell short of the hat-trick. He was stuck in work he didn't like, single and frustrated.

There just weren't that many ways to meet someone. Hooking up at bars was fine for 'flower princes', the Chinese term for playboys, but not for ordinary Zhous looking for a life partner. Most twenty-somethings still relied on their circle of friends and colleagues to make introductions, which limited options. Online dating had taken off in a big way, and websites with names like 'Cherished Love' or 'Beautiful Destiny' existed not to facilitate casual flings but were for those with marriage in mind. Groom seeking bride, bride seeking groom. When you signed up, questionnaires asked for information including height, education level, monthly salary and home ownership status. Speed-dating events were the same, each partner ascertaining marital compatibility in eight minutes or less.

Then there was the literal marriage market. Every weekend at public parks in Beijing and Shanghai the boulevards were lined with rows of adverts touting not goods but people. A typical one read: 'Beijing male, born 1987, undergraduate degree, height 1.73 metres, has car and flat.' It wasn't the lovebirds who posted them but their anxious parents, seeking a suitable match for their sons and daughters. In one such market next to the moat of the Forbidden City there was no one under fifty in sight, only rows of 'sellers' sitting on fold-away stools while 'buyers' browsed the adverts, jotting down telephone numbers to pass on to their child – who roll their eyes at mum and dad and rarely follow up on an arranged match.

Dahai didn't like that relationships were so commodified. He still believed in finding love but the reality around him felt more like a supply-and-demand market. At noon on 29 May 2012 he posted a song lyric on Weibo: 'I remember when we were young / Everyone was sincere / What we said was what we meant.' A female friend commented underneath it: 'One life is only enough time to love one person.' That evening he posted again, a short line in his best English: 'relationship is confusing, life is confusing, love is confusing.'

It was all confusing, really. To get anything worth having in China, he came to realise, either you had to play dirty or bend to the system completely. The rich second-generation flower princes had it all and there was no shortage of girls chasing them. His work-unit bosses sounded just like the socialist slogan banners around them. As for officials and businessmen, he simply assumed they were corrupt. The clean route to success was hard to see. It was enough to turn anyone into a cynic. Along with the other bare branches of his generation, Dahai was starting to snap.

*

There was no justice except keyboard justice. Dahai was still active on Weibo and followed each new story as it broke. In April 2012 Bo Xilai, a Politburo member and son of one of China's revolutionary 'eight immortals', was suspended and later put on trial for corruption after revelations that his wife had murdered a British businessman, Neil Heywood. As mayor of the western city of Chongqing Bo had been flying close to the red sun with his Maoist throwback policies, and some saw his downfall as a purge. Either way it exposed infighting in the top echelons of the Party and censors suppressed details. 'Chongqing' became a sensitive word online, so netizens talked about tomatoes instead – *xihongshi* being a homonym for 'red city in the west'.

In June it was a single photo zipping around the web. In the image a young woman called Feng Jianmei lay on a hospital bed, bags under her eyes, her skin sallow, exhausted. At her feet was a foetus, a second pregnancy forcibly aborted seven months into term after she couldn't pay the fine to Family Planning officers, one of many brutalities committed in the name of the one-child policy. And in August the object of hate was Yang Decai, an official caught on camera smiling at the scene of a traffic accident. Netizens spotted his expensive watch, performed a vigilante 'human flesh search' and found images of him sporting a collection of designer wristwear despite his modest official's salary. They called him 'Brother Watch'.

It was scandals like these that riled Dahai the most. While he was putting aside a thousand-odd yuan a month – pebbles at the foot of a mountain – corrupt cadres were lining their pockets. 'Bandits,' he called the government in private conversation. Each abuse of power was a new stone in the kidneys of his soul. And it wasn't just the leaders he was angry at, but all of society. One viral video from late 2011 was of a two-year-old girl called Wang Yue who was run over on the kerbside in southern China. In the seven minutes before a rubbish scavenger helped her eighteen people passed by, fearful of being blamed for the accident. Dahai was among the millions of netizens who shared the video. 'Reposting is power.'

It had seemed to him, in his first years on Weibo, that they were making a difference. Yang Decai was investigated and arrested for corruption. Victims of the Wenzhou train crash kept their legal rights thanks to pressure from netizens, who also rallied together to donate blood in the aftermath. 'Not in my backyard' environmental protests got results too, such as in the northern port city of Dalian in August 2011, when tens of thousands marched to shut down a PX chemical factory (though it later reopened). But the marches were always local, never national or in the capital where they would be dealt with harshly. Now he started to question if his disaffected generation would ever take to the streets. The only issue where major protests were given full licence was against Japan.

Patriotic education drilled home for the 'angry youth' what their grandparents had said at the dinner table all along: Japan was the old enemy whose spirit of aggression still lurks. 'Little Japan' and 'Japanese devils' are common epithets, and daytime TV war dramas show Japanese soldiers killing and being killed by Chinese troops in ever more violent ways. For most post-80s, once they get to college and learn independently about Japan their opinions change. Japan has plenty of soft power in China, from the anime cat Doraemon to hentai porn. The country is a popular holiday destination for twenty-somethings. But a minority cling to their xenophobia, and even for the majority there is a doublethink where they can be fanboys of Japanese culture and resent Japanese politics at the same time.

Every diplomatic clash sparked fresh outrage, and in 2012 it was the Diaoyu islands: two cragged hunks of rock thrusting out of the sea north-east of Taiwan at the scattered tip of Japan's sickle of southern islands. To China they were the Diaoyudao (literally 'fishing islands'); to Japan they were the Senkaku islands. Both claimed them as sovereign ground, even if their only inhabitants were sea birds. In April Tokyo's governor pandered to nationalism and said Japan would buy the islands from their private owner. In August a group of Chinese activists sailed from Hong Kong to the rocks as a statement, only to be detained by the Japanese coast guard. The waters boiled over.

On 15 September a crowd of thousands gathered in front of the Japanese embassy in Beijing. There were banners: 'Kick the Japanese out of the Diaoyu islands'; 'End Japanese imperialism'; 'China is destined to prevail'. There were chants: 'Japan is doomed to die!'; 'Little Japan, fuck your mother!'; 'Declare War!'. A few people surged forward to throw stones at the embassy windows. Others handed out Chinese flags and bottles of mineral water. The road was cordoned off by the authorities, creating a funnel for protesters as if it was a theme park. In other cities even bigger crowds marched, carrying Japanese flags with a cross through the red sun. Ramen restaurants were trashed and Toyotas were smashed. It didn't seem to matter that the owners and drivers were Chinese.

For these angry young men, there was more to their fury than frothing-at-the-mouth nationalism. The implicit criticism was that Beijing had let China be slighted by Japan. The implicit threat was that they could turn on their own government if it was seen as too weak. There were protests hidden within the protests: factions supporting Bo Xilai, and images of Mao as if to say that a stronger leader wouldn't have let this happen. At the root their real frustrations had less to do with Japan and more to do with social inequality and the daily sight of the rich and powerful taking all the spoils of growth. Many of them were from the lower rungs of education and work – losers in a rigged game – and took advantage of the sanctioned chaos to let off steam.

Dahai, who shared their frustrations, had no sympathy

for the rock-throwers. He thought the 'shitty youth' were just another mob. Where before he would have leapt at any opportunity to voice his anger, now his overriding emotion was apathy. He felt impotent to solve any of the problems he was once so passionate about. There were just so many outrages to get mad about, and nothing seemed to improve. He read and reposted less and less, and called himself 'numb' to it all. Only those without power shouted about injustice, he thought. Those with the power to do something about it kept silent and banqueted.

It was also a matter of age. Dahai turned twenty-seven during the protests, and felt that righteous anger – whether nationalistic or dissenting, or both – was a game for the early twenties. When he was fresh out of college he had grand ideas about how the common people should clean up, or even overthrow, their government. He had felt part of a netizen revolution. Already he looked back and realised how naive he had been.

Han Han, Dahai's favourite blogger (himself now thirty), had summed it up in three essay-length posts at the end of 2011. 'The final winners in a revolution,' he wrote in the first, 'are bound to be ruthless and cruel. To be frank, revolution is a word which sounds refreshing and exciting, promising instant results, but for China it's not necessarily a good choice.' 'Perfect democracy will never appear in China,' he continued in the second. 'Gradual reform is the best way out at present.' The third called for free speech as a starting point and finished optimistically: 'I have faith in the character of the people of our generation, so I believe these freedoms are bound to arrive sooner or later.'

Dahai agreed. Like Han Han, his first rebellious flush had been tempered by practical thoughts of the future. He now thought that China would only truly transform when the old guard died and his generation, the post-80s, took over. But it would be a slow change. By the end of 2012 he was thoroughly disabused of the belief that he could better his society. Instead he focused on improving himself.

Seven days a week he was down in the tunnel. Dahai's team of workers expected to meet the team digging from the other end by the following summer. As winter beckoned, he thought of what life might look like when his own angry youth was behind him – and whom he might spend it with.

SNAIL

Snail returned to China Mining and Technology University a year after he dropped out. There was some shame in re-entering the second year while his old classmates had leapt ahead. He kept his head down, avoided the Internet bar at the east gate, and three summers later won his bachelor's degree in Automated Electronics. At graduation he threw his mortar board up in the air for the group photo, with a grin on his face. He was now the first university-educated member of his family in all of its generations. But to stay in the capital he needed to work.

College graduates eking out a living in the cities have a nickname: the 'ant tribe'. Armed with a rolled-up degree and little else, they occupy cheap apartment blocks on the outskirts of Beijing and Shanghai in colonies of tens of thousands. Most of them are outsiders and a large portion are unemployed. Since the late nineties, in part due to a drive to create more college places, China has had more university graduates than jobs for them. Those who are gainfully employed still barely make enough to afford rent and noodles. Every morning they stream into the city from their far-out housing developments, like the ants who lend them their name.

Snail was lucky to find work through one of his college professors, who ran a tech company on the side to supplement his teaching salary. The firm designed, manufactured and sold a single product: a gadget that tests the gas level in coal mines (the professor's own invention). The company was just up the road from his old university, and had no more than twenty employees. Snail's entry-level position was as a paper-pusher, stamping forms to certify that all the screws had been tightened securely on each unit. His starting salary was 2,000 yuan a month. Instead of commuting with the ants from the outskirts, he plumped for the other option within his price range – underground.

Almost all high-rises in Chinese cities have a basement, generally one to three floors deep, once compulsory by building code as bomb shelters. To feed a boom of demand for cheap housing thousands have been converted into mazes of cramped flats, with little regard for comfort or fire safety so long as the rent is low. The rooms are often as narrow as one metre across, with just enough space for a single bed and a suitcase. A change to housing laws made it technically illegal to live in them but that is uniformly ignored. Of the twenty-odd million people in Beijing an estimated one million of them – mostly young graduates and migrant workers – live underneath the other nineteen million as a literal underclass. There is a name for them too: 'rat tribe'.

Snail's basement was below an apartment complex twenty minutes' walk north-east of his workplace. On the perimeter wall, painted characters were flaking: '*Warm and loving, virtuous and kind. Together enjoy a fragrant life.*' Spangly red banners hung over it: '*Improve the residents' disaster-relief consciousness*' . . . '*Safely together, you and us.*' Inside, four eighteen-storey buildings stood in faded green livery. Next to each of them was a low structure standing off to one side: a tunnel entrance leading down like the gates of hell for estate agents. Snail's hole was the one that read 'Building Number One Underground Housing', past a heap of locked bikes and a lonely warning cone.

Inside, the shallow steps turned sharply to the right underneath the building. There were bare electric bulbs and ventilation was minimal. The air stuck to your lungs. On the left was a small administrative office with a stockpile of fire extinguishers guarded by two middle-aged ladies, Mrs Zhang and Mrs Chang. Each kept a clinking ring of keys larger than the hand that carried it. There were fifty flats on the first basement floor, give or take, and the same another floor down – all partitioned by thin walls and narrow corridors to maximise the available space. At the far end were shared toilets and showers, next to a room with a trough-like basin in which to wash your face and clothes. The ceilings were just high enough for Snail not to stoop.

His room was three metres long and two metres wide, most of it taken up by his bed. To one side was a plastic table for his laptop and charger cables, and an open rack for his clothes next to it. He hung his favourite football team's scarf from the exposed piping above him. At the foot of the bed, by the door, was another table with an electric rice cooker and portable hotplate. That served as the kitchen. Snail boiled rice or noodles for most of his meals, mixed with stir-fried vegetables and a generous dollop of 'old spicy Mama' chilli sauce. The room cost 600 yuan a month.

Most of the other rat tribe were young migrants in Beijing with low-paid jobs, just like him. But his closest friends were a middle-aged couple across the corridor whom Snail called Auntie and Uncle. They had lived in the basement for almost ten years, and sold fruit and vegetables at the entrance to the complex: skinned pineapples in summer, hillocks of cabbage in winter, long stalks of spring onion, apples in plastic wrapping. It was all loaded onto a wooden three-wheel cart with scales dangling where the handlebars had been. Auntie greeted Snail every time he passed and every so often invited him for a meal in their room, which was larger and had a gas canister tucked underneath a hob to cook on.

Snail wondered who lived in the apartment above him, on ground level. He knew he was directly underneath a bathroom because every time they went to the toilet Snail could hear it and a moist patch in the corner of his ceiling grew larger. He glued paper over the stain to hide it but it was a losing battle. He had no idea whether his upstairs neighbours knew he was down there. Maybe they had passed him outside and nodded in greeting, oblivious that he was privy to their every bowel movement. There was no contact between below and above ground, and a stigma attached to basement dwellers that meant the other residents didn't stop to talk to him. To them the rat tribe was invisible.

For entertainment, he streamd TV serials on his laptop. One drama, *Beijing Youth*, followed four male cousins trying to succeed in the capital. Their given names were East, South, West and North by collusion of their parents (like Snail and his own three cousins, whose given names shared the same tree pictogram). In the first episode the eldest of them, East, gets cold feet seconds before stamping marriage papers with his long-term girlfriend. He dumps her, leaves his job and resolves to 'relive a second youth' by travelling around China. His cousins join him while their parents worry themselves silly. Eventually they return to Beijing and marry their girlfriends as a group on a mountain top.

At one moment in the show, East's father sums up the hardships of the post-80s and why they would want to break free. 'East's is the most unfortunate generation,' he says. 'When they were in school, university was free; when they were in university, primary school was free. When they hadn't started to work, jobs were assigned; when they entered the job market, they could only bash their heads to scrape together a living. When they weren't earning it was cheap to buy an apartment; when they had a salary flats were unaffordable.' Snail identified, but to him taking off on a voyage of self-discovery felt like a luxury only the city-born could afford. For him the goal was precisely what East wanted to escape – working in the city.

His own life was closer to another popular TV series which went by the English name *Dwelling Narrowness*. Set in Shanghai, it followed a young couple renting a shoe-box apartment while saving every penny to buy a property of their own. The Chinese title came from a phrase for cramped urban living conditions: 'snail home'.

*

After a year underground Snail's life fell into a rhythm. He worked long hours and was given more responsibility in his job. Sometimes he went on work trips to Shanxi province to field-test his company's canary in the coal mine. He scrimped on living costs and put aside a little more each month. Most encouragingly of all, his girlfriend from Anhui moved in.

Xiaoli was a childhood classmate – Little Beautiful, the girl he had sat behind in middle school and lobbed paper balls at. While he was in Beijing she had studied nursing in Hefei, the provincial capital of Anhui, then worked in a hospital. Her best friend had put them back in touch when Snail returned to university for a second time, and the two courted by instant message on QQ. They talked about such trivial things that he can't remember a single detail, but the subtext right from the start was whether they were compatible for marriage.

A favourite expression of anyone talking about marriage in China is *mendanghudui*: 'the doors match, the windows fit', meaning your partner should come from a background close to your own. Xiaoli was from the same corner of

China as Snail, although she grew up in Sixian town whereas he was born in the countryside proper (a difference only important to someone from the area). Their education had been in parallel. Their families knew each other. Xiaoli was understanding of Snail's past. It didn't matter that they hadn't met since they were teenagers. The doors matched, the windows fitted.

When Xiaoli came to Beijing Snail moved into a larger room in the same basement, next to Auntie and Uncle. It was a spacious four by four metres, with a double bed and even a high grating with a view of ankles trotting past above. As soon as she settled in Snail noticed how everything suddenly seemed cleaner. Xiaoli found a job at a hospital a short bus journey away and together they saved as much as they could. In the evenings she occupied herself by sewing a three-metre-wide embroidery of the famous Song dynasty painted scroll 'Along the River During Tomb Sweeping Festival'. It took her the best part of a year to finish.

Beijing is a city of seasonal extremes, and the rat tribe got the worst of it. High summer was sweltering and sticky, with no air-conditioning units. Winter was frozen and punishing as central heating wasn't installed in the basement, so Snail and Xiaoli had to rely on electric heaters to keep warm. Mrs Zhang and Mrs Chang hung thick green quilts over the entrance to keep the heat in, of the same kind that appear all over Beijing every November. But they also kept the damp in, and black mould crept up the basement walls.

A new word had emerged to describe the various kinds of down-and-out young Chinese, from ant tribe to rat tribe to snail tribe. It was first used in online forums in 2011 and about caught on quickly. Soon, everyone was calling themselves a *diaosi*. Literally the word meant 'penis hair' but 'loser' is the closest equivalent. It was used tongue-in-cheek by anyone with no money or prospects, almost as a badge of pride – these losers weren't responsible for their own low status as much as the society that kept them under. The post-80s generation embraced the term and Snail was no exception. But he was also trying to outgrow it.

That winter he got a phone call from his mother, who told him that he had been living with Xiaoli for a while now and he should probably propose. Snail thought that was reasonable and suggested the idea to Xiaoli that night. She accepted him and they set a date for a wedding ceremony in Anhui the following October. It might not have been the most romantic proposal, but Snail's prospects were looking up. Four years ago he had been a college dropout working as a KTV car-park attendant. Now he had a degree, a job and a fiancée. He might still be underground but Snail was finding the light.

FRED

Fred was following both elections. One was a rollercoaster culminating in a national vote that could go either way. The other was a foregone conclusion decided by committee months if not years before. One was a parade of blanket advertising, televised debates, town-hall speeches, media punditry. The other took place behind closed and guarded doors, where political factions argued and reached consensus. One would decide what some called the most powerful man on the planet, beholden to no higher authority than his own. The other was in America.

Fred was three years into her Ph.D. at Peking University when, in the autumn of 2012, she flew to the United States for a year abroad. Her doctoral research was on constitutional interpretation by the US Supreme Court and her mission was to plumb the libraries of Cornell University, an Ivy League college in New York state. It was her first time in America, and despite her patriotism she was excited to go to the country that was historically the enemy – a cognitive dissonance that she lived with quite happily.

China has more students overseas than any other nation. There are over three hundred thousand in American universities and more than sixty thousand in Britain. Getting in is big business in China, where educational consulting companies have sprung up left and right to coach kids through the application process. The memoir *Harvard Girl*, in which two Chinese parents outline the how-to regimen that got their daughter accepted into Harvard, was a national bestseller in 2000.

Most who get the opportunity to study overseas are from privileged backgrounds, like Fred. Some are the offspring of China's wealthiest businessmen and highest political elites (Xi Jinping's daughter was a Harvard girl). Cynics have dubbed them the 'just-in-case' generation, a strategy by high-powered parents to establish an escape route abroad should there be a crisis at home and a sudden need to flee. Either way it's prestigious to have a child studying in North America or Europe, and a foreign degree improves their market value back home.

For a few of the rich second-generation, college in the West is an opportunity to throw their money around away from the watchful eye of mummy and daddy. These are the ones who make the headlines: a speeding UC Irvine student who crashed his Ferrari; a twenty-six-year-old at Bath University who tried to bribe his professor to pass his dissertation. At one point their poster boy was Bo Guagua, son of the fallen politician Bo Xilai, whose party pictures from Oxford included Guagua lined up with four other students in academic gowns, pissing against the gates of Trinity College. The pictures were shared by netizens back home and Guagua became a symbol of the excesses of the 'Party second-generation', Fred's tribe.

Fred resented the prevailing stereotype of rich young Chinese as spoiled brats. She had met some like that, sure – the sort who drove luxury cars, wore the most expensive suits and blew 200,000 yuan on a single night. They were the high-profile rich who wanted to flaunt it and who felt they had the most to prove. But there were also the low-profile rich, who had the best upbringing and who worked hard to surpass expectations. Even Bo Guagua, to those who knew him, was entrepreneurial and driven. That many had studied overseas from as early as high school only meant they were more naturalised abroad. Now she was joining them.

Her flight landed in September, and Fred's first sight in America was of a tour group of Chinese visitors talking too loudly. She felt a twinge of shame that this class of tourist increasingly formed Western impressions of China. Yet when she settled into Cornell and walked around Ithaca, the town next to the university, her own first impressions of the US were entirely favourable. The air was cleaner, the grass greener. There were no concerns over food safety, no queue-jumping or pushing on buses. She could load the website of the *New York Times* without using a VPN. The breadth and length of the college reading lists impressed her, and she enjoyed a first taste of academic freedom without having to dodge around sensitive topics.

While the lives of young Americans are widely envied by

young Chinese, as the months went by Fred also saw a side to the US that jarred with the image of a land of plenty. It might have been her own projection from what she had read but she had never felt less safe than on the streets of New York. (Street crime is rare in China and guns almost unheard of, making Beijing a generally safe city to walk around at night.) There was also visible homelessness, all the more shocking in a country so much richer than hers. Signs of the economic slump were noticeable, from bankrupt shops to foreclosure signs. All of a sudden the idea of America on the decline and China on the rise, which she used to dismiss as a fantasy, began to feel more real.

Another detail from Cornell that stuck in her mind was a friendship she formed with a black fellow student. He sat behind her in lectures, at the back of the hall, and they talked while waiting for the lecturer to arrive. She told him about the beaches in Hainan, the smog in Beijing and what it felt like to be an outsider in the US. He said he understood, and told her about his nation's own problems with racial prejudice, police abuse and income inequality. The blemishes were showing on America's skin. But Fred was most interested to compare the two countries in November 2012, when in the same week that Americans voted for Barack Obama or Mitt Romney, China's government anointed its own new leader.

The occasion was the eighteenth National Congress of the Communist Party, a large internal gathering held every five years since the founding of the Party in 1921. The domestic media simply called it 'the big eighteenth'. In

America, everyone held their breath as Obama won his second term. In China, no one was surprised when Xi Jinping took Hu Jintao's place as General Secretary of the Communist Party and paramount leader of the People's Republic. The contrast could not have been starker.

While most of Fred's generation watched the US election with curious detachment, like some distant entertainment show, she was fascinated to have an inside view. She listened to pundits saying things about their leaders that couldn't be dreamt of on Chinese TV. It was eye-opening to see democracy in action. But the influence of corporate lobbyists and campaign funding gave her pause, as did a partisan deadlock between Democrats and Republicans. In those respects America's democracy seemed broken.

Despite studying it, she still saw electoral democracy as unfit for China. Already the early triumphalism of the Arab spring had entered its long winter, as Egypt and Syria descended into factionalism and chaos. From the Chinese perspective it was hardly a shining example of successful revolution, and state media took every opportunity to show the aftermath in its worst light. Fred admired free speech and judicial independence in the US, and hoped for both in China one day, but she didn't think that they were only possible with national elections. The more she learnt about US democracy the more strongly she felt that it wouldn't work back home.

Meanwhile, she got an education in views of China from the other side of the Pacific. When American classmates talked to her, Fred came to realise two things. First: no one knew much about China. Second: everyone had an opinion anyway. She fielded aggressive leading questions about the Tiananmen Square massacre and listened to vague diatribes about human rights abuses. They were all issues she had reasonable opinions about but in this context she became defensive. The same sense of American superiority seemed to underlie each conversation, along with the implicit question: why don't you hate your country? She tried to engage at first, but soon found it easier to feign a lack of interest.

Before long she began to withdraw from social life and spent her free time with her roommates, who were also Chinese exchange students. They were six thousand kilometres from home, transplanted into a different culture and using a foreign language – it wasn't easy to blend in. Instead of going to parties and drinking beer out of red cups she focused on study, viewing college overseas as an opportunity not to be wasted rather than an opportunity to *get* wasted. But her biggest complaint was the canteen food. Every day it was fried chicken, pizza, hamburger, hot dogs. Panda Express served something almost but not entirely unlike Chinese food, and the first time she saw a fortune cookie she didn't know what to do with it.

Most nights she cooked for herself: spicy tofu, boiled greens, chicken soup for the homesick soul. She immersed herself in lectures, seminars, long stretches in the library. She suffered from bouts of depression, and Cornell's grim weather only made her miss tropical Hainan more. For all of the novelty of America around her, she remained in a bubble. As the snows fell on drifts thick as lead, Fred bunkered down to weather the winter.

*

By the time the campus thawed, the end of her year abroad was in sight. She had spent Christmas break in Hainan, when everyone was busy with work. The fortnight of the Chinese New Year, meanwhile, had fallen in the middle of her own term. Her father came to visit in spring break and together they went on a sightseeing tour of famous American universities: MIT, Harvard, then the short hop across to the west coast to see Stanford and Berkeley. There had always been the possibility that Fred would return to America to study or teach after her Ph.D. But by June she only wanted to go back to Beijing.

The brain drain used to be a big problem for China. When Deng Xiaoping (who had studied in Paris as a young man) opened up the country to the rest of the world in 1978 it set in motion a small exodus of talented students over the following decades. Many of them stayed abroad and China lost its best and brightest. Now the trend is reversing and China offers some of the best opportunities. An increasing number of overseas Chinese students every year choose to apply their new skills back home – not drain but gain. As always there is a nickname for them: 'sea turtles', *haigui*, a punning play on the verb 'to return'.

Some Chinese sea turtles return more nationalistic than they left. Born into a confident era and comfortable with the idea of China as a strong nation, attitudes abroad only raise their hackles. For others, exposure to a new environment makes them more critical of their government. But for them all it is hard to readjust when plunged back into life in China. Colleagues and friends can be wary that returning students have been changed by the West, and in many ways they are right.

Fred found food for thought in the American way of life, but her world view wasn't blown wide open by it. She admired many aspects of the US that China lacked: friendly strangers, trust in society, assurance of legal rights. On the flip side there was a dynamism to China that she didn't sense in the States, a drive and an upwards movement. If anything, the two rival nations had more in common than they thought. Both had a strong sense of exceptionalism. Both wanted to be number one. Both were obsessed by personal and national quests for money and power. They were the same in opposite ways.

When she returned to Beijing, Fred had her share of reverse culture-shock. Her first reaction to the honking traffic and construction drilling was to be reminded of how far behind China still was. But her mixed feelings were eclipsed by a simpler human reaction: it was good to be home.

LUCIFER

Lucifer made up his mind to go solo on New Year's Day 2013. He was on subway line four, going home after spending the night at a Dutch girl's flat in the hutongs. At dawn he woke feeling that both his professional and personal life were disasters. It was a long ride and he had time and space to introspect. The Beijing subway is normally packed to bursting on weekday mornings: long queues on the platforms collapse like a house of cards as soon as the carriage doors open. But today the tube was clean and uncrowded as the rest of the city slept in.

Plugging in earphones, Lucifer considered his situation. The goal hadn't changed since he was fifteen: to become an international superstar. The challenge was getting from here to there. The market for Rustic hadn't been big enough, and a band singing in English would never go nationwide. All the hits playing on radio and TV were K-pop. His decision, which had been percolating for months, dripped out into his brain just as the dulcet female tones of the subway recording announced a stop. By striking out on his own he could sing in Chinese and make a bid for the big time.

Two weeks later he had cobbled together a motley supporting band for his solo act. Duan Xuan: the chubby lead guitar, prone to never-ending guitar solos while scrunching up his face like he was smelling a slug. Da Guo: the bassist, a skinny mulleted football-mad Radiohead fan who worked at the Chinese equivalent of Quora. Mao Mao: the drummer, with a basketball physique and a voice as deep as the pit of hell. Every other word out of his mouth was '*niubi*', a common slang that means 'friggin' awesome' but translates literally as 'cow vagina'.

Courting mass appeal, Lucifer wrote a new set of songs that he could imagine hearing on the radio. They were upbeat and cheery, with titles including 'Shooting Star', 'Hey Girl' and 'This Song is for You' – more pop rock than punk rock. The rest of the band lowered their standards of artistic purity, hoping to hang on to Lucifer's coat tails all the way to the top. As the former frontman of Rustic he was a minor celebrity in music circles and had made it clear from the beginning that he was the star. For their name he chose 'Li Yan and Band'. He set up a Weibo account too, THE LI YAN.

They played their first gigs at XP livehouse, a smoky dive tucked behind a roast-chestnut stand in central Beijing that was opened by the owner of D-22, Michael Pettis, months after his old club closed. By April the rest of China was ready to hear his new sound and the band went on tour. It was a more truncated tour than Rustic's, just a handful of cities. But there was one gig on the schedule, near the end, that Lucifer was anticipating more than all the others. It wasn't the biggest. In fact it was the most inconsequential by far, in a Podunk town in Hebei province. But that town was Gaocheng, where Lucifer grew up, and this was his homecoming.

The last time he had visited, over the spring festival, he returned to Beijing almost in tears. It was the same each year: despite his tales of winning the Global Battle of the Bands competition in London, his old schoolteachers and classmates saw him as the same misfit kid with the floppy haircut who dressed funny, on some wild-goose chase for stardom. They laughed at him when he told them he was famous in Beijing. His father didn't take his ambitions seriously and wanted him to give up the dream. By playing his music, this was his chance to show them all how far he had come.

*

On a balmy April afternoon, Li Yan and Band arrived at Late Youth, a bar carved into the outer wall of a football pitch near Lucifer's old school. The usual motivational slogans ran across the top of the stadium: '*All citizens, train your body.*' '*Help the country, help the people.*' On the bar door, a poster for the gig looked like it had been designed by a ten-year-old on Kid Pix: a jagged cut out of Lucifer holding his guitar plastered on top of drawings of leopards, monkeys and other jungle animals. The poetic title of the gig was 'This Dynasty of Youth's Morning'. Inside, the walls were plastered with Nirvana posters, coloured stickers, music quavers, fingers giving the V sign. Above the stage was a stencilled motto: '*We don't only have this perfunctory life, we also have music and aspiration.*'

They were greeted by Zhang Zhao, the portly owner of the bar, in his thirties and clinging onto his own late youth. They tuned in a perfunctory sound check then killed time while waiting for night to fall. Duan Xuan and Mao Mao chain-smoked and drank Red Bulls. Da Guo sat in a corner and picked out the bassline of Radiohead's 'Street Spirit'. Lucifer text flirted with two girls at the same time – one was a long-time fan from Tianjin, the other a stranger who had contacted him on Weibo. They all walked out back to look at the football pitch, empty but for school kids kicking a ball around at its dusty edge. Next year, Lucifer half-joked, they wouldn't be playing the bar, they would be playing the stadium.

At dusk, Gaocheng came. Lucifer had told everyone he knew in town to tell everyone they knew about the gig, and soon the place was packed with familiar faces curious to see the prodigal son return. There were mums and dads, teenagers trying to distance themselves from the mums and dads, small children running around like it was a birthday party, and grandparents looking confused in the middle of it all. A gang of Lucifer's middle-school friends were drinking beers at the back. His parents and former teachers were in the front row. Everyone was seated, and it was possibly the first gig ever to start at exactly the advertised time.

The warm-up act, Blue Pushpin, was the bar owner's own creation as manager: four men his age and a seventeen-year-old boy looking very out of place in a leather jacket and black T-shirt with a crossed-out swastika on it and the words 'NAZI PUNK FUCK OFF!'. The lead singer started by telling the crowd, 'We're going to sing some songs, see if they can move you,' and closed with a sickly-sweet pop number that had been playing on the radio nonstop. 'I'm a little little little little bird,' she crooned, 'flying very very very very high'. The pre-teen members of the crowd sang along and the parents broke into enthusiastic applause.

Next, Li Yan and Band took the stage. Lucifer had changed into his peacock outfit: those white-rimmed sunglasses, that loud floral jacket, a polka-dotted shirt and tight red trousers. They strummed chords, stroked cymbals, adjusted knobs. The crowd fidgeted. Lucifer breathed 'hey' into the mic and gestured for the master volume to go up. He didn't want just to sing some songs and move them. He wanted to blow their minds.

It turned out the audience was more confused than impressed. In the middle of the first song, Lucifer's dad began applauding, realised no one else was joining in, tried to change it into a rhythmic clap but couldn't find the beat and limply gave up. At one point Lucifer thanked his parents for coming, and invited his old clarinet teacher on stage. 'I started playing guitar in school,' he said. 'Now I'm twenty-four. I've been to America, I've been to England. I won a competition. Now I'm back in my home town.' He shed his jacket, turned to Duan Xuan and they started up another tune. The crowd was now clapping on the one and the three. As he played, Lucifer's eyes kept flitting to his father in the front row.

Near the end of the gig he jumped up onto one of the speaker boxes and struck his trademark pose – legs splayed, guitar head angled up sharply, just like in the poster at the entrance. When Duan Xuan's guitar solo crescendoed behind him, Lucifer leapt high off the speaker and landed on the floor in front of the crowd, dropping to his knees to close the song with one last rippling chord. But the lead for his electric guitar wasn't long enough and had snapped out mid-jump, drowning his big finale in white noise. He hastily plugged himself back in and glanced again at his dad, who was fiddling with his thumbs.

Folk went to bed early in Gaocheng and the show was over barely an hour after it had begun. There was no encore. 'When I was little,' Lucifer said into the mic before their final song, 'my father didn't let me play guitar. Now I hope everyone can get closer to their dream. A person should persevere with their dream.' The audience applauded and the lights flashed. '*We don't only have this perfunctory life*,' he quoted the slogan above him, '*we also have music and aspiration*. This tune is so you can sleep well tonight and face a better life tomorrow.'

Before the song ended, his father slipped outside to light a cigarette.

*

The last stops on Lucifer's solo tour were just as lacklustre. In Shijiazhuang two days later, they played at the Velvet Underground Club, where he used to go in high school. This show had the less catchy title 'In Love With a Mirage

Sea-Serpent's Building' (it loses nothing in translation). The lead singer of the support band was a first-year college girl who belted out 'Anarchy in the UK' in fishnet stockings, pleated black mini-skirt and Johnny Rotten T-shirt. The audience was only three people – technically a crowd. 'Shijiazhuang,' Lucifer berated his triangle of fans during a break between songs, lost for words. 'Oh, Shijiazhuang, Shijiazhuang.' As a consolation prize over kebab skewers after the gig, he made out with the girl in fishnets.

Undeterred, Lucifer enrolled the band in a Pop Idol style reality TV contest called *China Superstar*. Along with the dating shows, singing and performance talent competitions were now on every channel. This one was a mainland spin-off of a popular South Korean show, with audition rounds, celebrity judges and an intensive boot camp called 'superweek' before the top twelve flew to Seoul for the final. As ever, the motive for contestants was exposure as much as the grand prize.

Their audition was in Wuhan. Inside grey studio headquarters appropriately named the Hubei Province TV Big Building, a fifty-foot-high banner advertising the show wafted in the breeze while a scrolling digital ticker tape in the registration hall repeated 'You can be the next international star' on loop. The first step was to shoot their introductory video, to be aired alongside the audition. 'Hey guys, we are Li Yan and Band!' Lucifer told the camera on the fifth take. 'The reason why I'm participating in this show is very simple. It's because I want to become' – here he switched to English for show – 'a *superstar*.'

Back in the waiting room a dozen other acts killed time until it was their turn to perform, while a cameraman shot behind-the-scenes material. A bespectacled man practised Thai boxing moves. A cherubic boy band looked bored in matching white, blue and pink jackets. A troupe of silky bodies with long flowing hair, flesh barely covered by frilly hotpants and tight-fitting tops, turned out on closer inspection to be an all-male cosplay group. A middle-aged Monkey King in full regalia swung his golden staff. A seventy-five-year-old pensioner, Mr Huang, hummed the patriotic song he was to perform, 'I Love China'. And a Chinese Elvis impersonator called Jiang Zhenwei stalked the room, complete with thick-swept quiff and heavy golden necklace.

Eight hours after they arrived, Li Yan and Band were called into the recording studio. It was a mess of wires and swooping camera cranes, with a grid of stacked TVs showing each of the angles. A blue neon circle hung halo-like above the pristine stage floor. There was a drum kit and microphone stands, against a backdrop of the Wuhan nightscape. Ten-foot-high characters spelt the name of the show in sparkling electric blue. The three celebrity judges sat at a sleek white table with a star behind it and two pink neon columns to either side. Each band had two songs to wow them with in order to get through to the next round. Lucifer was up first.

The judges weren't impressed. One thought his music style was copied from other bands. Another told him he was overdressed, 'like all four seasons at once'. The most famous of them, the Taiwanese rock star Wu Bai, crossed his arms to form an X and eliminated them from the competition with the words, 'I'm out.' When the show aired two months later, their spot had been cut down to thirty seconds, using Lucifer's quote 'I want to become a *superstar*', one shot of him goofing around in the waiting room, and five seconds of his music before Wu Bai cut him off..

That night, Li Yan and Band were already booked to gig at Vox livehouse, the Wuhan venue which Dahai loved going to at university. Lucifer's mood had plummeted, the Band was losing faith and none of them felt like performing. But there was a large audience this time and energy was high. 'Today we went on a TV show,' Lucifer complained into the microphone during a lull. 'They didn't like us so much. But I think they were wrong.' The crowd was only half-listening. They wanted another song, and who was Lucifer to deny his fans.

DAHAI

'Miss Dong, you never forget to smile
Even if like me you long to grow old.'

The words of the song reverberated down the tunnel before disappearing into the undug earth at its end. Dahai sneaked down here at night sometimes, to sit on a pile of rubble and make the most of the acoustics. He came with his new workmate Xiaohai – 'small ocean', the work unit's nickname for him as he was a head shorter and three years younger than Dahai. Xiaohai was singing 'Miss Dong', a new tune by the young Beijing folk singer Song Dongye, in a husky baritone while Dahai clumsily picked out the chords on acoustic guitar.

'Miss Dong, it's so beautiful when the corners of your
mouth curl down
Like the clear water under Anhe bridge.'

Neither of their own love lives were thriving. For over a year Xiaohai had nursed a crush on a girl but didn't tell her. He wanted to earn more money then make an expensive romantic gesture, to prove both that he cared and that could make something of himself. But he delayed too long and she married someone else. That was the lot of the *diaosi*, the 'penis hairs', the losers. He could only sing on.

'Miss Dong, I'm also a complicated animal
I say things aloud, but repeat them in my heart.'

Dahai wasn't faring any better. Except for a fling with a nurse he had been single for two years, while many of his peer group from university were married and some already had kids. He was losing faith that there was someone out there for him. It was the high buildings around him made him a loser, he used to say, while he struggled below. He couldn't help but feel a pang of solitude when the chorus of the song came around.

'But all those possibilities are just a lie, Miss Dong
You're not a woman without stories.'

It wasn't unheard of to get married without money and property. That was called *luohun*, a 'naked wedding', but it was the exception rather than the rule. Parents often helped to buy a flat for their child or bought it outright for them. It was an investment, in the ballooning property market but also in their son's marriage prospects as well as their own retirement (when they would expect to move in). For some brides, the flat was a must.

'You've fallen in love with a wild horse, but my home
has no grasslands
That makes me feel so hopeless, Miss Dong.'

Dahai had no grasslands, no home of his own, but he was getting closer. A different division of his construction bureau was building a complex of apartments in the north-east of Beijing. When completed they would be sold to work-unit members at heavily discounted prices. It was a way off yet, but a crumb was as good as a feast for his hopes. Another pocket ace was his Beijing *hukou*, the urban registration that allowed him to buy property in the capital more easily. The second chorus, accompanied in the original by a high female voice, was more upbeat.

> *'But all those possibilities might be true, Miss Dong*
> *Who can take the trouble to comfort our unwitting*
> *youth?'*

At heart, Dahai was a romantic. Society might confuse marriage with house-hunting but that was their problem not his. As with his proud use of the word 'penis hair' to describe himself, he felt he was the victim of his low status rather than the one to blame for it. He hoped to find some-one who looked beyond the material. Someone to face the same direction as him and share his challenges. They could be losers together.

> *'I want to cast aside all reason along with you*
> *Walk with me, Miss Dong.'*

*

At the beginning of 2013 Dahai's work unit was reassigned. It was common for teams to switch between projects shared by the state-owned umbrella company, and workers had no say in where they were sent. Dahai had been digging the railway tunnel in Beijing for the last four and a half years. Now he would be laying a water pipeline in the highlands of Shanxi province. It was all the same to him.

Shanxi – literally 'western mountains' – is two provinces west of the peaks that encircle Beijing. From the provincial capital of Taiyuan, Dahai's work unit drove three hundred kilometres south to Huzhuang village in the Taihang mountain range, where the roads gave out. It was a dramatic landscape, with fields of cows and bulls, hills rolling higher and higher, a wide lake down the valley and herds of mountain goats that blocked the road out of sheer spite. The work-unit dorms were cut into the hillside up a dirt track from the village.

Iron gates, freshly painted red, opened onto a dirt court-yard with a single basketball hoop. Behind the yard, two rows of bungalow dorms with blue corrugated roofs showed their backs to the cliff-face. It could have been a village school but for all the heavy equipment and pick-up trucks. Here the red slogans painted across the top of the buildings had a local twist: *'The work unit pays respect to the people of Shanxi.'* *'Honour the commitment to your contract.'* *'Leave a positive legacy.'* Dahai's dorm room was underneath the bit about commitment.

They rose at six each morning, had steamed bread buns for breakfast, filled their Thermos flasks with tea and bundled into the open back of a truck to drive to the worksite, an hour up into the hills. The project, already half-way complete, was to connect the pipeline all the way to Taiyuan. In the craggier sections it was a feat of landscape engineering and involved explosives. As team leader Dahai was the one to press the button from a safe distance and watch the hills boom.

In the evenings, when he was sick of stir-fry in the work dorms, he walked to the village to eat home-style dishes in a cheap family restaurant. It was the only one in miles, and he wolfed down flat Shanxi noodles mixed with vegetables, black fungus and pork chunks while watching the owner's dog (called 'Money') chase chickens around the yard. The clean mountain air gave him a sense of space that he sorely lacked in Beijing. But when the wind whistled and the lights went out early, it was desolate. Most of all, Dahai missed an Internet connection.

The old communities online were disappearing anyway. Weibo had peaked in 2011 and Xi Jinping's regime began to declaw it in earnest. In the summer of 2013 some of the most politically vocal verified micro-bloggers or 'big Vs' – each with millions of followers – were arrested. Soon after, a new diktat decreed that whoever posted a rumour shared over five hundred times or seen more than five thousand times was criminally culpable. The first victim was a sixteen-year-old who was detained for posting about a local abuse of power. Weibo stopped being the hub of the national conversation. But it was also dying a natural death, as blogs had before it, to be supplanted by the next technology.

WeChat is a social app similar to WhatsApp, designed for smart phones, and by 2013 every millennial in China was on it. As well as text messages you can send voice messages, emoji, moving stickers and gifs. You can link it with your bank card and pay for coffee by scanning a code at the counter. Chats can be between two friends or in groups of a hundred. If you want to pick up a girl, the first thing to do is to get her WeChat. There are broadcast-only public accounts, and a feed where friends share photos and links. Dahai still had mobile data on his smart phone, and he could see pictures of what everyone back in Beijing was doing just by scrolling down.

Not long after he arrived in Shanxi, and just after the Chinese new year, the girlfriend of one of his university classmates from Wuhan gave him the WeChat 'namecard' of her own college friend, a young woman who was living and working in the north-east of China. Introductions like that were a common way to find potential partners, vetted by married friends who now wanted to hook up everyone else. Dahai added her and they began to court by WeChat.

There was no signal inside the dorms, and the only place where Dahai could get bars was at the top of the hill behind the compound. Every day after work he slogged up to thumb messages to her, his hands freezing in the cold without gloves on. Right from the start he tried to impress her with his credentials. A stable job at a state-owned work unit. A better salary than many. Those Beijing residence documents. The possibility of a flat in the apartment complex under construction by his company. He sent her an image of a floor plan. She reciprocated with selfies.

One day in spring, their local driver told him and his workmates about a Taoist priest who kept a temple higher in the mountains. Like many Taoist priests he told fortunes, and apparently all the bosses of the work units who passed through went to see him – perhaps to receive auspicious news about an upcoming promotion. Fortune-telling is common in the Chinese countryside and is often as much about creating good karma through the temple visit as about what you're told. The driver, meanwhile, was making his own fortune. He said he could take Dahai up there another day, for a modest price.

When Dahai went he discovered the Taoist 'temple' was just a regular courtyard home with a makeshift shrine room at the back. The priest himself was pushing seventy and barely came up to Dahai's chest, with the requisite long white beard. He ushered Dahai into his living quarters to give a reading, where the priest's son, in his forties and mentally disabled, sat in the corner. The priest made a point of explaining that it was heaven who had made his son an idiot in retribution for his telling the future with such blasphemous accuracy. His predictions were anodyne – good fortune, future windfalls – but when it came to affairs of the heart, two prophecies stuck in Dahai's mind.

'You will find love in the north-east direction,' the priest told him.

Dahai perked up. The girl he was flirting with on WeChat was from the north-east.

'By the end of this year,' went the second prediction, 'you will be married.'

Dahai gave him a hundred-yuan note for his trouble.

Although not naturally superstitious, Dahai was shaken by the priest's words. He hadn't even met this woman but his mind was leaping ahead. They had longer conversations on the phone and he already felt like he knew her. She was soft-spoken, with an artistic temperament that impressed him. They started calling each other by their nicknames and signed off messages with endearments and cute emoji. He would look at the pictures she had sent of herself, smoke a cigarette, and realise he had finished it without taking his eyes off her.

In the summer, when the weather finally turned, she mentioned she was thinking of making a trip to Pingyao, an historic old town and tourist destination in Shanxi not far from Dahai's worksite. Dahai said immediately that he would join her, and asked his boss for three days off work. They set a date for 22 June. When the day finally came he was giddy with excitement. He borrowed his boss's car and thought of her all of the way to the airport, running over and over in his head how he would greet her when they met face to face.

Her name was Xiaoxiao.

XIAOXIAO

Xiaoxiao booked her flight to Shanxi the same day that
Dahai said he would accompany her. She had received his
first WeChat message just days after the distressing Spring
Festival visit to her grandparents – timing she didn't treat
as a coincidence. He was sweet and funny, always ready with
a grinning emoji or a goofy moving gif. He even played
guitar, or so he claimed. The trip to Pingyao was entirely a
ruse to create a natural opportunity to meet.

Her job prospects in Harbin weren't so thrilling any
more. The cafe in the converted synagogue where she
worked had closed in May after the local government
claimed the building as a historic site and kicked all the
businesses out, only to sell it to a developer who turned it
into a music hall. Xiaoxiao was indignant but resigned: that
was how China worked and there was nothing she could
do. She thought about taking back the management of
Remember, her old clothes shop, and toyed with the idea
of opening an online store on the shopping site Taobao.
Mostly she wanted to get out of Harbin, and planned an
itinerary to make good on her childhood dreams of travel.

She first saw Dahai as soon as she walked out of arrivals

at Taiyuan airport on the afternoon of 22 June 2013. He was taller and skinnier than she had imagined, less rugged than he came across in his profile picture. He didn't notice her at all: his sight line was a good foot higher than it should have been as he searched the crowd. She came right up close to him before he looked down and gave a start. Later he would tease her about it.

They were both nervous during the drive to Pingyao. Dahai tried to fill the silence with the dumbest small talk, but Xiaoxiao was too excited herself to recall a word he said. She spent most of the journey looking out of the window and playing with her phone. At dusk they arrived at their romantic courtyard hostel, the kind that sprouted all over Pingyao's old town when it became a tourist destination. There were potted plants, tiled eaves and hanging lanterns that washed the courtyard at night with soft red light. They settled into their room (two single beds) then went to a restaurant nearby to eat.

An hour and several bottles of Yanjing beer later, Dahai was more at ease and Xiaoxiao found the sweetness underneath his blabber. The age of the camera phone had arrived and it was Xiaoxiao's habit to document every moment of her life, then post it on her WeChat social feed. She had already taken dozens of snaps of the hostel and restaurant, and of her food from twenty different angles. Now they took pictures of each other and selfies of them together, nestling their heads in close while Xiaoxiao held the lens high above them. When the meal was over Dahai recorded a video of Xiaoxiao across from him.

'Xiaoxiao,' he asked, 'do you like me?'

She was wearing a soft blue-and-white striped top and rested her chin on her left wrist, elbow on the table as she leaned in. Her fingers arched over her lips to hide her smile, but the crinkle of her eyes still showed.

'I don't like you,' she teased.

'Why?'

Seven seconds went by in silence. Xiaoxiao just looked into his eyes.

'Why?' he asked again.

Five more unanswered seconds. Xiaoxiao reached for her bottle of beer and took a token sip, giving Dahai an imperceptible shake of her head as if to say: you idiot.

'How could you not like me?' he persisted. Xiaoxiao broke eye contact and looked over her right shoulder, then back to him and realised she was going to have to say something.

'Love me, take care of me, never abandon me.'

Dahai thought for a moment. 'That's not what I asked.'

They clinked the necks of their bottles and he stopped recording.

On the second day they went exploring. The old town of Pingyao is a picture-postcard maze of cobbled alleyways, crammed with temples and historic residences. Zhang Yimou shot the film *Raise the Red Lantern* here, and the lanterns were everywhere. Dahai and Xiaoxiao bought a ticket pass and he used a pamphlet to give her a guided tour while she took digital reams of photos: ornate archways, hanging calligraphy scrolls and landscape paintings, eroded stone lions guarding doorways, moss growing between cobbles. And of Dahai in a checked shirt with a leather bag slung over his shoulder, shaved head and thick glasses, map open as he pretended he wasn't lost.

They left the morning after and drove back to Dahai's work unit in the mountains, where his leave was up. On the way they stopped over at a prince's mansion a few kilometres outside Pingyao, the 'House of Wang', for some more sight-seeing. Xiaoxiao had the time to kill: she was jobless since the synagogue had been requisitioned and would stay with him for three days before continuing south on her savings. While Dahai blew up the landscape she got bored in the dorms with no one around. She made paper cuttings of phoenixes and flowers out of red paper, and watched films that Dahai had downloaded onto his laptop.

Dahai used rare moments of signal at his worksite to send her texts and she climbed the hill behind the dorms to pick them up, just as he had done for hers. 'I'm your obedient darling,' he wrote. 'Thinking of you.' 'This time is just too busy for me.' 'Later we'll go to Tibet together.'

On the sixth day he returned before sunset, and they walked to the lake nestled into the valley. Sweetcorn was growing by the banks, its broad green leaves just beginning to bud. Reeds poked out of the water like straws while the sun dropped behind them. As they strolled, Dahai filmed Xiaoxiao from behind.

'Wife,' he called out, as if testing the word. Xiaoxiao spun around to look at him with an inscrutable expression.

'Let me interview you,' he continued. 'What do you feel up here in the mountains?'

'Very lucky,' she said.

'Why?'

'Because you're here.'

'Do you like it here?'

'Yes. Why don't we settle here?'

'Not me. You settle here.'

'I might just do that.'

'Then I'll sell you to the mountain people.'

Xiaoxiao picked a dandelion, turned to Dahai and blew the soft white seeds at him. She moved in closer to brush them off his face and they kissed. That night, Dahai sneaked out of his shared dorm room and into hers, and they disappeared under the blankets.

Neither of them expected to be moving so quickly after less than a week. But both of them saw their meeting as *yuanfen*: the fate that brings lovers together. The word was originally a Buddhist notion of destiny but is now used by lovers all over China who believe that they were meant to be. For a boy from Hubei and a girl from Dongbei to come together in the mountains of Shanxi – that was *yuanfen*. On the seventh day Dahai drove Xiaoxiao to the train station, and they parted.

Her next stop, coincidentally, was the city where Dahai went to university: Wuhan on the banks of the Yangtze. That was where her college classmate Baobao lived, the one married to Dahai's friend who had introduced them in the first place. Xiaoxiao stayed with them on the outskirts, took videos of their cat riding a skateboard and texted with Dahai.

'Whenever I think of you, I feel like crying,' she wrote.

'You're not allowed to cry, honey,' he messaged back, and she saw he had changed his profile picture to one of them together. 'Even though we're not together, we can each separately work hard for our future, for our life together.'

On the twelfth night of Xiaoxiao's trip, Baobao dragged her off the couch and suggested that they go for a street-side barbecue. They took a taxi to a place she knew in town and sat on cheap stools around a table on the kerb. While they were ordering a car pulled up next to them. One of Baobao's friends emerged from the driver's seat. Xiaoxiao turned to watch the passenger door open and out came Dahai, clutching a bouquet of flowers and grinning at her sheepishly. He had taken another two days off work just to surprise her, planning it in secret with Baobao and her husband.

They all ate together, turning over strips of raw beef and lamb with tongs before they stuck to the portable grill. Afterwards they went to a karaoke parlour near his old stomping grounds, and sang for four hours straight before bundling into a cab back to Baobao's. Over dinner Dahai wrote Xiaoxiao a note in his messy characters: 'In this world all chance encounters are reunions from a long time ago. Do you believe it?' Xiaoxiao replied below in her neat hand: 'I believe it. I love you.' They both signed their names and the date, 3 July.

On the fourteenth day, Xiaoxiao and Dahai went to the train station together. He returned to his work unit; she moved on. The next city on her checklist, Suzhou, was billed as China's Venice: a water town full of canals, gardens and rickshaw drivers haggling over the price to get to the canals and gardens. From there she went to Shanghai, where she walked the Bund, explored artisan shops in the French concession and took selfies in front of the Pudong skyline. And then back to Wuhan, to see Baobao again and tell her all about it.

Xiaoxiao's final stop wasn't originally in the plan. She had been to Beijing before, but Dahai said he would join her there and introduce her to his parents. He had already stretched his work unit's patience and knew they wouldn't give him any more time off, so he risked his job and left without telling his boss. In Beijing he showed her the military compound in Miyun where he had grown up. The railway line where he used to crush bullets was now overgrown with sharp yellow grass, the storeroom was empty. They had dinner with his mother and father, and on the twenty-ninth day they set off again, this time to meet *her* parents.

Two days straight they drove into the north-east. Xiaoxiao fed Dahai at the wheel while they listened to Coldplay songs on the stereo. They stopped at a cheap hotel overnight, then passed Harbin and the dipping rigs of the Daqing oil fields, and the grasslands near Inner Mongolia dotted with churning wind turbines. At dusk they pulled up outside Xiaoxiao's family home in Nehe. Dahai was so nervous that he barely said two words over dinner. It was 22 July, exactly a month after their first night in Pingyao. They left the next morning, barely twelve hours after arriving, and drove all the way back to Beijing while Dahai ignored his boss's calls.

The couple had all they needed now. Both sets of parents had been visited. Their ID cards and other necessary documents were ready (part of the point of their trip to Nehe was to pick up Xiaoxiao's birth certificate). Their minds were made up. It was drizzling on the morning of 26 July when they arrived at the Miyun marriage-registration office. There were two entrances to the building: one for marriages, one for divorces. After going through the motions, a squat lady behind a counter looked them over briskly and stamped their red wedding booklets. On the thirty-fifth day after they first laid eyes on each other, Xiaoxiao and Dahai were married.

That afternoon Dahai checked his messages to discover that in his tunnel in Beijing, the two digging teams had finally broken through to each other.

SNAIL

Snail and Xiaoli waited almost a full year to marry after getting engaged. In China it's the bureaucracy of the marriage registration that ties the knot. A ceremony comes later if at all, and is purely for show. The key is getting the passport-sized red booklet that is legal proof of marriage, and to register within days of making the decision to marry is common. But the document has to be processed in the same place as one of the couple's residence papers, and for both Snail and Xiaoli that meant a return to Sixian in Anhui. They decided to hold the ceremony with their families at the same time and do it all together.

When they arrived in Sixian town on Friday 3 September, the plan was to register straight away. But Snail's grandmother pointed out that it was too close to Ghost Festival, the fifteenth day of the seventh month in the lunar calendar, when relatives burn paper money for departed loved ones – an inauspicious date for getting hitched. Xiaoli wanted to wait until 9 September as the word 'nine' sounds like 'for ever' in Chinese. They compromised by sitting out the weekend and went on Monday 6th ('six' sounds like 'going smoothly'.)

They were the first couple at the registration office that morning. In the lobby they filled out their forms: name, date of birth, ID card number, known diseases. They trundled from room to room for medical check-ups, getting a sticker for each exam to fix onto their forms like it was a children's treasure hunt. Next a bored-looking photographer sat them down in front of a red background for the joint photo that would appear in both of their booklets. He told them to look up, took a couple of snaps without warning and bundled them out with a receipt. Four hours after they arrived a clerk checked the paperwork, processed their payment, placed their booklets under a machine and down went the red stamp that marked them as man and wife.

When they looked inside at the photograph that immortalised their marriage, Snail was mortified. He was gurning at the camera like he had missed his medication. Xiaoli had a cemented grin like a killer in a line-up. This was the image all of their relatives and friends would to ask to see as soon as they got back. It was a travesty. They pleaded to the clerk for it to be redone, but the computer said no. Snail joked to Xiaoli that they should get divorced then remarry with a fresh photo. They could do it that day without leaving the building.

The photo shoot that really mattered came later that week. Bridal photography – literally 'wedding dress photos', *hunshazhao* – is arguably the most important marriage ritual in China and often the first thing an engaged couple does – sometimes long before actually getting married. On summer weekends China's beaches, lakefronts and lavender fields teem with hundreds of brides and grooms striking poses, while photographers circle like seagulls. There are studios which specialise in fake romantic backdrops from the Eiffel Tower to the Pyramids, and richer couples travel to have their wedding photo taken at the real thing – partly to remember, mostly to show off.

Snail hired a company to do theirs, which cost 2,000 yuan or a month's salary (cheap at the price compared to other options). The team included a stylist, a make-up artist, a lighting boy, the photographer and three assistants. Xiaoli bought a wedding dress with a bush of frills at the bottom, and Snail rented a white suit to match. The studio had various sets to choose from. They went for the Victorian dressing room, complete with white fur settee, slatted wooden blinds and a violin and bottle of whisky placed on the mantelpiece above a fake fireplace. Snail and Xiaoli sat back to back on the settee, her hands demure in her lap, him squinting into the camera with his glasses off. Both of them were heavily Photoshopped after, to remove Snail's spots and whiten Xiaoli's skin.

By the time the picture was blown up a metre wide and framed above the bridal bed, preparations for the wedding feast were underway in the village of Tangzhangcun. The bed wasn't the only new addition: the house where he had grown up was unrecognisable. Like many migrant workers in the cities, Snail's father had saved up to demolish and rebuild the Miao family's crumbling ancestral bungalow. The outer wall and earth courtyard were preserved, along with the kitchen outhouse and storeroom. But the main building was now a two-storey block covered in glittering white tiles. There were large windows, a balcony, a tiled roof with solar-panel cylinders to heat the water and two ceramic dragons on top of the eaves that guarded it all.

The village was dotted with these two- or three-storey buildings, some of them knocked up in a matter of weeks for as little as a few wads of 10,000 yuan. They were status symbols of the family's earning power, a game of one-upmanship with the neighbours. Part of the point was to help a son or daughter attract a spouse (and to retire in after they did). But for all of their showy exteriors the inside was always the same: unheated, with bare walls and sparse wooden furniture. Xiaoli brightened the living room by gifting Snail's parents her tapestry of 'Along the River During Tomb Sweeping Festival'. The marital bedroom upstairs was a nod to the tradition that a bride moves into the groom's house, even if they would hardly ever use it.

There is nothing formal about country weddings in China: no speeches or taking of vows, no exchanging rings and no kissing the bride. Sometimes there is a procession through the village, clanging cymbals as the couple pay house calls. Often there is live music by a travelling band with the kazoo-like pleadings of a *suona* trumpet. Mostly it's an excuse for a party, more for the parents than for their children. This was a chance for Snail's mum and dad to show the neighbours how well their family was doing, with a married son who had graduated from university and found a white-collar job in Beijing. It was now early October and a week of national holidays had just begun. Many of the villagers had come back from their work in the cities to help with the autumn harvest of sweetcorn and soybeans. But the harvest would wait until after the feast.

Food was the priority, and lots of it. There were over three hundred people in the village and everyone was invited (those who weren't would turn up anyway). Snail's parents were footing the bill, most of which would be recouped by cash gifts from the guests. It was crucial to appear generous. They hired two local chefs, and a dozen or so relatives and close family friends came over the day before to help. In town they bought giant shanks of beef and mutton, small mountains of fruit and veg, chickens and fish by the bucket. They balanced each haul in the back of their three-wheel motorised cart, vrooming into the market then inching home to avoid tipping over.

For the centrepiece of the meal they killed two of their own pigs, and not a part of them went to waste. The organs were removed and set aside for later, the faces skinned and the ears lopped off. The lungs were cleaned by plugging a hose into one of the severed tubes, washing the blood out the other end. The trotters were a trickier proposition, as they were covered in bristly white hairs. The Anhui solution was to dip and roll them in a pot of boiling tar, then dunk the dripping trotter in a bowl of cold water so the tar hardened suddenly and could be peeled off, the hairs coming out with it.

In the courtyard, a giant iron wok was set up over a coal-fired stove and filled with water. When the steam rose in billowing clouds, in went every piece of pig: chops, shanks, hocks, ribs, jowl, heart, liver, lungs, kidneys, tongue, ears and skin. A couple of bungs – the rectum with large intestine still attached – were in there somewhere too, for especially lucky guests. The chickens were boiled, the fish fried in oil, the greens washed and cut, the fruit chopped, the plates and chopsticks stacked, the bottles of hard spirits counted. Each dish was meticulously planned and it was all pre-cooked so that the following day it could be reheated and served with garnish.

When everything was finished there was nothing left to do except watch the stars come out. The chefs and helpers ate the first haunches of pork for dinner, smoked and drank and played cards, then went to bed early to wait for the sun to rise high in the sky and the village to arrive.

*

According to custom, Snail and Xiaoli spent the night apart – him in the village, her in Sixian town with her parents. At first light, Snail bundled into a borrowed car with his cousins to steal the bride away to her symbolic new home. They were bearing gifts: a selection of harvest crops, fruit and delicacies. Normally the groom would also bring red envelopes stuffed with money, but Xiaoli's parents knew Snail couldn't afford it and let him off. While he was en route, they rang with a last-minute request: two live carp. Panicking, Snail diverted the car through the fish market. He jumped out to buy the fish without even stopping to bag them, holding them by their slippery tails away from his rented suit as they flapped and gulped.

The next trial to pass was at Xiaoli's front door. In this stage of the ritual the bride is locked inside with her family and best friends, and as a token of her reluctance to leave her parents she isn't supposed to come out without a fight. The groom must break down the door to get her, or at least make a show of it which generally ends with pleading. With his cousins Snail banged on the door and begged to be let in, while Xiaoli's friends called out questions from behind for him to answer. 'Who will be the boss in your household?' *'Xiaoli will.'* 'Who will keep watch over the money?' *'Xiaoli will.'* 'Will you be obedient?' *'Yes!'* Three for three. They let the groom in to collect his prize.

Snail presented the gifts to Xiaoli's mother and father, including the wriggling carp (now in a plastic bag), and the two parties sat down for tea. Xiaoli was already in her wedding dress but barefoot. There was one more tradition to honour before he could whisk her off. Snail got down on his knees and washed Xiaoli's feet in a tub of warm water, then gently slipped on her red socks and matching shoes. In centuries past she would have been dressed all in red, even the veil, and carried to her new family in a sedan chair as part of a loud procession. That had been replaced by a white wedding gown and a black sedan car, but the red footwear was a wink and a nod to the old ways.

Back in the village, guests were beginning to trickle in. Six large round tables were set, both in the courtyard and spilling outside next to the hand-pumped well. Each table seated ten, which meant that only sixty people could eat at a time – but the guests knew to come in a steady trickle from late morning until mid-afternoon rather than all at once, and were happy to stand around while they waited their turn. Each seating was served twenty-one shared dishes: four pork, four stewed, four pan-fried, four deep-fried, four cold and one soup. Balanced in the middle of each table were two litre bottles of *baijiu*, the sorghum liquor, as well as soft drinks for the children. No one went home hungry, and few went home sober.

Outside the entrance to the courtyard was a small wooden desk, where one of Snail's uncles sat with a large red ledger open in front of him. Each family presented a red envelope to him when they arrived, and he wrote down the sum of money they had given next to their name. This was one of the master books of weddings in the village, noting what each household gave to help cover costs. The amount varied according to closeness of relation: a relative or in-law might give a large sum (666 and 888 yuan are auspicious, if fiddly, amounts), while a friend would be expected to give at least a couple of hundred and a young acquaintance could maybe get away with fifty. Everything was reciprocal: part of the point of the ledger was so that each guest would have a record of what they might expect from the Miaos when it was their turn to host.

Snail and Xiaoli's families ate together at a special table inside the house, but while they sucked on pork trotter and slurped chicken soup the bride and groom barely had time to wolf down a few morsels. Xiaoli had changed into a red dress for the feast, another nod to tradition. Their duty was to make the rounds and greet the guests, toasting every seating in turn. The rule of drinking *baijiu* in China is that anyone can toast anyone else, clinking the rim of their cup lower or higher than the other's according to status. At each table, everyone wanted to toast the groom. After downing his tenth glass of spirits on an empty stomach Snail was pretty far gone, and begged the guests to excuse him for sipping beer instead.

By dusk most of the guests had left, leaving behind a few stragglers and a small landfill of leftovers and empty bottles. Snail and Xiaoli finally ate their own wedding meal, while their parents and closest relatives had seconds for dinner. In the evening there was just one more tradition to endure, the 'teasing of the bride'. In front of him, Snail's cousins and other male friends ribbed and baited Xiaoli with playful japes – often suggestive allusions to the wedding night – that turned her face the same colour as her dress and shoes. Snail was busier processing the alcohol in his liver than what was being said about his wife.

All of these ritual elements of the wedding were, in the end, lip service: customs to honour that were devoid of any deeper meaning. Like other people his age Snail enjoyed paying tribute to countryside practices from an age long past, but found it so far removed from the modern China he lived in that he couldn't connect the two. It was hard to conceive of a time when a red-veiled bride would be carried to her husband's village. There were new conventions now, such as the Photoshopped bridal photo shoot. Still, it felt good to make a show of it all. They stayed another five days in the village, and Snail helped his father and mother reap the harvest, then they took the new high-speed train back to Beijing.

Nothing had changed in the city. Their underground flat and daily grinds were waiting for them. Another winter fell, the damp crept in and the black mould returned. Shortly after the Chinese New Year in February, Xiaoli told Snail she was pregnant. His reaction was a mixture of excited resolve and blind terror: he would be a father as well as a husband now, and his own childish days were behind him. Yet their joy was short lived. In May Xiaoli stopped feeling sick in the mornings and suddenly lost her appetite. She told a colleague at the hospital where she worked. A doctor examined her and broke the bad news. When they talked about what might have caused the miscarriage, he asked if her living conditions were cold or damp.

MIA

Chinese New Year is a time to take stock. Like Christmas it's a natural break, a chance to reunite with family and eat far too much before beginning the next year refreshed. Also like Christmas, as childhood magic fades the festival becomes less about you being treated by your parents and more about your parents getting to see you. The first year when the difference sinks in is another threshold of adulthood, and for Mia it was the spring festival of 2014, the year of the horse.

She was twenty-three: young enough that each passing year could bring a reinvention, old enough to wonder where she was headed. One month after being offered the full-time position at *Harper's Bazaar*, she quit in order to become a freelance stylist. But the idea of being her own boss was more exciting than the reality of not having a reason to change out of her pyjamas in the morning. Clients were hard to find. There were long dead periods with no work. She got acne which she hid with a facemask that she pretended was for the smog. By February she was ready to go home.

All around China, everyone else was doing the same. The week leading up to the Chinese new year involves a logistical nightmare called the 'spring transport' as hundreds of millions of Chinese who work away from their home crush into trains to return before the holidays. The first day the advance tickets go on sale is bedlam. Queues at the stations can stretch to several kilometres. Inside the trains themselves, the metal-floored sections between carriages are carpeted by the sleeping bodies and burlap bags of migrants who could only get a seatless ticket. For those travelling to Xinjiang it's a fifty-hour trip. But flights are easier to book, and Mia instead flew the four hours to Urumqi Capital Airport.

When she told her friends where she was going some of them jealously assumed it would be hot, their heads filled with images of the Xinjiang desert. But Urumqi is further north than Beijing, not far from Western Mongolia, and its winters are frozen. When Mia landed it had snowed recently, and the streets were white and crisp with frost. Vendors in fur hats were selling last-minute supplies from wooden carts: paper cuttings, fireworks and firecrackers, red envelopes. For the Uighurs it wasn't their festival – they had their own, Rosa at the end of Ramadan and Corban at Eid al-Adha – and they went about their business as usual. Every Han-owned shop in town was shuttered.

This new year was a special one for Mia. It was the astrological year of her birth: two cycles of twelve after 1990, the horse had trotted around again. Your birth-sign year or *benmingnian* is supposedly full of challenges and it's traditional to tie a red string bracelet around your wrist or ankle for good luck to help you through, keeping it on all year.

Images of horses were everywhere. It's a popular sign, symbolising vigour and hard work, and the word 'immediately' in Chinese literally means 'on horseback'. From corporate adverts to personal greetings, the requisite pun was to wish 'success on horseback' or 'make a fortune on horseback' in the year ahead.

It was also the first Spring Festival that Mia was fully financially independent, with savings of her own from *Bazaar* and her freelance work. On her first day at home she gave a gift of 10,000 yuan to her parents, no small amount for her. It's common for Chinese children to give money back to their parents (if not a regular cut of their salary) just as it's taken for granted that mum and dad might move in with you when they retire. That is partly out of filial piety, but also a sense of reciprocity: they did pay for your upbringing and schooling, after all. As a kid it was Mia who was given red envelopes with lucky money inside. Now her father took the wad of cash off her and tucked it away in a drawer without a word.

However grown-up Mia felt, the holidays would always be an excuse for her mother to pamper and overfeed her. It was easy to regress when she was waited on three meals a day, with her laundry taken care of and a bowl of fruit and snacks constantly replenished in the living room. Over the course of a week she binge-watched forty-four episodes of *Under Zhengyang Gate*, a TV drama about three generations of a Beijing family who lived in a hutong courtyard a little too picturesque for Mia to find believable. After that she rewatched *I Love My Home*, the nineties sitcom which she used to love, and old episodes of *Friends.* Most of all she indulged her favourite hobby, sleeping in.

But while she slipped into her childhood groove, Mia's family knew nothing about her actual life. The clubbing, the photo shoots, her gay best friends – they wouldn't be able to accept any of it, so it was simpler not to tell them. She had stopped trying to bridge that gap long ago. Each generation was separated by too many experiences that the other couldn't grasp. They didn't even know what she did for a living: 'freelance stylist' wasn't in their vocabulary. Mia had taken a part-time reporting job at a stolid newspaper called *China Textile News,* mostly for the health insurance but also so that she could lie to her family that she had a 'work unit' as a journalist.

From her perspective, being home was reassuringly familiar. Her parents had moved flats since she was a child but apartments in Chinese high-rises all look the same: two bedrooms, a cramped hallway, smells wafting from the kitchen air duct and a rack of slippers next to the front door. One new addition was a collage of old photos of Mia: a baby in a yellow raincoat; a growing child with her mother's arms around her; a girl of eighteen with curled waves of hair and an angelic face in soft focus. It looked nothing like Mia now, who had highlights, tattoos and piercings. But it was how they wanted to remember her.

*

The heart of Spring Festival is the family reunion dinner on New Year's Eve. That afternoon Mia and her parents drove across town to her paternal grandparents' flat to celebrate it together, as her grandparents were too frail to come to them. Theirs was another carbon-copy apartment: two bedrooms, cramped hallway, rack of slippers next to the front door. On each stairwell landing the sound-activated lights clicked on with a clap of hands or a stomp of feet, and the grimy walls were plastered with all the usual adverts for drivers, refitters, plumbers, 'massage'.

On the blue-grey metal door itself, a red paper-cutting of the character for fortune – *fu* – was tacked upside down. (The custom owed its origins to another homophone: 'upside-down fortune', *fu daole*, sounds the same as 'fortune has arrived'.) Calligraphic couplets printed on red paper strips hung to either side of the door frame, another seasonal must. The couplet on the right-hand side read '*Ten thousand wishes come true, every step higher.*' Balancing it on the left was '*Smooth sailing, good fortune every year.*' There was a four-character phrase across the top for good measure: '*Luck and money filling the house.*' The inside of the door was livened by another paper-cutting, of two galloping horses.

Mia's aunt was there – the Chinese medicine doctor she had lived with during high school – and was rolling dumplings in the kitchen. Mia's mother went to help. Most of the other dishes had been prepared already but the main feature of every new year's meal is the dumplings. Each one was hand-rolled by nestling a fingerful of minced pork and chives in the middle of a flat pastry circle, then skilfully pinching it closed until it was a perfect flat-bottomed crescent with serrated thumbprint edges. Side by side the two women rolled them at a prodigious rate, one every few seconds like they were on an assembly line. When over eighty were wrapped they arranged the dumplings in concentric circles on a bamboo tray, and that was only the first round.

Mia, meanwhile, had her own work to do. If she was going to succeed on horseback it was all about building a network of connections. New Year's Eve was the perfect occasion to send well-wishing messages to contacts in the industry, and her iPhone was the only tool she needed. It was labour-intensive and she bunkered into a sofa corner to get an early start. Like the dumplings, each WeChat message had to be individually crafted and stuffed with well-chosen emoji. If it was hurried it would look copied and pasted. There were hundreds to get through, and every reply had to be replied to in turn. A typical message read: 'Wish you smooth progress, success in the year of the horse, more and more happiness in your job 😄🐴💗💗💗❤❤❤.'

Her grandparents watched TV next to her, with nothing to do but enjoy the consolations of old age. At eight o'clock sharp the Spring Gala came on: four hours of live song and dance until the countdown to midnight. There were celebrities, sketches, cross-talk comedy and without fail a patronising display of China's ethnic minorities dancing in colourful folk dress. Sometimes a foreign singer was invited on (the year before it was Celine Dion; this time it was Sophie Marceau). Everyone agreed it was cheesy and stupid – but they watched it anyway. Each year upwards of 700 million people tuned in, making it the biggest show in the history of television.

Early in the programme, the hosts introduced a fifteen-year-old girl (the daughter of a famous dancer) who would spin in circles continuously for the entire four hours, on a platform to one side of the set. There was no explanation as to why, or reprieve if she got dizzy. Just as she started to twirl, her dress blooming out like a carousel, Mia's aunt and mother carried in the first of the food from the kitchen and everyone's attention was distracted.

There was enough to feed an army. Chicken feet, boiled shrimp, eggs soaked in green tea. Cold beef cuts, fish garnished with sour potato strips, cakes of dried blood. Triangles of steamed tofu, sticky balls of glutinous rice studded with sesame seeds. A tin hotpot bowl that bubbled on an electric heater was a lucky dip of cabbage, lamb strips, fish balls and miscellaneous innards. Plates of boiled dumplings magically refilled themselves. It was tradition to hide a coin in one of them, bestowing good luck or a hospital visit on whoever ate it. Some families used chilli paste or sugar instead, though Mia's folks didn't bother at all. Everyone was too busy eating, while a shaggy white dog looked from face to face helplessly.

Mia's grandfather dominated the conversation. He was a wire-thin eighty-eight-year-old with a stooped frame that looked like the wind could blow it over. Most of his teeth were missing and his voice was weak and wavering but that didn't stop him holding forth all night about his favourite topic, the Sino-Japanese War. An orphan from

China's north-east, he had suffered terribly when the Japanese invaded and occupied his homeland in the thirties. In the fifties he moved to Xinjiang as a car mechanic for the People's Liberation Army, and he had absolute faith in the Communists as China's saviours. Every other sentence he uttered began with either 'those Japanese devils' or 'our Communist Party'. His ageing wife had heard it all before, and kept her silence.

Through a toothless smile he asked his granddaugher about her work unit, pleased that she was earning. 'You've got to be independent,' he told her. 'That's what Marx and Engels said.'

'We know, Grandpa,' Mia sighed. Everyone else nodded and grunted, lost in their food bowls or watching the spinning girl. Mia was sending replies whenever her phone buzzed, but Grandpa was just getting warmed up.

'Your grandpa wants you to learn two things from him,' he said. 'I do exercises every morning, and I wash my own clothes. Medical fees are too high, your health is the most important.'

'*Yes*, Grandpa.'

'We old people have a saying. Hope is with you young people. The world in the future is you young people. We are old, finished.' He chuckled, raspy as nails. 'We give the future to you young people. What I'm saying is the world is yours, in the peaceful nation.'

Mia wasn't even listening any more.

In between courses her mother made a show of tying the customary red bracelet onto Mia's wrist. By the time

the meal wound down, it was eleven o'clock and Grandpa
wanted to go to bed. He had seen in enough new years in
his time and preferred an early rest. Before he turned in he
had some final advice for Mia.

'Some young people criticise the Communist Party,' he
began. 'What do they know about politics? What do they
know? They don't know anything.'

'Grandpa . . .' she tried to head him off, but it was no
use.

'Xi Jinping said we mustn't forget the common people,
the old hundred names. You mustn't have the wrong political point of view or the wrong direction in life. Your
grandpa doesn't have much to say, just this basic principle.'

'I know, Grandpa!' Mia rolled her eyes.

'I participated in the Chinese Revolution,' he went on.
'I learnt these principles under the Communist Party. So
today I'm telling you that . . . the Communist Party gives
you work, gives you wages, lets you survive, lets you work,
organises things for you. So be hard working.' He paused
but couldn't think of anything else to add. 'That's right.'

'I've got to go,' Mia said, and with her parents she
finally escaped. The girl was still spinning on TV.

Midnight was nearing, and they went to Mia's second
auntie's flat in another identical high-rise nearby: two bedrooms, cramped hallway, rack of slippers. More couplets
hung outside the door (*'Spring reflects that winter has gone,*
welcoming a prosperous age' and *'The stallion and spring*
arrive together, developing grand prospects'). The same
spread of dishes was being polished off on the dining table

next to four empty bottles of *baijiu* and two tubs of home-brewed sweet red wine, a Xinjiang speciality. It was a premonition of the next few days, when Mia would do the rounds of all her relatives' homes until every belly was bursting and every liver broken.

Second auntie's husband, a soldier, was already red in the face. Sitting next to him was his daughter Zoe, Mia's cousin, who lived in Shanghai. Zoe was the same age as Mia and they looked alike. But Zoe used skin-whitening products and wore fake furs, a material-girl style which Mia had nothing but disdain for. The adults at the table, though, all doted on Zoe. The conversation turned to her boyfriend, who was wealthy and had Shanghai residence documents.

'Does Xiaorui have a boyfriend?' Zoe's father asked Mia's father, using her Chinese name. He had no idea. Mia said she didn't, and her mother cast her a withering glance.

At ten minutes to twelve everyone put on their padded coats and piled outside. Other families did the same, until the public square in front of the block was teeming. Snaking strips of red firecrackers lay out on the concrete, while boxes of fireworks were set into snowdrifts by the side. Over the last few days there had been a steadily rising volume of bang and crackle, like an orchestra warming up. But now Urumqi was silent as the crowd counted off the seconds until the fiery overture began.

When midnight struck, the city exploded. Spitting firecrackers ate the street in scorch marks, while fireworks whooshed and popped above. The night lit up with red, green and white. It sounded more like a war zone than a holiday. Every face was turned skywards as if to find the first good fortune of the new year up there – until one by one they turned back, and went in from the cold to finish their dumplings.

Mia was still thumbing emojis on WeChat.

LUCIFER

Lucifer took a good long look at himself and liked what he saw. The mirror had a portrait frame around it after all, and was lined with dressing-room bulbs. Shenmei Stylists ('Appreciating Beauty') was that kind of hair salon. Plastic chandeliers blinged up the ceiling, and celebrity faces greeted customers from a rack of fashion magazines: Prince Harry on the cover of Chinese *GQ* next to doe-eyed models and square-jawed metrosexuals. At most street-side barbers in China a haircut sets you back around ten yuan. Here a gent's cut cost fifty, eighty or a hundred and twenty yuan depending on whether you chose a 'skilful', 'senior' or 'chief' stylist. Every day before opening, the staff – clones of the same waxy-haired eighteen-year-old – lined up on the kerb for a pep talk by their boss, joining hands and chanting motivational phrases back in unison.

Li Yan and Band had floundered after their rejection on the TV talent show in Wuhan. Da Guo, the bassist, left to join his girlfriend in Chongqing. Lucifer found an equally skinny bassist called A Guo to replace him. When the drummer Mao Mao and the lead guitar Duan Xuan jumped ship, Lucifer replaced them too. He changed the name of the group to Lusifa – the Chinese transliteration of Lucifer – but gigs were few and far between. The band went through four more incarnations before it fizzled out.

The truth was, if Lucifer couldn't succeed in music or performance he didn't know what he would do. He had no other skills, and to throw his lot into the job market would be to begin at zero. He was twenty-four and still living off loans from his mum and dad on top of pocket money from gigs. Sometimes he said that if he didn't become a star, he would kill himself. But his self-confidence was only ever momentarily shaken. He knew the path to fame was paved with disbelievers, like the TV show judges or his family. And he reminded himself that Psy recorded seven albums before breaking through with the hit 'Gangnam Style' which still blasted from speakers in hair salons all over China, including the one he was in.

The good news was that he was no longer a *beipiao*, a Beijing drifter. His father bought a flat in Lucifer's name (as much an investment for himself as a home for his son) in the far southern suburb of Daxing, a two-bedroom in one of the apartment blocks that were sprouting around the edges of Beijing as the city expanded like a pancake being spread. It was an hour and a half by subway from the city centre, a natural colony for the 'ant tribe', and Lucifer was bored stiff. Soon after moving in he sprained his ankle playing football with some kids and could only hobble around. Stuck on the outskirts, it wasn't long before he missed his drifting days.

That summer of 2013 was hot and sweaty even for

Beijing, and Lucifer went stir-crazy cooped up in Daxing. He started smoking, put on weight and watched a lot of daytime TV (his favourite show was a clip compilation of car crashes). His dresser table was a mess of pain medication, empty bottles of water, unopened bottles of whisky and loose tissues. He used the 'people nearby' function on WeChat to find and flirt with women in the area. He picked up one girl in the queue at McDonald's, impressing her with the fact that he owned a flat, and took her home that night. But his spending money was running out and he had nothing to do with his time. Lucifer needed what he had never tried before: a job.

His first brief-lived attempt at gainful employment had been the summer before, and he had won the job on TV. The set up was similar to a dating show – contestants tried to impress a panel who could accept or reject them – only instead of matching lovers it paired young job-hunters with bosses from various companies. Lucifer brought his guitar along again and even played the same song, 'I Love You Girl', with one small change to the lyrics. '*I love you boss*,' he sang. '*You're in the miracles. I want to be your boy when you're sad and blue.*' It worked. He charmed over the representative of a Mercedes Smart car dealership, despite not knowing what a Smart car was. But when he started work he spent more time fantasising about owning a car than trying to sell one. He may have loved his boss but after a month he left her.

In Daxing that autumn, he tried again. Brother B, the goofball vlogger, had introduced him to a media firm that made high-end video adverts. The job paid 3,000 yuan a month, part time, and the office was an achingly cool all-white pod-chair open-plan affair. The boss, a high-powered thirty-something executive, was an amateur musician and hired Lucifer in part because he wanted to start a vanity band with him. They would be called Boss and Boy. Lucifer strung him along, asking for long paid holidays using his sprained ankle as an excuse, and threatened to resign twice in order to get a pay rise before he left for good after three months. That was the way of the 'strawberry tribe' – pretty outside, soft inside – who couldn't hold down a job. Office work just wasn't for him.

Soon after, Lucifer had a heated exchange on WeChat with his brother, who was eight years older with a stable job and a family. His brother reached out in a long text message to encourage him to give up the dream and get serious.

'You're no kind of older brother,' Lucifer replied angrily. 'Don't count on me to do anything for you as a little brother either.'

'You prick, you think you're so fucking *niubi*,' his brother wrote. 'Who are you kidding? You're not a child any more.'

'Fuck,' Lucifer shot back, 'don't fucking swear at me. You're also not a fucking child, to use such fucking filthy language.'

'You really think you're a star,' came his brother's sarcastic reply.

'Your artistic level is too low,' Lucifer thumbed. 'I've always been a fucking star.'

His brother texted back just two letters in English: 'sb'. *Shabi*. Stupid cunt.

Lucifer complained to his parents and made peace with his brother the next day. He wasn't going to lose faith that easily. But the plan had slipped, and for the first time there was a voice in the back of his mind that questioned whether he would make it. Looking at his reflection in the mirror at Shenmei Stylists hair salon that winter, he knew he needed to get his act together.

*

In the spring of 2014, Lucifer found his feet. He landed a job scheduling events at Hot Cat Club, a smoky piano bar in the hutongs that attracted a mix of locals and expats. On Wednesday nights there was stand-up comedy, called *tuokouxiu* in Chinese (a transliteration of 'talk show'), where fodder for jokes ranged from dating pressure and the gender gap to the one-child policy. At the weekend there was live music, and the occasional burlesque night: 'Vamps, Vixens and Weimar' for German cabaret, 'Sirens and Seductresses' for songs of thirties Shanghai. They paid Lucifer 4,500 yuan a month, which he supplemented by teaching guitar to private pupils, and he got to play his own album over the sound system.

He moved out of Daxing and rented a three-by-four-metre shoebox apartment at the back of a hutong maze close to Hot Cat. He exchanged the springy single bed for a double (you never know who might stay over) and lived on fried rice when he ran out of money. When his parents transferred him 15,000 yuan to deal with an administrative cost on the Daxing flat, he used it to buy an upright piano instead. Every day he practised twelve-bar blues and boogie-woogie, reinventing himself as a bluesman. He read the biographies of singers – Tom Waits, Leonard Cohen, Fats Domino – translated into Chinese, and analysed the secrets of their success as if to build a composite formula. He started going to the gym and stopped eating dinner, a diet regimen to lose his puppy fat.

Besides international fame, the other element missing from his life was a partner. Ever a skirt-chaser, Lucifer didn't want for flings. In May he had a dalliance with a bargirl at School bar, although he suspected she just wanted a free bed to sleep in. And in June he flirted with a rich second-generation girl who drove a BMW and treated him to meals out. But he wanted something stable and found his new-found self-discipline lonely. One of his public updates on WeChat was 'Please God, give me a girlfriend'.

Soon after his twenty-fifth birthday, for a lark, Lucifer went for a consultation with a professional pick-up artist. As conservative modes of courting gave way to twenty-first-century mores, Beijing along with other big cities had a small but burgeoning scene in 'chasing women studies'. They had all read *The Game* (the Chinese subtitle is 'from stay-at-home loser to fashionable boy') but tailored its techniques to work in China, where the secret was often as simple as pretending to be richer than you really were. One tactic was to display a rack of expensive magnums of champagne at a private table in the club, which in fact were only rented and remained unopened.

The ends differed from the West too. While for some of the wannabe alpha males the goal was to get laid, others were learning skills in order to attract a wife. The website of the PUA group that Lucifer consulted ('Bad Boys') used statistics for its marketing pitch: 'According to the 6th (2011) national census the male population is 686,852,572 or 51.27%; the female population is 652,872,280 or 48.73%.' That means there are 105 men for every 100 women, it continued in a bold red font, and 23,150,000 surplus bachelors. The real message was implied: with competition this fierce your game had better be good.

Chen Guang, a cherubic twenty-two-year-old with artfully gelled hair and a penchant for waistcoats, met Lucifer in Maan cafe, an industrial-scale brunch joint that served scrambled eggs and hash browns by the thousand. Chen Guang's name meant 'the brightness of the sun at dawn' – just like his smile (or that was the line he used on girls). He explained the three assets a PUA needed to cultivate: a neat appearance, conversational and emotional skills, and the euphemistic 'displayed value'. He also listed the five types of men that women go for: Alpha Males, Divas, Mystery Men, Shining Boys and Poets from Afar. Lucifer, apparently, was a Poet from Afar. For just 4,800 yuan he could join a three-day course called 'Male God Plan Development' that would give him a full make-over and provide wingmen for nights out in the Worker Stadium clubs. Lucifer declined.

For a whole three weeks that summer he had a legitim-
ate girlfriend, a cute college graduate who had a thing for
rockers. They dressed up in matching breeches and flat
caps, like Bonnie and Clyde, and Lucifer posted their
couple selfies on his WeChat and Weibo feeds. But she was
into sex, drugs and rock 'n' roll whereas Lucifer's lifestyle
was now piano practice, gym and motivational reading.
After she left, he reminded himself of the line in Lady
Gaga's autobiography: a lover will be gone in the morning
but your career will always be there. A part of him still
pined for the days when he was a minor rock celebrity.
More than ever he missed the old gang.

Ricky Sixx was so different you wouldn't recognise him
on the street. He had cut his glam-metal locks and switched
his leathers for faded jeans and T-shirts. He got a job as an
estate agent, scootering prospective tenants around central
Beijing to show them into cramped apartments. When he
got bored of that he teamed up with Li Fan – himself in a
new band, Bed Stars – and together they opened a hole-in-
the-wall guitar shop at the east end of Drum Tower East
Street, called Foxy Guitars. It was barely big enough to fit
the two of them in between the rows of Gibsons and Fend-
ers, while the floor was a spill of wires and empty cigarette
packs. On the far wall was a frayed Rustic poster.

They had talked about getting the band back together
before, but relations between Lucifer and Ricky were still
strained and the idea never got off the ground. The year
before they had even posted a come-back announcement,
but it didn't last longer than one gig. Now the time was

ripe. Lucifer had tried life in the 'working grunt tribe' but, like Ricky, he just wasn't cut out for it. After the freedoms of the last seven years, a nine-to-five job felt like defeat. He couldn't afford to escape for ever. Reality would bite again. But for the moment he was still young and could rock on.

FRED

Back in Beijing after her year abroad, Fred felt everything had changed. That was how it went when you were away for long. China years are dog years: they fit more in. It wasn't just the new buildings and different street shops, the inflated prices and unfamiliar memes. The whole atmosphere was different. Xi Jinping had been officially sworn in as China's leader in the spring of 2013 and soon announced his first catchphrase, the 'China dream'. No one knew exactly what that meant or how it would differ from the American dream, but the promise was of a 'great rejuvenation of the Chinese nation' and there was a first flush of excitement about new leadership.

As Xi planted his feet under his desk, it became clear that the China dream wasn't about individual wishes being fulfilled. It was a central programme to strengthen China's economy, military and governance under the consolidated control of the Communist Party. As Party Chairman, as well as Chairman of the Military Commission and head of half a dozen other key bodies, Xi Jinping was pulling all the strings. One early decree called Document No. 9 listed what were later called the 'seven unmentionables' to go unspoken in academia and media: constitutional democracy, universal values, civil society, neoliberalism, a free press, historical mistakes by the Communist Party and questions about socialism with Chinese characteristics. But Xi's first priority was to tackle corruption.

The wealth of some apparatchiks was hard to miss: the Audis, the watches, the banquets, the *baijiu*. One official was revealed to have forty-seven mistresses. Public dis-affection at the injustice of it all was boiling over, and mass protests over local abuse of power were commonplace. Corruption has a dynasties-old history in China (as do anti-corruption campaigns) where it is entrenched and difficult to battle. Chiang Kai-shek once said of the Nationalists, 'Fight corruption and lose the party; don't fight corruption and lose the nation.' Xi was fighting cor-ruption to save the Party. His anti-corruption crack squad announced they would target officials of both the highest and lowest ranks, 'tigers and flies'. In practice, observers noted, Xi was also purging enemies and buttressing his power base.

Fred's father, the Communist Party official, was some-where between a fly and a tiger. He had risen higher in the ranks, which had its dangers as well as its perks, but both her parents came from intellectual backgrounds and were careful to toe the line. Indeed they relished the prospect of the Party cleaning itself up. Meanwhile the net tightened around them, even on distant Hainan – the mountains were no longer high, the emperor no longer far away. Every so often they would tell Fred about an official they knew who had been arrested. The biggest difference to her father's life was that banquets with colleagues were now limited by edict to four dishes and a soup.

Fred supported the anti-corruption campaign along with the rest of the nation, but she was no longer on the extreme left and had early reservations about Xi Jinping. She still thought a single strong Party was necessary for China, but would have preferred there to be more checks and balances on his power. She didn't like the restrictions on freedom of speech and civil society that Xi was doubling down on, including Internet censorship. In that respect her time in America nuanced her worldview: having studied an independent judiciary and witnessed a free press, she wanted those and some other unmentionables for China when the time was right. Nor did she see any contradiction in her position. She could be behind the state in full knowledge that it wasn't perfect. She could be both a patriot and a critic. Above all, she reserved the right not to be defined by politics when there was more than that to life.

Now entering her eleventh year at Peking University, if all went well Fred would finish her doctorate the following summer. After that the road of higher education ended and she would have to figure out an actual living. She was twenty-eight and had been single throughout: the textbook definition of a 'leftover woman'. Part of the point of the term was to encourage educated women not to be picky about finding equal matches. In China it was often explained that 'A' men married 'B' women, while 'Bs' married 'Cs' and 'Cs' married 'Ds'. That left two groups out: the 'D' men – bare branches who couldn't compete – and the 'A' women, who didn't want to marry the 'Ds'.

Fred was happy to hold out but it wasn't always easy. One cruel barb popular on campuses summed it up. There are three genders, the joke went: male, female and female Ph.D. So when in her final year at Beida she got together with someone she liked, Fred was nothing but glad. They had been classmates for years – he had joined the Politics department as an MA student at the same time as she did – and took tea with Pan Wei together before growing closer during parallel doctorates. They flirted in a subtle way that was all but indistinguishable from excessive courtesy. While she was at Cornell they video-called, negotiating the thirteen-hour time difference across the Pacific. When she got back they officially became a couple.

He was short and delicately built, with gentle eyes and round spectacles, like a Chinese scholar from the thirties. His style of conversation was just as formal, and he prefers to be called here by his *zi* or ceremonial middle name, sometimes called a 'courtesy name', a relic of the educated classes in imperial China. Even his *zi* – Jun – is a word straight out of Confucius, meaning gentleman. (See Analects 2:12: 'A gentleman is not a pot'.) The other reason why Jun stood out was that he was from Taiwan.

*

Throughout her school education, Fred had only ever thought of Taiwan as another Chinese province – an island belonging to China just like her own Hainan. She knew its history: how it was a former Dutch and Spanish colony called Formosa brought into the folds of the Chinese empire during the Qing dynasty. How the Japanese had taken it after war in 1895 and influenced its development and culture. How the Nationalists had fled there in 1949 when the Communists won the civil war. But her textbooks all pushed the line of 'One Country, Two Systems' and on every (politically correct) map Taiwan was a coloured province like any other that made up the People's Republic of China. It was only at college that she found out that the people of Taiwan felt otherwise and used a different name: the Republic of China.

As a politics student she learnt about the intricate stand-off between the mainland and Taiwan, without questioning the doublethink that declared Taiwan *was* the mainland. She learnt about their two political parties: the Nationalists or KMT (the 'blues'), who were in power at the time and hoped to establish closer economic and diplomatic ties with Beijing; and the Democratic People's Party or DPP (the 'greens'), who wanted more independence and self-reliance. Even knowing the facts put her ahead of other young mainland Chinese: for most of her generation Taiwan wasn't on the radar. But it was only through Jun that Fred discovered how it looked from the other side.

At his prompting, she looked up the websites of Taiwanese media and was amazed at how openly they discussed politics. She read books from Taiwan too, where titles banned in China could be openly published. They used traditional or 'complex' characters (the mainland has used simplified characters, which are easier to write, since the fifties) and opened from the back – reading downwards from the top-right corner whereas most Chinese books read left to right – but they were still perfectly understandable. Elections were openly debated and political freedom ran to the core of Taiwanese identity. Fred's default position had been that democracy wouldn't work in China. Singapore was the go-to example outside China's borders of a successful authoritarian state better suited to Asian realities. But here was a functioning Chinese democracy just offshore.

In practice there was little to extrapolate: the Singaporean model worked in Singapore, the Taiwanese model in Taiwan, but both were small and self-contained. China was a different equation and there were no flawless examples. Corruption was also Taiwan's bane: its former Prime Minister Chen Shuibian was arrested as soon as he stepped down and sentenced to twenty years in prison. The KMT under Chiang Kai-shek had committed its own atrocities on the island's native population, chief among them a massacre of civilians on 28 February 1947. But while many young Chinese raise their hackles at the suggestion Taiwan isn't part of China, young Taiwanese reciprocate the feeling. In the spring of 2014 the elastic reached snapping point.

The pro-independence camp or 'greens' had worried for years that Taiwan was a frog in slowly warming water. The problem wasn't military – even if Beijing did have an awesome array of missiles pointed at them – but economic. Two decades ago Taiwan had been the richer between them, one of the 'four Asian tigers' along with Hong Kong,

Singapore and South Korea. But now China had outpaced them all, and with economic clout came political leverage. When the KMT signed a trade agreement that tightened the knot between Taiwan and the mainland there was public outcry. On 18 March, after the agreement was forced through despite promises to review it, hundreds of students stormed the Legislative Yuan, Taiwan's parliament, and barricaded themselves inside.

Their demands were about the trade agreement, but the demonstration was as much a statement of independence in the face of stronger sway from Beijing. As the cause won popular support it was dubbed the 'Sunflower Movement' – a nod to previous youth protests in Taiwan with floral names. The students briefly occupied the Executive Yuan, Taiwan's cabinet offices, but were cleared out by riot police with water cannons. In April the occupation peaceably dissolved, but the bad blood lingered. The Democratic People's Party was tipped to win the next election and leaders of the Sunflower Movement said that the seeds of dissent would spread again.

In mainland China the protests went unreported or were spun as illegal riots, but Fred followed them in the Taiwanese press. She had some sympathy for the students – she came from an island apart from the mainland herself – but didn't condone their actions. Nor did Jun, who while in favour of self-rule thought engaging with Beijing was necessary for Taiwan's future. Fred had her own patriotic stake to consider, as greater independence for Taiwan held its dangers for China. What if Xinjiang and Tibet tried to split off as well? Or other nations saw China as weaker for territorial losses? Once again she was dragged back into politics. It was hard not to be, in a country like China.

Fred and Jun shared another interest which they could both get behind – ancient Chinese culture. There are few vestiges of antiquity in modern China, where the iPhone is better loved than the I Ching. Historical buildings and relics were destroyed during the Cultural Revolution, when traditions of thought such as Confucianism and Taoism were also victims. In the more forgiving eras that followed any cultural revival has been secondary to breakneck modernisation. Children learn to recite the most famous Tang dynasty poems in school and everyone knows about the four classical novels – but few have read them, and for all the boasting about five thousand years of continuous history it is difficult to connect the dots.

Taiwan, meanwhile, has since 1949 considered itself a legacy-holder of Chinese civilisation. Uninterrupted by the upheaval of Communism, for many the island is where Chinese culture truly continued. The traditional characters in books and on street signs are more faithful heirs to the first oracle bone pictograms. The cadences of language aren't infected by sloganeering Mao-speak. The architecture is inspired by Chinese and not Soviet tradition. Most young Taiwanese are still more interested in video games, but at least the traces of old culture are around them. Jun was steeped in it. He was even the disciple of a *guoxue* or 'traditional national studies' master in Taiwan, who taught him everything from classics to calligraphy.

To spread the lore, Jun set up his own traditional studies school in Beijing. He ran it out of his apartment near Beida and kitted the place out accordingly. Calligraphy scrolls and landscape paintings adorned the walls next to an etching of Confucius, hands folded in his robes. Opposite the Sage was a photograph of Jun's own master, a kindly looking old man with a beard and overflowing white eyebrows. Classes of half a dozen fee-paying school students sat cross-legged on wicker mats around low wooden tables while Jun lectured them on their heritage. University students could audit for free while drinking ceremonial tea out of antique teapots and cups. The school was called Ancient Chinese Treasures National Studies Schoolroom. Its motto, printed on the information pamphlets that Jun handed out, was 'Cultural Revival, Harmony Across the Straits'.

In the summer holidays after Fred's final term at Beida, they travelled to Taiwan together, so she could see across those straits herself. They spent ten days there, mostly in the capital of Taibei where Jun was from but also walking the mountainous interior. In tea plantations they sampled Iron Buddha and other fine oolongs, and bought boxes of hand-rolled tea leaves as gifts for friends and family. Fred admired the architecture and basked in the natural beauty. In many ways it reminded her of Hainan, her own island, and she came to tacitly support Taiwan's de facto independence. With each new experience out of the mainland, her perspective widened and her politics softened.

Back in the honk and smog of Beijing, Fred submitted her doctoral thesis and received her Ph.D. She was a student no more. There was no dorm for her at Peking University, no lectures to attend. Her library card was handed in, her ID card had expired. The academy that had sheltered her for so long cast her out onto the street with three degrees and a head full of knowledge. Now she faced a long-delayed and entirely different prospect: employment. Independence wasn't as simple as it sounded.

DAHAI AND XIAOXIAO

There was no honeymoon for the newly weds. Theirs was a 'lightning marriage', *shanhun*. Neither Dahai nor Xiaoxiao thought they were the type to rush, but when it was happening to them it only seemed natural. Now Dahai was overdue at work (his boss was furious with him for eloping without permission for the time off) and two days after they registered as a married couple he returned to the mountains of Shanxi province. Xiaoxiao travelled with him but soon fell ill from the unheated nights. Dahai applied to switch back to his old railway tunnel worksite in Beijing, and in the autumn they moved into the city together to begin their married life.

It was also a 'naked wedding', as they didn't yet own a flat. That winter they rented a cramped studio a few subway stops away from the tunnel. On the way home at the end of each shift, pebbles and earth fell out of Dahai's clothes. But at the beginning of 2014 the apartment complex built by the other division of Dahai's work unit was finally completed, and he had first dibs. As these flats were only for employees of the construction bureau and not on the property market, they were sold at cut rates. Dahai bought one on the cheap (his father helped out), and they could move in after the Chinese new year.

When they first visited their marital home it was all unpainted walls and cold bare floors, while a team of workers bustled around installing insulation, wiring and floorboards. The complex wasn't far south of Beijing Capital Airport, and every few minutes they could hear the dull thunder of a plane descending or watch them from the balcony. Theirs was the sixth and top floor – any higher and Chinese building code requires a lift to be installed – and had a spacious ceiling. They had stairs put in to create a split level in one corner, just big enough to squeeze in a spare bedroom that diminished to nothing with the slope of the roof (handy for guests who weren't too tall). There was a car park in the basement and they even had a Buick to put in it, a hand-down from Dahai's uncle.

Flat: check. Car: check. Disposable income: check. A year ago Dahai thought of himself as a 'penis hair', a loser. Now he had all three of the 'haves'. He had been promoted again, from 'assistant engineer' to 'engineer' – an equally meaningless job title as he was still overseeing construction work – and he was earning 8,000–9,000 yuan a month, a decent haul. His naked wedding had been clothed. Now, with Xiaoxiao, they were promoted to a new class of losers: the 'mortgage slaves'.

Xiaoxiao didn't miss the label of 'leftover woman' either, even at a certain loss of her independence. She tried to find work in Beijing, but every employer she applied to turned her down. As a new bride in her late twenties, managers assumed she would be taking maternity leave soon and there were no laws in place to prevent the discrimination. For the time being she bit her tongue and waited. Their apartment was still empty, so she ordered a sturdy wooden dining table, chairs and a sofa. On the shopping site Taobao she bought rug throws, tablecloths, lamp shades and curtains, embellishing them herself like she had in her shop in Harbin. She draped prayer-bead necklaces over side tables, hung a wooden Tai Chi sword above the radiator and placed an African drum in a corner. Her 'artistic youth' tastes were becoming bourgeois.

There was one more pilgrimage to make. With Dahai she drove to Beijing's blue IKEA warehouse, and they walked through a hundred potential versions of their home. In China a trip to IKEA is as much about the day out as what you bring back with you, and at the weekend it can feel like a theme park. Shoppers sprawl on beds and sofas for a nap (the only true test of comfort). Families sit down at showcase dinner tables for make-believe meals. Couples have real domestics in fake kitchens. The restaurant serves meatballs and spaghetti, the shop sells Swedish glögg wine. Xiaoxiao and Dahai filled their crinkly carry bag with Sedlig cutlery, Färgrik dinnerware, Gestalta wooden figurines and Finansiell decorative horses. As they trundled out with trolleys of flat-pack furniture and armpits full of rugs, it felt as if they had been baptised into the middle class.

The final housewarming arrival was the cat. He was sleek and blue-grey, a British Shorthair, and Xiaoxiao found him through an advert online. They called him Fugui, 'riches and honour', for the positive auspices – though the first thing riches and honour did was to methodically scratch all their new furniture. Now it truly felt like they were settled, with a nest to call their own even if their marriage was still only on paper. The months went by until 22 June 2014, the first anniversary of when they had met in Pingyao. It was a special occasion, because that was the date they had set for their formal wedding ceremony.

*

Urban Chinese weddings differ from traditional country ones in their mix of Eastern and Western customs, but both share an ostentation that is mostly for the benefit of the parents. Dahai's mum and dad hadn't approved of their son's flash marriage at first, but now accepted their daughter-in-law and invited Xiaoxiao's parents to join them for a joint party. Everyone came: extended family, old friends, colleagues, bosses, military brass. Half of Dahai's work-unit team piled into a coach which took them from their dorms to the venue. His parents funded and planned the whole affair, and clearly wanted to show off. Dahai knew that meant it would be unendurably corny.

For the occasion they rented the banquet hall of a hotel in Miyun near Dahai's old military compound. The ceremony would be in the late morning, followed by lunch. At the hotel entrance an inflatable pink archway had been erected, with blow-up hearts to either side and bulbous English letters swaying in the wind: W E D D I N G. Across the top a banner congratulated two complete strangers on their marriage – leftover from the last wedding the hotel had hosted – until an employee was told and switched it for one with the right names, Yu Hai and Liu Xiao.

To get inside guests first had to pass three collectors of red envelopes, like the heads of Cerberus: one to take the money, another to keep the record, a third to usher them in. Next they shuffled through an antechamber decorated by toy bride and groom figurines sprinkled with white rose petals on a purple-sequined table. To each side were block letters as high as a child: 'L' and 'O' to the left, 'V' and 'E' to the right. When they emerged into the main hall they were met by a giant wreath of fake leaves that hung over-head, fishbowls full of petals dangling from it on pearly strings. A raised catwalk ran up the middle, shiny silver and lined with flowers, to a stage lit up by theatre lights. On a screen at the back Dahai and Xiaoxiao's wedding photos were projected – artistic snaps taken in a forest near their home. Twenty-four round tables filled the rest of the room, each glass lazy Susan loaded with snacks: baby tomatoes, jujubes, peanuts, seeds and sweets.

While the hall filled with people, chatter and heat, Xiao-xiao waited in a room upstairs. With her were two make-up artists, three high-school and university classmates and a chatroom friend from Xi'an whose Internet name was Vampire. Xiaoxiao fiddled with her dress – a lace-topped fountain of white she had designed herself – and debated with Vampire whether to pin on a sprig of forget-me-nots or whether the bouquet of white roses she was carrying was enough. At ten to eleven they went down and waited in the antechamber. The ceremony began at exactly 10:58, as the digits 5-8 when spoken, *wuba*, sound (with a generous stretch of the imagination) like *wofa*, 'I make money'.

A master of ceremonies had been hired to keep the wedding moving along – a lucrative profession in China. Their host was in his early twenties, with slicked-back hair and slicker manner, dressed nattily in a waistcoat with red bow tie and a carnation in his breast pocket. He had the gift of the gab and a habit of dragging out his words, alternating between slow and fast pace like an auctioneer.

'Laaadies and geentlemen, guests and friends,' he greeted the crowd. 'Gooood morning! Today is the year 2014 AD, June the 22nd. Here, in the city of Beijing, the suburb of Miyun, the couple Mr Yu Hai and Ms Liu Xiao are joyfully combining in maaarital uuunison. Today's proceedings will begin in 5 . . . 4 . . . 3 . . . 2 . . . 1 . . .' He leapt up onto the stage to introduce himself, accompanied by epileptic lighting flashes and dramatic music. 'Your host Lei Wu is taaaking the staaage!'

The audience applauded while he fired them up, his language dripping with all the poetic phrases that were an occupational hazard. Dahai and Xiaoxiao were 'flying like two birds in the sky, intertwining like two branches on the ground'. Every other sentence ended with 'wish them ten thousand good wishes!' When he finally invited the groom to 'solemnly climb the stage', Dahai jogged up in a black suit clutching a bouquet of flowers. His friends waved strips of colourful paper on sticks to either side of the catwalk, cheering him on.

'Yu Hai,' the host asked, 'as you stand on this happy stage, what are your thoughts and feelings?' He thrust the microphone into Dahai's face.

'I'm very, very excited,' Dahai replied quietly, looking terrified out of his wits.

'He's very, *very* excited,' the host echoed for those who couldn't hear. 'And who does the groom want to see the most? Please shout her name, and tell us those three words!'

'Liu Xiao, *I love you*!' Dahai said louder, and the host led a fresh round of applause.

The music changed to a choral falsetto when Xiaoxiao walked in. She stopped underneath the ceiling wreath, like they had rehearsed, and waved to her friends while the host waxed lyrical about her beauty. Dahai took the mic and sang a song ('Every time I'm lost in the darkness of night, you're the brightest star in the sky') while walking down the cat-walk to his bride. When it was over the host invited him to say a few words.

'I'm a little nervous,' Dahai began, 'so I'll just say something that everyone can understand. I will love and protect you until I die,' he told Xiaoxiao. 'I will walk this road together with you, and not abandon you.'

A circle of friends had formed around them under the wreath, and broke open confetti poppers to coat the lovers in sparkling paper hearts. Xiaoxiao and Dahai walked up on stage together – getting more facefuls of confetti along the way – while the host told a parable about a man on the moon who fates two lovers to meet by tying them together with a length of invisible red string. At the denouement of the story a pair of flapping white wings appeared on the big screen behind Dahai and Xiaoxiao, and the Enya song 'May It Be' came on the sound system.

'Groom,' the host told Dahai. 'Please look into your loved one's eyes and say your marriage vows. Say to this beautiful, graceful woman in front of you, regardless of sickness or health, poverty or wealth, are you willing to look after her for a lifetime and together build a beautiful future? Say it with me: *Are you willing?*'

'I AM WILLING!' Dahai shouted back.

'Groom, please remember that in your bride's heart you are a mountain she relies on. In the future, just as your parents loved you, you must love her, look after her, and give her a beautiful tomorrow. *Can you do it?*'

'I CAN DO IT!'

'Bride.' The host turned to Xiaoxiao. 'Look into your loved one's eyes, and give your marriage vows. Say to this handsome, elegant, diligent and wise man in front of you, regardless of sickness or health, poverty or wealth, are you willing to look after him for a lifetime and together build a beautiful future? Say it with me: *Are you willing?*'

'I am willing,' Xiaoxiao said softly.

'Bride, you must remember that in your groom's heart you are a beautiful flower. Look after him, encourage him in his life and work, give him a warm and loving home. *Can you do it?*'

'I can do it.'

Next came the exchanging of the rings, another Western tradition incorporated for ceremonial show. After putting a ring on Xiaoxiao's finger, Dahai kissed first her left hand ('It represents yesterday,' the host explained, 'their beautiful early love, the depth of their feelings') then her right hand ('It represents today, the exquisiteness of their life together, the happiness of their success in love'). While his head was bowed, Xiaoxiao took the opportunity to wipe off some confetti that clung to his sweating forehead. The screen behind them now showed two interlocking golden bands. The music was the theme from *The Lord of the Rings.*

There were also Chinese wedding customs to honour. Each of them poured out a cup of 'wish-granting sand' into a tray, though Dahai was too self-conscious to remember to make a wish. They clasped their hands together and bowed to their parents. And most crucially of all they offered a cup of tea to each other's parents, a ritual after which you can call your in-laws 'mother' and 'father'. Again the host led the proceedings. 'Baba, Mama, please drink this tea,' he told Xiaoxiao to tell Dahai's parents. 'Eh, good daughter,' they were instructed to reply.

Dahai's father gave a speech of his own too, but years of smoking had made his rasping voice barely intelligible and the whole room muffled giggles. His People's Liberation Army superior followed him, wishing that Dahai would grow to be as clever and diligent as his father and Xiaoxiao as beautiful and virtuous as her mother-in-law. The guests yawned through that one. There was just one all-important ritual left: the checking of the paperwork. Dahai's work-unit leader was handed the bride's and groom's wedding registration booklets on a tray, like they were hors d'oeuvres. He read them out into the mic, right down to each of their eighteen-digit ID numbers, to certify that the marriage was real. The final phrase in each booklet was, 'Their wedding is in accordance with the marriage laws of the People's Republic of China.' With those romantic words, the knot was tied.

'In thirty, forty or fifty years' time,' the host said at the end of the ceremony, 'there will be a day when you are walking on the street, and you will see a pair of wizened, white-haired people. That will be Yu Hai and Liu Xiao, walking hand in hand, shoulder next to shoulder. Respected guests, laadies and geentlemen,' he slowed down dramatically before the closer, 'I can now announce that their angelic wedding is satisfaactorily cooompleted.'

Finally, the guests could eat.

Once everyone had left, and there was no one else for Dahai and Xiaoxiao to clink glasses and make conversation with, they could relax at last. They were both utterly exhausted, having been on show all day long. Back home that evening, as soon as they changed out of their stiff clothes and fell onto the red sheets of their wedding bed, they went straight to sleep.

SNAIL

Snail was moving up in the world. With Xiaoli he had left the sunless basement and found a flat on the seventh floor of a gated residential block on the outskirts of north-west Beijing, even further out than his old university. It was his graduation from the 'rat tribe' into the 'ant tribe' – above ground but just as anonymous. The reason for the move was not a happy one: the loss of their unborn child the spring before had prompted them to find healthier living conditions before trying again. But there was also progress to celebrate as they moved into a bigger place with an actual window, let alone a view.

Luxuriant City, their new apartment complex, was two bus rides away from an outer subway stop that no one knew of except the tens of thousands of commuters who relied on it every day. There was little luxuriant about it besides the name, which was plastered in Chinese and English all around the outer walls as if to make up for that fact. Inside, a dozen cream buildings rose up in between wide boule-vards, with a pimpled security guard at each gate. In the summer crickets chirped in the grassy verge and children played hopscotch on the paving. Snail and Xiaoli rented a single room in a three-bedroom flat they shared with four other people, recent college graduates and one bachelor in his forties.

It was a considerable rent hike, from 600 yuan to 2,200 yuan a month. But Snail had traded up jobs too, joining a bigger tech company which made the electronic devices that waiters use in restaurants to punch through customers' orders. Snail worked in the logistics department, overseeing how the machines were put together and making sure they passed spec. Sometimes he was sent on business trips to the southern factory city of Shenzhen, where the components were made, to sort out problems on the supply chain. The university degree that he had won at such effort was finally paying off. He thought back with horror to the days when he was a KTV car-park attendant.

His offices were at the opposite edge of Beijing, in Daxing district to the far south. To get there he had to pass underneath all of the city. Every weekday he set his alarm for 6am, and by 6:50am he was out of the door. He took buses 118 and 114 to the subway, where he switched lines twice, then took another bus, number 580, to his company in time to start work at 9am. The trip took two hours door-to-door both ways, and the hours at work were just as long. Overtime was expected, as was being called in to work on Saturdays, for which he wasn't paid extra. Often he didn't get back home until 10pm, with just enough time to reheat dinner and set his alarm before going to bed to start it all over again the next day.

Snail's favourite way to pass the time on the subway was

playing games on his tablet – not roleplaying games but swipe-and-slash apps, slicing fruit and crushing candy. One of them was 2048, an arithmetic game popular in China at the time in which numbered tiles on a four-by-four grid are combined to add their value: 2 and 2 into 4, 32 and 32 into 64, 256 and 256 into 512. The object is to collect the ballooning values in one corner to reach 2048, processing new small-value tiles before they overwhelm the screen. Snail liked it because he finally got to use the maths skills he had learnt at school.

It all came down to the money. In this job Snail earned 7,000 yuan a month. Xiaoli had found a new nursing job which was an extra 2,000 yuan. Living frugally they could put away 5,000 yuan in savings every month between them, but it still didn't feel like enough. By the summer of 2014, after four years of working in the capital, Snail had amassed what he saw as paltry savings: a shave over 100,000 yuan in the bank. The priority, especially if they would have a child, was to buy an apartment of their own. But the going price for property even on the fringes of Beijing was 30,000 yuan per square metre. A decent-sized place would cost about 1,000,000 yuan. Snail would need to put a third down – at least 300,000, three times what he had – and then pay in roughly 3,000 yuan a month for the next twenty years.

Any way he calculated it, it was a daunting task. Like the game he played on his tablet, the numbers combined until they became too big for him to handle. 5,000 times twelve is 60,000. 60,000 times five is 300,000. That meant in five years he should have enough for a downpayment. But all the while smaller numbers appeared at the edges that must fit inside his earnings: unexpected bills, administrative costs, out-of-insurance health care, rent hikes, money for his parents. 100 goes twice into 200, which makes 400 and multiplies by twelve to turn into 4,800, while a stray 1,600 becomes 3,200 to treble into 9,600 that combines with the 4,800 that has doubled, and new numbers are popping up all over and the pace is constant and there's no pause button until the maths fails and the screen is full and . . . Game Over, Player Kill.

One early morning on his commute into work, Snail saw a beggar sleeping on the side of the pavement. The beggar was lying in the foetal position, and two dogs to either side of him were napping next to their owner. Snail thought it looked comical: three figures in a row, curled up like bananas, connected by leads and snoozing in the balmy spring air. Meanwhile he had to hurry past and work for ten hours before commuting back home. In that moment Snail felt envy. He imagined the beggar must be sleeping very deeply, with nowhere to rush to, no family responsibilities to worry about, no pressure to earn a higher salary. It looked like a peaceful life.

*

By the summer, Xiaoli was showing and Snail knew he had to come up with a plan. When she told him she was pregnant this time, early in the year, he sneaked online while she was sleeping to prepare himself. He found a bulletin-board post on a discussion forum that said the combined average costs of raising a child to eighteen were roughly 2,000,000 yuan. It all just seemed too much. Not for the first time he considered whether his family could stay in Beijing.

The thorniest problem was his residence status, the all-controlling *hukou*. Snail's papers marked him as from the countryside of Anhui, which put him at a disadvantage in the city in several ways. There were more restrictions if he wanted to buy a flat. (For one he needed five years' work experience with insurance, but while he had worked for almost as long his old company hadn't given insurance so in practice he was starting from scratch.) His access to health care was limited. And a greater concern still was schooling. Even if born in Beijing, his child would inherit his and Xiaoli's classification of rural residence and couldn't enrol in regular city schools, but instead would have to attend significantly less good schools that were exclusively for the children of migrants.

It would be so much easier if they were in Anhui. Snail figured that they could buy a big flat in Sixian town for about 400,000 yuan, well within reach – or in the country-side they could have their own house built for a fraction of that. Snail could find work in a nearby city or in the provincial capital, Hefei. Even if his wages would be lower, living costs would be cheaper. Their child could go to the best school in the region – maybe even Sixian Number Two Middle School, to walk down Tsinghua University Road and Renmin University Boulevard like this father had before him. But it wasn't only out of practical considerations that Snail felt tugged back to Anhui. In his heart it was the homeland.

After nine years in the capital, Snail was still conscious every day of the gulf between city and countryside. However settled he felt in Beijing, there was a splinter in his skin that told him he didn't belong. China is supposedly a classless society – certainly a socially mobile one where you can transform your status by making enough money – but the real class divide is between rural and urban. The matted syllables of his Anhui accent gave Snail away. In the eyes of Beijingers he would always be a country boy. Every province has its associated stereotypes and people from Anhui are seen as poor and coarse, the cleaners and delivery boys of the city. Urban migrants are routinely treated as secondclass residents and the gap is only widening as more arrive. Snail questioned if it was possible to truly cross it.

From the other perspective, that of the countryside, the measure of a young person's success was how far he or she got away from the field. By that criterion Snail had made it: he was in Beijing no less, and earning a monthly salary beyond his family's expectations. Yet Snail began to wonder, was that the only definition of success? What of wellbeing, happiness, a sense of community? He was putting aside money, for sure, but he was working himself to death and it still wasn't enough. He felt no attachment to Beijing beyond the opportunities it afforded him. Since he first began to study for the college entrance exams he had been told that life was about moving upwards: better grades, a better university, a better job, a better apartment, a better life. Now he had those things, but he was just as much a slave.

In July Snail went back to Anhui for two weeks, to see his mother but also to scope out property in Sixian town. The harvested maize was in the storage vat and the summer crops were budding: sweetcorn and soybean in the fields, watermelon, chilli pepper and mint in the smaller garden plots. The nights were chilly but when the sun shone it glared down on his ancestors' earthen grave mounds as if the gods were warming those buried bones. The pond where he used to catch crabs and snails was now overflowing with litter. The good earth that Pearl Buck wrote of was no longer so good, and there were fewer farmers to till it. But the people who did remain hadn't changed.

As Snail chatted to his old neighbours and school-teachers, their reaction to his idea of buying an apartment in Sixian was just as he imagined. If he was returning to Anhui they thought he must have failed in Beijing. This 'public opinion', as he called it, would be a major loss of face. There was marital discord over the decision: Snail wanted to make the move but Xiaoli was adamant that they should stick it out in Beijing. She didn't want their child to grow up in the provinces only to face the same trials to get out that Snail had undertaken. He saw the logic in that, and they planned to stay in the city for the time being.

He knew the plan would change, and change again. They would move out of Luxuriant City, and move again. He would switch jobs and apartments and subway lines. Meanwhile China was changing around him too. While he had grown up playing with toy guns, the new generation of 'post-00s' were already using smart phones. Gaming culture, too, had moved on from Snail's dissolute days: now everyone was playing *League of Legends* not *World of Warcraft* and Snail couldn't keep up with them.

Whatever the struggles to come, it was all so that his family could have a better future with every passing day. They were a unit now, the three of them: two on the outside, one within. In that respect it didn't matter where they lived. Wherever Snail went he would carry his home on his back with him. In October, at the first bite of another winter, his daughter was born. In keeping with the horticultural theme of Snail's surname, the pictogram of grass growing over a field, they called her Guoguo – the character for 'fruit', twice.

She would grow on the fields he sowed.

LUCIFER

When in the autumn of 2014 Lucifer auditioned again for a TV talent show, he told himself that this time was the last – make or break. He was in his mid-twenties now, and felt conscious that most of the music stars he emulated had succeeded when younger than him. He didn't like to dwell on what he would do if his ambitions came to nothing.

This show was called *Rising Star* and was the latest in a string of solo-singing contests cloned from abroad that also included *The Voice of China*. It would be aired on CCTV 3, a nationwide channel, and was a big deal. Getting through to the final rounds would be a guaranteed name-maker. Lucifer felt light-headed on a cocktail of excitement and anxiety as he walked to the recording studios, which were three blocks away from his flat (he didn't tell the studio that and still accepted a complimentary hotel room nearby). They were taping roughly twenty first-round contestants that evening – the auditions were held at night so those with day jobs could make it – and Lucifer was so nervous in the waiting hall that he methodically shredded a stack of paper cups into a small landfill of cardboard strips.

Shortly after 9pm, having waited for three hours, it was

his turn to go in front of the judges. Under the glare of the lights and attention of the cameras, he poured his story out to them like wine. His first guitar lessons in Gaocheng; his father's early disapproval; the time he smashed a glass over his head to show that he meant business; Rustic's early gigs at D-22; the Global Battle of the Bands final in London; his bid for solo fame. 'My wish is to realise my dreams,' he told them, 'like Lady Gaga did.' He had chosen his outfit carefully – white leopard-print trousers with an artistically torn left knee, red socks, brown leather shoes and a shirt with white and black stripes – to complement the song he was going to perform, 'Zebra'.

It was a song with personal meaning for him. He had written the melody back in college in a flash of inspiration, then put new words to it when he was beginning his solo career. '*When I wanted to start everything over again,*' he sang, '*I suddenly lost all of my courage.*' He had noticed by then that he always split the crowd: some people loved him, others hated him. Mostly, he thought, they didn't understand him. '*You say I'm a zebra. You say I'm white stripes on black. I think I'm black stripes on white.*' In the end he didn't want to be what other people said he should be. Lucifer didn't know if he was white or black, good or bad, winner or loser. Maybe that wasn't what was important. '*Nobody can know the answer.*'

Sure enough, the verdict was a hung jury. The two female judges said yes, but the male judges wanted to see the rest of the auditioners perform before deciding if he would make it through to the next round. While the production assistant was explaining this to Lucifer, in a studio set next door the three foreign friends he had invited to be his official 'behind the scenes' supporters stood in front of two stage doors. One was blue, with a large arrow pointing up. The other was red, with a downwards arrow. Depending on which door Lucifer came out of his friends would know if he had been accepted or rejected, and their reactions would be recorded by a handheld camera thrust in front of their faces. But Lucifer didn't come out of either door. Instead a stage hand ushered him quietly out of a grey side exit, to the bewilderment of his friends.

The assistant told Lucifer he would have to wait until all the other contestants had auditioned, then the judges would re-tape their verdict as if it had been spontaneous. In the waiting hall there was a free and endless supply of boxed dinners and miniature bottles of 'Mongolian Cow Yoghurt', the main sponsor of the show. Lucifer killed the hours by goofing around with his foreign friends, including a lawyer and comedian from Australia called Andy and an Italian musician with dreadlocks who went by the stage name Fulvio Boogie. Andy had brought his violin along and played 'Eine Kleine Nachtmusik' to soothe the nerves of a terrified girl about to go before the judges. Fulvio had brought spinning balls on string, and whirled them around furiously while apologising that they weren't on fire. They all took turns on Lucifer's guitar and had a singalong to Bob Dylan's 'The Times, They Are a-Changin''.

It was 1:30am when Lucifer was finally called back to hear the judges' ruling. By then he was a wreck, but tried to hide it. Once again his friends were lined up behind the scenes in front of the two stage doors, blue and red. Not only did they have to pretend that no time had elapsed but the whole faked anxious wait while Lucifer auditioned had to be reshot, as a producer had spotted that Fulvio Boogie's T-shirt featured a graphic design of large-breasted naked women having an orgy (he was given a polo neck to replace it). When it was time to find out the verdict, all eyes were on the doors. Andy took out his violin, poised to play either Vivaldi or the funeral march.

All of a sudden Lucifer came bursting out of the blue 'yes' door. Triumph! But the joyous first chords of 'La Primavera' faded into silence as soon as Andy saw Lucifer's scowling expression.

'Don't celebrate,' Lucifer said in English. 'They didn't accept me.'

As it turned out, he had provoked a heated discussion among the judges. But after a dramatic pause for the benefit of the cameras, the main judge said that Lucifer didn't have what it took to go through to the next round.

'Even though you didn't pass,' he said, 'I hope you can still keep your excited attitude to life.'

Lucifer thanked him and asked for a favour. 'Can I go out through the blue door?'

'Sure you can,' the judge said sarcastically. He didn't see why not.

On the way out, Lucifer turned to face the judges again. He wanted to have the last word.

'Everything bad is good,' he told them.

So long as he came out of the blue door anyway, he felt like he was winning. The show never did screen his audition.

*

Lucifer's hands were idle once more. He left his job at Hot Cat club after half a year, and over the months to come he tried out various new career paths. He had always been keen to give acting a go, and in the spring he starred as the romantic lead in a commercial short film, a love story set in Lhasa promoting a brand of mobile phones (the lovers texted a lot). He wrote a song called 'The Light of Dreams' that another campaign bought, for a French cosmetics brand. And he landed a role in a long TV advert for Schwarzkopf hair products, in which he played a clarinet player who was struggling until his dangling fringe was cut and styled, giving him the confidence to excel. ('I feel like a new man,' Lucifer wrote on his WeChat public feed about the haircut.)

Advertising seemed to be a logical line of work that would pay his bills. He tried his own hand in the industry, and started a one-man company that produced video and photo campaigns for brands. He called it Li Yan Space and rented an office in Daxing, the suburb where he was living again. Just around the corner from the office building was Beijing's second IKEA store, and he went there for lunch whenever he felt like Swedish meatballs. But he failed to attract any paying clients and closed business three months later. He was constantly running out of money and even considered taking an actual full-time job, as music director for an advertising firm that had given him an offer.

But Lucifer wasn't going to give up his dream so easily. He was still playing solo shows, although their frequency was dwindling along with their success. Meanwhile Rustic had re-formed and were gigging regularly – first to small crowds in XP, then bigger bookings at MAO livehouse and Dos Kolegas, a bar further out next to a drive-in cinema. They knew it wouldn't last – another split-up felt almost inevitable – but while it did they rode the wave. Their biggest show yet, a little over a week after Lucifer's rejection on *Rising Star*, was at Yugong Yishan as part of the livehouse's tenth-anniversary celebrations. The line-up brought together all of the biggest acts in the scene, and Rustic was the first set.

Ricky Sixx had transformed back into his glam-rock former self, having shaved the sides of his head to create a floppy mullet, in his leather trousers and a mesh vest with war paint smeared on his cheeks. The crowd was already dense, and he sprayed out a mouthful of beer to baptise the moshpit. Lucifer had totally reinvented his look again, wearing a long flasher mackintosh with oily slicked-back hair. The yellow glare of the set lights silhouetted him against the venue's logo, a socialist worker with pickaxe raised. Next to it were the four Chinese characters of its name, 'The Old Fool Who Moved the Mountain' – the proverb of the man who succeeded in the impossible out of sheer stubbornness.

'I want to tell you friends something,' Lucifer addressed his acolytes below the stage, while Li Fan ticked an impatient drum beat behind him. 'Compared to how you were living before, the rock 'n' roll life is the healthiest and best way to live, don't you think?'

The other life, the nine to five, was no comparison. He wanted to wake up to something different every day, to be free. His elders kept telling him he needed to get real. But there was a courage in persevering against the odds – lifting his pickaxe and moving that mountain.

'We are all young,' Lucifer panted into the mic, picking the first chords out of his guitar. 'For us all, youth is an art. Youth is our fashion.'

That was his life philosophy if anything was: youth was an attitude. It wasn't a bracket of years, or a style. It was the art of optimism. The will that no matter what happened yesterday, it wouldn't affect tomorrow. The readiness to seize what came, come what may. The energy not to stop and the faith to hold the course, without a roadmap.

'We are all just fucking – Chinese princes.'

There would be more failures, he knew. Blows to his confidence and concessions to reality. But he would keep on going until he succeeded or until all hope of it was extinguished. Tomorrow he might be someone totally different, and that was his prerogative. Rising star or fallen angel, so long as he was on that stage while the throng thrashed underneath, Lucifer was doing fine.

'This song is about what we're striving for in youth,' he said. 'It's called "Rock 'n' Roll for Money and Sex".'

The money and the sex were waiting for him. There was no doubt in his mind. He would be an international superstar.

FRED

Armed with her Ph.D. Fred sent off applications to a slew of colleges in Beijing to teach politics, but there were few academic positions for the taking. She tried the think tanks, but during the vetting process one of them found out that her boyfriend was Taiwanese. They said they would have to investigate them both more closely, and Fred pulled out. She tapped her father's and mother's Party connections in the top universities, but in the end she was hired by a small state college low down her list to which she had fired off a boilerplate enquiry.

China Youth Politics University is the official higher education institute of the Communist Youth League. It is a modest campus in Beijing's university district next to the multi-lane traffic of the third ring road, just across from China Minorities University, and could be mistaken for a residential compound. The manned gate is like that of any apartment complex and the teaching and dorm buildings are ordinary red high-rises. At the centre is a small rock garden and pavilion, with jutting stone formations around a low pool of water. Next to it is a yard full of exercise equipment with Chinese characteristics: jogging and cycling machines that offer no resistance, metal disc-spinners to limber up stiff shoulders and monkey bars more reminiscent of a playground than a gym.

On 1 September 2014, a Monday, Fred started class. Exactly eleven years ago she had been the first-year college student; now she was teaching them. She specialised in Western political philosophy, covering seminal thinkers of the European and American tradition – Max Weber, Emile Durkheim, Samuel Huntington – along with the ins and outs of constitutional democracy. It was a freer academic environment than she had expected, although the red line was still there: all courses and textbooks were officially approved. Free thought and the Party lived together in an unhappy marriage.

Past the rock garden and exercise jungle is a bulletin board with posters pinned up behind glass. At the top are six bold characters: 'Countering Harmful Education Warning Propaganda Board'. Below is a twenty-panel cartoon charting the principles of rule of law enshrined in China's constitution. Each maxim is in a speech bubble, spoken by a friendly amoeba-like blob wearing a mortar board: '*All power belongs to the people*' . . . '*Cherish basic rights*' . . . '*Support the leadership of the Party*' . . . '*Deepen propaganda education*'. Another poster next to it lists the twelve 'core values of socialism': Patriotism, Respect, Honesty, Friendship, Freedom, Equality, Justice, Rule of Law, Wealth and Power, Democracy, Civilisation, Harmony.

That was the doublethink of the Chinese state: a single Party system called democracy a core value. Students ignored the bulletin board, of course, but the message was hard to escape: the twelve words were also stencilled across the car-park wall, and one of the teaching buildings was emblazoned with 'Love the Country'. Fred was conscious that where before she was receiving the propaganda, now she was part of the establishment that delivered it. She also noticed that while at Beida her peers had mostly leaned towards the free market and Western models, her pupils now gravitated to nationalism and the ideal of Chinese exceptionalism. It was in part a self-selecting function of the university's specialisation, but also a trend that the new youth were more confident in China's strength.

The jingoism was never more apparent than during the National Day holidays of 1 October 2014, when the nation got a week off to celebrate the sixty-fifth anniversary of the founding of the People's Republic. There was a special flag-raising ceremony on Tiananmen Square, true believers hung smaller flags outside their homes, and state television had a field day. As with bombastic military parades, while many of the elder generations shed a patriotic tear, among young Chinese there was a combination of cynicism and genuine pride in their country – often at the same time. Most people simply took advantage of the holiday, also called 'Golden Week', to go on shopping sprees and invade tourist destinations en masse.

Fred went back home to Hainan. On the island of her childhood she ate her favourite seafood dishes, walked and fished in the hills and breathed in the clean(er) air. But that year's National Day was eclipsed by events in another far southern island city, as students occupied Hong Kong in what became the biggest democracy protests on Chinese soil since Tiananmen.

*

Ever since the handover from Britain to China in 1997, by many measures Hong Kong had remained apart from the mainland – and by others was increasingly dependent on it. Residents felt they were Hong Kongers not Chinese: they drove on the left, spoke Cantonese, shopped at Marks and Spencer, queued. Mainlanders were cast by a few as 'locusts', crossing over the border to snatch up iPhones and property. For decades there had been a sense of superiority while China lagged behind, but now big brother to the north was richer and more powerful. With that came anxiety over whether guarantees to preserve Hong Kong's free press and special political status – a fully autonomous region with its own Chief Executive and passport control – would hold up. Every 4 June a candlelit memorial defied Beijing, commemorating the Tiananmen killings, and small pro-democracy assemblies were common. The seed was in the earth, waiting for rainfall.

One of the newest activist groups was 'Scholarism', made up mostly of high-school students. Their first major protests were in August 2012 against curriculum changes that emphasised 'moral and national education': Beijing wanted Hong Kong's schools to look more like theirs. An even more heated debate was over elections slated for 2017, which would be the first time in history that Hong Kongers could elect their own leader. But the Party balked, ruling that candidates would be chosen by a nominating committee and must be 'people who love the country'. In September 2014 Scholarism protested outside the central government offices and another citizen group, Occupy Central with Love and Peace, joined the demonstrations. Police panicked and fired tear gas into the crowd. The rain had fallen, out came the brollies to protect against the gas, and the 'Umbrella Movement' was born.

On 1 October, while the Chinese flag was raised at government headquarters a (literal) stone's throw away, the heart of Hong Kong was clogged. Thousands of protesters blocked three central arteries, two on Hong Kong island and one in downtown Kowloon on the peninsula. The occupiers claimed the road with piled-up crowd barriers, while makeshift stalls gave out free bottled water, biscuits, waterproofs and umbrellas. Banners that hung from pedestrian overpasses called for 'Free and Fair Democracy' alongside quotes from Vaclav Havel and John Lennon. One slogan was 'Keep Calm and Be Alert'. C.Y. Leung, Hong Kong's Chief Executive, was depicted on posters as a vampire and a wolf – a pun on his nickname, 'the wolf'. From one overpass a stuffed-wolf toy from IKEA was hanged on a string – the toy's name in Swedish, Lufsig, sounded in Cantonese like a filthy expletive.

The intensity of the protests waxed and waned. In daytime the occupation zone in the central commercial district was all but empty except for hardcore campers, like an abandoned street fair. On the malls around them, adverts loomed over the slogans of dissent, for Stuart Weitzman designer clothes and Piaget watches. One message for Ovolo hotels simply read 'There's something happening here'. But after dark, when everyone got off work, the causeway became jammed with bodies. On the night of 4 October, tens of thousands of them gathered for a peaceful rally. They sang protest songs by the local band Beyond, waving the torch function on their smart phones like lighters at a concert. Joshua Wong, a seventeen-year-old leader of Scholarism, fired up the crowd in Cantonese. 'We young people,' he said, 'feel that we must go out onto the streets because this is our home . . . The three of us [leaders] standing here are still in school. We're standing here to strive for democracy.'

Fred felt the contrast to her generation on the mainland. She was following news of the protests closely on both domestic and overseas websites. As with Taiwan she had some sympathy for the cause. She admired the students' passion in defending the big ideas – free speech, universal suffrage, liberty – even if she didn't agree with the practicality of it. The occupiers resisted the term 'revolution' and their concerns were limited to the future of Hong Kong, but in spirit they had picked up the torch of Chinese youth rebellion from 4 May 1919 and 4 June 1989. The difference was that it was the fringes revolting, not the centre.

Fred's considered reaction was that civil disobedience didn't do anyone any good. For meaningful political reform to happen, she still felt stability was paramount. It was certain that Beijing wouldn't give in to allow fully free elections in Hong Kong, and in many ways the protests harmed that cause. If they escalated to threaten national security or territorial integrity, the government would shut them down with ruthless force if necessary. While most of the students were the model of civility, in other aspects of the rhetoric there were clear streaks of anti-mainland sentiment that she resented. The roots of young Hong Kongers' dissatisfaction also included unaffordable property prices and a widening wealth gap, and Fred didn't see how bringing the city to a standstill helped.

The view from Beijing was much more unforgiving. State media stressed the unlawful nature of the protests, speculated about involvement of 'hostile foreign forces' and (correctly) pointed out that the British had themselves denied Hong Kongers the vote for a century and a half. The *People's Daily* decried democracy as 'a poison in Taiwan and a disaster in the Arabic world' that 'would create chaos in China and cause the people to suffer'. In one state television news report, when a foreign pundit mentioned the word 'Tiananmen' the live feed suddenly went black. But there was never any real chance of protests spreading to the mainland. Fred's relatively nuanced opinion was rare. Many if not most mainland Chinese saw the Hong Kong protests as unpatriotic, ungrateful and illegal. Among the most critical were young Chinese the same age as the protesters.

By December, the demonstrations sputtered out. The occupation had thinned dramatically and fell out of favour with the public. Local business owners and taxi-drivers complained, their livelihoods affected by paralysis at the city's centre. There were counter-protests by mainlanders in support of Beijing, and other Hong Kong residents felt that a functioning city was more valuable than a meaningful vote. Dialogue between student leaders and local government got nowhere, and none of their demands were met. On 15 December the occupation sites were cleared peacefully by the police. The umbrellas didn't last to Christmas.

*

The pendulum of Fred's politics had swung dramatically. When she first arrived at Peking University in 2003, eighteen years old, she had been swept along by the progressive ideas of the Chinese political right. Soon after, still impressionable, she had turned sharply left to follow Pan Wei's creed of Chinese exceptionalism. Now she had settled at equilibrium. Not nationalistic but patriotic. Not an ideologue but a realist. Socially liberal, politically conservative. She knew her government needed to reform, and that it didn't behave as well as it should either to its own people or in the international arena. But she also felt that China's path to modernity would be different to the West's. After sampling the whole spectrum, the only ideology left was pragmatism. In the end Fred's politics were mainstream for her generation: change in China must come by evolution, not revolution.

The trouble was that evolution is slow, and Xi Jinping's China was moving further away from meaningful change. Fred had always felt that rule of law was the best place for reform to start. But in October the Party promoted the vaguer formulation of 'ruling the country according to law': rule *by* law, to serve their own agenda. That same month Xi said at a cultural forum that art and literature should 'embody socialist core values', and later his education minister banned the teaching of 'Western values' in universities. Clampdowns on civil society, NGOs and the Internet became the new normal. Groups organising outside the system were imprisoned, from human rights lawyers to feminists. The military was bullish in the South China Sea. It was certainly a strong and stable leadership, but Fred was worried: she didn't know what Xi wanted or where it was all going, and feared a small war in Asia.

As to the system itself – Leninist capitalism and single-party rule – she might have shrugged her shoulders, paraphrased Winston Churchill and said it was the worst form of government for China except for all the others. It wasn't just a matter of her family's stake in the Party's survival; it was about her own stake in the nation's future. There were such monumental challenges ahead: a slowing economy, regional instability, a demographic crunch as a generation of workers retired and the supply of cheap labour ran out. In her eyes the leadership, for all its flaws, was still negotiating those challenges – and avoiding the frankly terrifying alternative of a power vacuum. It was corrupt and messy and had skewed priorities, but the nation was still taking two steps forward for every step back. As Deng Xiaoping said, they would cross the river by feeling for the stones.

The metaphor applied to her own life too. She signed a five-year contract at China Youth Politics University, but teaching proved dull and she toyed with the idea of leaving academia. She hated the patina of smog that choked Beijing and thought about returning to Hainan, or even of moving with her boyfriend to Taiwan. At the end of 2014 he proposed – or rather suggested that their parents meet before he and she got formally engaged, which was the traditional way of doing it. They set a date the following spring for their engagement (at least she wouldn't have to act surprised) and another in the autumn for the marriage.

At twenty-nine Fred thought of her future as she did her nation's. There should be goals but no fixed plans, as the only constant was change. Principles but not dogma; the best course was whatever worked to keep getting richer, stronger, better. The teenage growth spurt and formative twenties were over. Now it was time to be responsible and find a role in the world. It would take a while yet and there would be tough times to weather, like the long Beijing winter ahead of her. But she could be patient, and wait for spring.

MIA

Mia was slurping a cappuccino in the cafe from *Friends*. The 'Central Perk' logo was frosted on the window front and the interior was a near perfect recreation of the set, right down to the upholstery. Catch phrases were painted on one brick wall ('How U Doin'?', 'Could I BE any more . . .', 'WE WERE ON A BREAK!') and a blackboard behind the counter listed hand-cooked muffins named after each of the characters (the Rachel had pink icing). At the back was *that* sofa, facing a TV screen where episodes of the series played on loop. There was even a smelly cat.

The only minor inconsistency was that the facade fronted not a bustling New York street but the sixth floor of an empty shopping mall in downtown Beijing. The cafe's red-brick walls gave out above two and a half metres to the open piping of the mall's high domed ceiling. The view from the window nook was of an escalator. From her high corner table Mia half-watched an episode ('The One with All the Poker'), but it was hard to suspend her disbelief and maintain the illusion. She turned back to her friend, a former colleague she hadn't seen in a while. She had some big news to share.

Mia had thrown herself into the year of the horse with a work ethic to match. She got more bookings as a freelance stylist and her old editors at *Harper's Bazaar* hired her for several big features. There was 'Shopping Girl', a six-page spread shot in Joyce's, a glistening high-end clothing store in the business district, with two models as tall and pale as the mannequins they posed by. There was 'White Bride', a wedding-supplement shoot where the bride in question, frosting in her hair, clutched by turns pale lilies, a milk-white parrot and a very disgruntled-looking snowy cat. And there was work for other Chinese edition glossies: *Madame Figaro*, *The Bund*, *Cosmobride*. All of a sudden Mia was in demand.

She took other work too. An advertising campaign for *The Voice of China* singing competition and a subway poster for Momo, a dating app with a reputation for facilitating one-night stands. As well as styling models for photo shoots, she also dressed celebrity clients for red-carpet events: first an actress, then a talk-show host, then another young actress whose break-through role was a fox spirit in one of China's never-ending film treatments of *The Monkey King*. Mia's biggest commission yet was to be on the team that dressed Yao Chen, a celebrity actress, for her new TV show *Divorce Lawyer* (about a beautiful but aloof divorce lawyer in Beijing who, surprise, finds love).

Mia still worked one day a week at *China Textile News*, chiefly for the health insurance. Twice a year, in spring and autumn, her job was to cover Beijing's Fashion Week. The theme of spring 2014, sponsored by Mercedes-Benz, was

'The Golden Age' – an expression first popularised by the novelist Wang Xiaobo. The opening ceremony was a parade of gilded pomp at the opulent Beijing Hotel, the front rows stuffed with officiating cadres while the hosts talked about 'disseminating fresh messages from within the world of fashion to the international audience beyond'. The final show was a supermodel contest with a line-up of models as young as sixteen, and included swimwear and wedding-gown rounds. Mia couldn't take it any more, bought her own insurance and resigned.

By the autumn she was busier than ever. She styled Li Na, the Chinese women's tennis champion, in an advert for a new line of Tiffany's jewellery. She went to Bali as part of the team for a bikini shoot, and showed off her own beach body on her WeChat public feed (it got plenty of likes from her male friends). She was an on-camera stylist for the first series of *China's Next Top Model*, a copy of the American and British equivalents. And she dressed a celebrity client who was the host of an online talk show about Western astrology called 'Astrology Goddess'.

When Yugong Yishan held their tenth-anniversary gig in September, Mia went along and watched Lucifer rock 'n' rolling for money and sex. It was a chance to let down her hair and remember her rebel years. On principle she didn't buy the expensive entrance ticket and rang up her ex, Set-light, who still worked there and got her stamped in. She didn't even let a text from her mum spoil the night: 'Next year you will turn twenty-five. Girls go downhill from here.

Don't become an old lady. Youth is capital.' There was no point in replying.

Her party friends rang her up too, her 'meat and booze' girls, to try and get her out to the clubs like in the old days. But Mia was in a different stage of life now, and turned them down to focus on her career. After a few months they stopped calling. Her work was so busy she was hardly ever at home, and often squeezed in just five or six hours' sleep a night. In her precious downtime she worked out, and signed up for a year-long Muay Thai boxing course at Glee Gym. Her instructors were two stocky Thai fighters, endlessly amused that her English name sounded like the Thai word for wife. 'Mia!' they shouted whenever she came in, breaking down into fits of giggles.

On top of Muay Thai she also dabbled in Krav Maga, the defensive martial art that fuses techniques used by the Israeli army and club bouncers, favouring a jab in the eyes or a knee to the balls to end fights quickly. After a trial class she started dating her instructor, a diminutive Chinese boy who had discovered Krav Maga after getting bored with the graceful but slower-paced Wing Chun kung fu. To celebrate Singles Day as a couple he cooked her dinner (pig's trotters with rice) at his parents' home where he lived, and they watched the American TV show *The Walking Dead* on his laptop.

But Mia was already looking ahead. It was her habit on auspicious days in the Chinese lunar calendar to pray at Yonghegong, a Buddhist lama temple two blocks north of her flat. For a modern girl Mia was surprisingly superstitious.

Once, in Temple of the Earth Park, she thought she saw a ghost. Praying wasn't about Buddhist faith for her – she was a devout believer in making her own destiny. It was more about the introspective ritual of it all, though it didn't hurt to hedge her bets. And so on the first day of winter according to the ancient agricultural way of marking the seasons, she pilgrimaged to Yonghegong in the hope of accumulating good karma.

It was early in the morning, but the crowd was already dense. Mia wore her blue Tsinghua University hoodie and clutched a pack of incense sticks, sold on the street of shops outside the temple that blared '*Om mani padme hum*' out of speakers on repeat. The first oblations to offer were at the ticket hall (twenty-five yuan), and the faithful were tested again at the X-ray bag check. Finally inside the compound, she paid her respects in a full circuit of the temple rooms. Outside each golden-roofed prayer hall was a stone brazier filled with smouldering dunes of hot ash, into which worshippers plunged their incense sticks. At the first brazier Mia lit three sticks and held them up to her forehead, bowing three times while facing north, east, south and west before thrusting them into the ash, her silent prayer still burning as she moved on.

The second prayer hall housed three Buddha statues, for the past (Dipamkara), present (Sakyamuni) and future (Maitreya). Mia thanked the first two for everything she had in her life so far – and asked the third for even more. The next hall was being used by robed monks to intone a morning prayer, but in a side room was the Buddha of financial fortune (Jambhala), one of the more popular idols that was swamped by the crowd. Next to it was a jet-black statue of a mythical dog-like beast, a *pixiu*, that also represented money-making. Mia rubbed its head and asked for good fortune in her career.

In the fourth hall was the Buddha of medicine (Bhaiṣajyaguru), where Mia prayed for her grandma and grandpa's health back in Urumqi. But the most impressive statue, and the most important prayer, was in the fifth and backmost pavilion. Here the Maitreya Buddha rose twenty-six metres high, carved out of a single white sandalwood tree trunk, next to a Guinness World Records plaque. There was nothing beyond it. It guarded the future.

The towering Buddha looked down on the twenty-four-year-old, unimpressed. He had heard it all. They came by the thousands every day, waving incense at his toes and bowing their heads like pigeons – begging for money, success, love, sex, promotion, retribution, high exam scores. Mia stared him in the oversized eye.

'Buddha, I promise I will work hard,' she intoned, figuring that the enlightened don't help the lazy. 'Make me stronger, so I can achieve what I want to.'

Later she articulated the prayer.

'I don't know what I want, but I know I really want it.'

*

In the following spring Mia dumped her Krav Maga instructor boyfriend, and made a decision that would end one chapter of her life and begin another. She had come to

Beijing from Xinjiang six years before, to widen her horizon and get as far away from home as possible. Now her sights were set on new frontiers, and as a freelancer there were no ties to hold her to the capital. The idea of moving to Shanghai came naturally. It was an international hub – a city that looked out to the West whereas Beijing looked inwards to China. She wanted to live in the French Concession where she could walk along leafy boulevards, shop in trendy boutiques and drink martinis in fancy bars.

Back in Central Perk, she told her old colleague about the new plan. So much had happened in a year, and she knew the next would bring many changes more. She would have a different life and fresh challenges all over again, in a new city. But whatever the crises and opportunities, she would roll with the punches and give a few of her own. There was no five-year plan. There wasn't even a five-day plan. Her daydream was of a beach house in LA or Malibu, where she could sun herself every day. For now, the future only meant tomorrow. She didn't know what the next quarter-century would bring, for herself or for China. But it was hers to meet fighting.

A month before leaving for Shanghai, Mia got a new tattoo: a mermaid on her upper left arm with the words 'Salty Soul'. Shanghai means 'on the sea' and Mia liked to say she had a soul that loved the ocean. One day she would cross it. She also treated herself to a gift, having finally saved the money to buy a Louis Vuitton handbag. It was just large enough to hold both her knuckle dusters and her iPhone, in a new phone case that read 'BITCH: Beautiful

Independent That Can Handle any thing.' She had the inside of the handbag inscribed with white capital letters: MIA. A friend had told her that in Italian it meant 'mine'.

XIAOXIAO AND DAHAI

This time the married couple got their honeymoon. Xiaoxiao had always wanted to go to Tibet, but that was remote
and expensive so instead they travelled to Yunnan province
in China's far south. Yunnan – 'southern clouds' – has
mountains, forest, valleys, gorges and grasslands, as well as
a mouth-watering cuisine. Street stalls sell goat's cheese
pancakes and roasted insects by the cup. The region is
known for its ethnic minorities, and local performers put
on song and dance shows in bright folk dress for the benefit of domestic tourists, even if not everyone appreciates the
cultural appropriation.

After their official wedding ceremony they flew to
Kunming, the provincial capital, and borrowed a friend's
car to drive to Dali, a lake town on the backpackers' trail
for both Chinese and foreigners. From there they went to
Lijiang, its beautiful old town protected by UNESCO
but prey to souvenir shops selling Naxi minority trinkets.
Lijiang, with its canal-side bars and courtyard hostels, has
a reputation among young Chinese as a destination for
bohemian stoners and erotic casual encounters. But the
second-time newly-weds followed the tourist itinerary. They

rode horses in the grasslands, set loose floating candles in the canals, and bought hemp ponchos and silk scarves dyed in hippy colours.

Xiaoxiao had finally made it to the opposite edge of China from her birthplace, her dream since she was little. She couldn't help but feel a twinge of disappointment: where she had imagined the exotic and adventurous, instead there were entrance tickets and fridge magnets. The coloured silk scarves were of the same kind she could have bought on Taobao, and were probably made in the same factory. Her best memories from the trip were of the food. She wasn't so sure she wanted to go to Tibet any more, out of fear it would be the same. After two weeks they flew back to Beijing, bearing gifts of bamboo chopsticks and Buddhist-style peach-stone bracelets for their friends.

In September 2014 they both turned twenty-nine. According to the old way of counting age in China, *xusui* where at birth you are one year old, that meant they were thirty. It was the age Confucius had in mind when he said, 'At fifteen I set my mind on study; at thirty I took my stand'. Dahai and Xiaoxiao had a joint celebratory dinner at a post-80s-generation themed hotpot joint called Number Eight Courtyard. From the outside it looked like any other cheap eatery, except it was exclusively for customers born after 1980. ID cards were checked at the door, strictly no one older was allowed in, and post-90s could only enter if accompanied by a responsible post-80s. They didn't have a policy for post-00s.

Inside was a lovingly reconstructed classroom from

Xiaoxiao and Dahai's childhood. The tables were wooden study desks with chipped plates, tin mugs and an ashtray (it had always been Dahai's dream to smoke in class). Class rules were printed at the front – punctual assembly, no talking over the teacher – and on the walls were all the familiar posters of every Chinese school: Lu Xun, Lei Feng and a chart for the daily eye-rubbing exercises that brought back memories. Behind the cash register was a blackboard and lectern, and when all the diners were seated a school bell rang. One of the owners (born 1982) banged a wooden baton against the lectern.

'Hello, students!' he said. 'Welcome to Number Eight Courtyard. There is just one important rule here. There is one word you can't say: "waiter". We are teachers. Does everyone understand?'

'*Yes, teacher!*' the class chorused back.

The menus were in the desk drawers: a multiple-choice questionnaire to mark up with a stubby pencil, choosing which meat and vegetables to go in your hotpot. When one student piped up with a smart remark the teacher brandished his baton at him, then switched it for a long wobbly saw. Later the saw was upgraded to a machete, and after that a plastic Kalashnikov. Everyone laughed along in bittersweet nostalgia for their school days when the rod was no joke.

After the meal was finished, the teacher led the class in a singalong to the theme tune of the nineties cartoon *Little Dragon Club*. There was a musical quiz for other childhood theme songs – *The Calabash Brothers*, *Slam Dunk*, *Ultra-*

man, Doreamon – and Dahai was quickest to answer one of them. His prize was a packet of *tiaotiaotang* candy powder, the kind that fizzes on your tongue. As they left Xiaoxiao bumped into a high-school classmate from her home town who was coming in for the next seating. Neither knew that the other was in Beijing. They hadn't seen each other in ten years.

*

The decade had passed Xiaoxiao and Dahai by as if without warning. Depending on perspective it seemed like either yesterday or a lifetime ago that they were fresh out of high-school. Now they were almost thirty, married, with a car, a home and fixed income – 'like grown-ups', they said, before realising that they had been for a while. Sometimes it felt like they didn't recognise their nineteen-year-old selves, or the plans that other them had made for the future they were now living. Not a cliché about dreams left behind but a feeling of something setting, like molten metal cooling into a groove as it runs.

Dahai's anger at authority, for one, had been tempered by his new responsibilities. Once he had imagined he was a superhero, standing up to his bosses both at work and in Party central. Now his goal was to become one of those work-unit leaders – if you can't beat them, join them. Before he had posted subversive comments online about the government. Now he bought a hardback edition of the collected speeches of Xi Jinping, titled *Governance of China*, and even admired 'Daddy Xi' (a popular nickname) for his strong-man fight to clean up corruption. Dahai still didn't like the system. The difference was that his livelihood now depended on it, and at this age he knew he wouldn't do anything rash like join a protest. He was the first to admit that he had compromised.

Xiaoxiao saw compromise in her life too. Her first small business, the clothing shop Remember, had been priced out. The second cafe she worked at had been closed down by local government, and she hadn't tried a third time. She still nursed an entrepreneur's fantasy of opening a combined coffee-and-clothes shop in Beijing, but the business rents anywhere central were prohibitive. The truth was that in marrying Dahai she had swapped those aspirations for a considerable degree of dependence. She kept looking for employment and worked briefly as a barista, but in the end settled for a stable office job in Dahai's work unit which he helped set up. With the tunnel finally finished, their new project was to extend a subway line to Beijing's far east.

Ten years also meant that Dahai was overdue to dig up his diary. On the eleventh anniversary of its burial in May, he and Xiaoxiao returned together to the mountain behind his childhood military compound. It wasn't only them who had changed but the mountain itself. Where before there was a solitary pagoda at the top, now the whole hillside had been transformed into a tourist site. There was a row of ticket windows and electronic turnstiles; a tiled square with a water feature; two giant golden Buddha statues (one standing, one reclining); a line-up of fifteen busts of historical Chinese figures; a stele perched on top of a stone tortoise; and a golden sculpture of a hand taller than Dahai, thumb and forefingers closed in a gesture of meditation. At least the new cable car saved them a steep climb.

At the top, the path to the summit led through a series of interconnecting caves, newly decked out with fairy lights and brightly coloured Taoist god statuettes. Next they walked along the back of a miniature fake Great Wall that zigzagged up a second peak, until the old pagoda was in sight. It was covered in scaffolding, in the process of being renovated and given a new paint job by a dozen workers. The team leader didn't want to let them through, but Dahai found a way onto the site around the back and they picked their way over gangplanks, past supply pulleys and a cement mixer, and across an arched stone bridge to where the plot of pine trees still stood.

This is where he stopped. Which was the right tree? There were a few dozen possibilities and X did not mark the spot. Dahai unfolded his collapsible spade and started to dig at random. Later he switched to a full-size spade that had been left behind on the construction site, while workers on their lunch break gathered around him to gawk and take pictures. But it was no use. After an hour of futile archaeology in the beating sun, the earth yielded nothing but roots and stones. Perhaps someone else had found the box by accident and was reading the pages he had written. Or maybe he was looking in the wrong place entirely. Dahai never did find his diary that day. He shared a cable car with Xiaoxiao back down the mountainside, and they went home.

They wouldn't miss the uncertainty of the twenties, as they found their path and partner in life. In that respect youth was a time for embracing bad decisions in order to figure out what the right decisions were. They hoped the thirties would bring just as much excitement, surer in the knowledge of who they were. And they could only imagine what the view would look like from forty or fifty or eighty. Would they have transformed again entirely? Would they obsess over fading memories? Or laugh at how little they had understood? Would they have money? Would they be happy? Would they still be together? Would their child have a better future than they did?

They planned to wait until the year of the monkey before having a baby. (Xiaoxiao didn't like the year of the sheep, an animal often regarded as feeble.) When news came that the one-child policy had finally been scrapped, it felt like the end of an era. From 2016 all couples could have two children. Along with other urban families it didn't make a difference to them, as they still planned on having just the one. Xiaoxiao was resolute that she wouldn't pamper or over-pressurise her child, as had been the fate of her generation. The next lot would inherit a different China entirely. And in time their own little monkey would grow up, and be young like they were, once.

*

They celebrated the Chinese New Year at their own home. Dahai's parents came over from Miyun, and so did his brother Xiaoyang with his wife. They invited their English friend as well, the one who was writing a book about them. There was spicy sausage from Hubei, sun-dried for weeks, and generous shots of Moutai-brand *baijiu* for the men. The Spring Gala on TV was co-hosted by an animated ram, and at various points viewers were told to use the 'shake' function on WeChat to compete for digital red-envelope cash prizes. Everyone in the room except the parents shook their phones like crazy all night long.

For Xiaoxiao it was another New Year's Eve away from her parents. She knew that when she had a child of her own it would be more difficult to visit, so near the end of the festival fortnight she flew back to the north-east. In Harbin she visited the site of her old shop, and remembered Remember. Her home town of Nehe was frozen as ever, minus twenty degrees at night. She ate apples and pears from crates in her parents' fruit storehouse like she had as a kid. She enjoyed her favourite local barbecue dishes and drank boiled Coke poured from the kettle. She walked past her primary school and the sweet shop next to it, now shuttered for the holidays.

The fifteenth and final night of the holidays was Lantern Festival. It was a day traditionally marked by eating *yuan-xiao*, sweet glutinous rice balls filled with red-bean paste in hot water, and by solving riddles. It was also a night for lovers, who would sneak out to light lanterns together under the first full moon of the new year. That evening Xiaoxiao's extended family gathered in a restaurant for one last big meal. While they slurped their glutinous rice balls the fireworks started – a final chance for the residents of Nehe to paint the skies red before festivities ended.

After dinner Xiaoxiao split off from her elders, who were going to bed. She wanted to walk into the centre of town, and two of her friends and a cousin came with her. She pulled on her winter furs, tightened her scarf and went out into the street amid the crackle and patter of firecrackers. They headed in the direction of the park, where the biggest crowd was gathering. Along the way other groups and couples joined them, walking south down the main road. Above them was an opposite current: thousands of wish lanterns flying north on the wind. Xiaoxiao had brought one with her, and at a crossroads within sight of the park she unpacked it, careful not to tear the thin red tissue paper. The corners had to be prised apart from flat, until the wire frame opened and the gossamer walls bloomed into a cube. Into a tin cage suspended at the open base she nestled the firelighter, whose heat would give the lantern its lift.

The design had barely changed in two thousand years. The story goes that in the Three Kingdoms era the general Zhu Geliang invented a flying lantern while under siege, writing a message inside it to plead for reinforcements. Now they were sold in convenience stores for a clutch of yuan, set loose by friends and lovers on special occasions. They were known as *kongming* lamps, after the general's ceremonial title, but also as sky lanterns and wish lanterns. Some wrote their wish on a strip of paper tied to the wire, others on the outside itself. Most silently intoned it as the lantern carried their thoughts into the sky – and prayed that the open flame inside didn't catch, leaving them to watch as their wish crashed and burned.

As a fire hazard it was illegal to set them flying on the street. That was only allowed in the park, from where the stream of twinkling yellow lights was coming. A fire truck was on alert just up the road from where Xiaoxiao opened hers. But her cousin was an off-duty policeman and he said it was OK. His armpit bulged with more flat-pack lanterns, which his on-duty colleagues had confiscated and given to him instead.

She kindled the firelighter and pinched the delicate upper corners of the frame as it filled with hot air. When the sides began to swell, she let go. The lantern bobbed down and for a moment looked like it was going to kiss the concrete, but a gentle touch kept it aloft. It hovered sideways before lifting into the night.

There it joined the sky river with the others, a thousand wishes on the air like migrating fireflies. Each lantern carried a heart beating softly inside its paper chest, fragile and buoyant, buffeted by the wind. Each light was watched anxiously by whoever had wished on it, to see how far it might fly. Xiaoxiao watched hers until it disappeared.

Then she turned, and walked on.

Dahai on the tracks inside his military compound,
the mountain where he buried his diary behind him

Xiaoxiao prepares for her photoshoot; the name of her clothes shop in Harbin is on her phone case

Fred reads on the stone boat by the side of 'Nameless Lake'
in Peking University

Gamers indulge in a late-night session at the internet bar
where Snail became addicted

Lucifer struts his stuff at MAO livehouse in Beijing

Mia takes a break in her favourite cafe in Shanghai

Author's Note

The problem with making big statements about China is that you can immediately think of an example that suggests the opposite. To generalise is to be an idiot, William Blake said. But single dots can form an image, and six notes can make a melody. I hope that through these individual stories, I show rather than tell what it means to be of a particular generation of young Chinese at this moment in the country's history.

Their generation is also my own. When I first came to live in China in the Olympic summer of 2008, I was twenty-two. I studied Mandarin at Peking University, embarrassing myself with bad tones and cramming characters in the library, a process akin to smashing your head over and over again with a very ancient and beautiful brick. For two years I ate a lot of noodles, travelled widely on cheap trains and kept a blog called *Six* about a (different) half-dozen of my peers. Their stories fascinated me, and in 2012 I moved into the hutongs to write, when I began research on this book.

I decided early on that I would not appear in these pages myself. I could have talked about my interactions with the characters – going on TV with Lucifer, helping Mia's spoken English, Fred's curiosity about my own politics – but I prefer not to intrude into their stories, having arrived so late in them. That does not mean that their lives are not still filtered through my foreignness. Writers who use 'I' have the luxury of reminding the reader that they are an alien element in the bush, and that the way the material is selected and presented is inevitably tinted by their own experience and perspective. Instead, inadequately, this note will have to serve.

It is also crucial to remember that the people I write about can only represent themselves. There are over 320 million Chinese in their teens and twenties in mainland China. Here are six. They are not spokespeople for their generation, and while they come from a variety of backgrounds their lives don't reflect many facets of young Chinese society, let alone of ethnic minorities and the diaspora. For one, they all get a university education and all end up in Beijing – the aspirational kind of young Chinese in the city that I wanted to write about in the first place.

I found the six variously: Snail in a *World of Warcraft* forum, Lucifer at a gig, Fred through her teachers, Mia on a geo-location app, Dahai and Xiaoxiao through their wedding photographer. I travelled to each of their home towns with them, and saw other key locations with my own eyes. Later set scenes I witnessed in person – Spring Festival in Xinjiang, protests in Hong Kong, the wedding in Beijing – while earlier ones I pieced together from interviews, and gigabytes of old photos and videos. Every quotation is checked against recordings or notes. This book is the product of meaningful time over three years spent with people of my own age in their own language, much of it not 'getting material' but building trust and getting *them*.

But non-fiction never nails the whole truth. I am ultimately relying on others' memories and on what they tell me, which will not be everything. I have tried to signpost recollection as distinct from cold fact, but reconstructing the past is an exercise in sculpting jelly. I confirmed details with third parties where I could, but otherwise let my characters tell their own stories, then took apart the jigsaw and reassembled it. Where I write of someone's thoughts or feelings, going inside their head as it were, it's because they expressed those sentiments directly to me – still a big liberty to take. At the kernel you can never truly know someone else, and words on a page are only shadows on a cave wall.

One reason why I wrote this book is because I felt that the popular portrait of young Chinese was painted with too few brushstrokes and far too large a splash of hyperbole. I wanted to show them as diverse, exposed to complicated influences and encompassing a range of political opinions – as well as having the right not to have any. Above all as a generation of individuals, with more hopes and fragilities in common with us all than we might think. This is a transition generation, the thin end of the wedge that will change China, whether slowly or suddenly. Millennials coming of age as their nation comes into power.

Finally I hoped that the book could be not only about China, but more simply about being young. As such, it resonates personally. When I first visited China less than a month after leaving university, I had no idea that the country would define my twenties, let alone that I would turn thirty here. Writing about young Chinese negotiating early adulthood, their characters and careers developing alongside mine, I can't help but connect it to my own story. In that respect, I have shared the journey with them.

Acknowledgements

My deepest debt of gratitude is to the people I write about in this book. The six of them have showed great generosity in sharing themselves and their time with me: welcoming me into their homes, digging up old memories and photos, and putting up with endless questions that frankly must have been a pain. Their trust to let me tell their stories is no small gift. Dahai, Xiaoxiao, Fred, Snail, Lucifer and Mia: 我永远是你们来自远方的朋友，心里知道你们都会成功。

There are a handful of China hands who have been supportive from the beginning. Jeffrey Wasserstrom was possibly the only person besides my family to read my blog back in 2008, and has given me advice and opportunities ever since. Evan Osnos bought me a beer on a rooftop during my first trip to China and was nothing but encouraging. Orville Schell was inspiring with his example and generous with his support. Rana Mitter, Isabel Hilton, Jonathan Fenby, Tania Branigan, Rob Gifford, James Miles, Gady Epstein, Barbara Demick, Jeremy Goldkorn, Kaiser Kuo, David Moser, Jeremiah Jenne, Sun Shuyun, Lindsey Hilsum, Paul Mooney, Bill Bishop, Jo Lusby, Paul French, Graham Earnshaw and Ian Johnson all gave guidance whether they know it or not.

ACKNOWLEDGEMENTS

During research, and as an author in search of six charac-
ters, I relied on help from a number of people who know
better than I do. Whether it was information, a promising lead
or a key insight this book would not be what it is without:
Michael Pettis, Charles Saliba, Matthew Neiderhauser, Ami Li,
Mary Bergstrom, Sim Chi Yin, Charlie Custer, Yang Xuefei,
Joel Martinsen, Pan Wei, Xiang Guo, Wang Hui, Josh Sum-
mers, Ryan McLaughlin, Max Duncan, Nels Frye, Ye Fei,
Jocelyn Ford, Mary Kay Magistad, Brendan O'Kane, Robert
Foyle-Hunwick, Eric Fish, Jemimah Steinfeld, Mengfei Chen,
Helen Gao, Becky Davis, Te-Ping Chen, David Wang, Candy
Yang, Evelyn Yu and Yang Zhazha.

Indeed this book wouldn't be anything at all if it wasn't for
Rebecca Carter. I couldn't have wished for a more attentive
agent, who took a chance on a twenty-six-year-old in an
Oxford pub and has been a rock ever since, along with Cullen
Stanley, Rebecca Folland and all of her colleagues at Janklow
and Nesbit. Kate Harvey was a patient and careful editor at
Picador, and since she moved on Kris Doyle has been a delight
to work with. Thanks also to Paul Baggaley, Ansa Khan Khat-
tak and Nicholas Blake for seeing the book through, and to
Christopher Cherry for his wonderful photographs.

To my friends in China, I won't list you here but you have
made Beijing my home. For their contributions to my sanity
during the writing slog, in particular I want to thank Anthony
Tao for the scotch, Alex Taggart for the bass, David Lan-
cashire for the Bach, Snail home hostel, Beetle in the Box cafe,
the Anton library, Badr at Cuju bar and everyone who has let

me crash on their couch, especially Katrina Hamlin and Adam White in Hong Kong.

Tom Pellman, Magdalena Navarro and Ben Carlson are true friends, and gave invaluable comments on the draft. Karoline Kan not only fact-checked the manuscript but helped me to discover much of what's in it. Christina Larson and James Palmer have been wonderful neighbours, ever supportive of the book – and introduced me to Ginger the dog, who kept me company while I wrote it. Rosalyn Shih read every word, and has given me more joy than I can put into words.

I wouldn't have wound up living in Beijing at all if I hadn't taught English in Qinghai province in the summer of 2007, surviving bat bite, bus crash, karaoke and Dico's burgers to emerge addicted to China. My five travel companions were the best company I could have possibly hoped for, and three of us got the bug for life. Nor could I have spoken a word of Chinese without so many wonderful teachers over the years. Thank you to all of my Chinese teachers at PKU and IUP, and to Deng Min who has been a patient tutor since, helping me decipher accents and communese as well as sharing her compendious knowledge of Chinese culture along with her own inimitable world view.

There is some inanimate software to tip my hat to before I'm done. Freedom for Mac, I am a procrastinating lost soul and you are my saviour. Chrome Nanny, you are gracious in not judging my crippling need to self-bind. Habitica, without you and my teammates in your pixelated realm, I would still be on the couch.

ACKNOWLEDGEMENTS

The last thanks I give are the first I owe, to those who would never ask it – my family. Right from the cot my brother, Tom, has been a friend and an example to look up to, which I treasure all the more for my glimpse at a generation of only children. My mother, Danuta, has given me love, comfort and wisdom from the bottom of her deep heart. My father, Timothy, taught me show not tell and less is more, and this book is dedicated to him.